Creating Corporate Reputations

Creating Corporate Reputations

Identity, Image, and Performance

GRAHAME DOWLING

OXFORD
UNIVERSITY PRESS

OXFORD
UNIVERSITY PRESS

Great Clarendon Street, Oxford OX2 6DP

Oxford University Press is a department of the University of Oxford.
It furthers the University's objective of excellence in research, scholarship,
and education by publishing worldwide in

Oxford New York

Auckland Bangkok Buenos Aires Cape Town Chennai
Dar es Salaam Delhi Hong Kong Istanbul Karachi Kolkata
Kuala Lumpur Madrid Melbourne Mexico City Mumbai Nairobi
São Paulo Shanghai Taipei Tokyo Toronto

Oxford is a registered trade mark of Oxford University Press
in the UK and in certain other countries

Published in the United States
by Oxford University Press Inc., New York

© Grahame Dowling 2001

British Library Cataloguing in Publication Data

Data available

Library of Congress Cataloging in Publication Data

Data available

ISBN 0-19-924163-5 (hbk.)
ISBN 0-19-925220-3 (pbk.)

3 5 7 9 10 8 6 4 2

Typeset by Hope Services (Abingdon) Ltd.
Printed in Great Britain
on acid-free paper by
T.J. International, Padstow, Cornwall

That nothing is so weak or unstable as a reputation (for power) which is not based on one's own forces.

(Niccolo Machiavelli, *The Prince*.)

Character is the result of two things—Mental attitude and the way we spend our time.

Character must be kept bright as well as clean.

(Anonymous.)

Who steals my purse steals trash; 'tis something, nothing.
. . .
But he that filches from me my good name
Robs me of that which not enriches him,
And makes me poor indeed.

(William Shakespeare, *Othello*.)

Exhibit P.1. Introducing a company

"I don't know who you are.
I don't know your company.
I don't know your company's product.
I don't know what your company stands for.
I don't know your company's customers.
I don't know your company's record.
I don't know your company's reputation.
Now—what was it you wanted to sell me?"

MORAL: Sales start **before** your salesman calls—with business publication advertising.

McGRAW-HILL MAGAZINES
BUSINESS•PROFESSIONAL•TECHNICAL

PREFACE

One of the most famous industrial advertisements of all time is reproduced here as Exhibit P.1. McGraw-Hill expresses the belief that a company's reputation exerts a powerful source effect in industrial selling. Salespeople discover this every time they meet a potential customer. Over the following years, this advertisement has become famous because it cleverly summarizes the communication task of most private and public sector organizations. In effect, the McGraw-Hill ad challenges managers to answer three basic questions:

(a) What are the reputations that people hold of your organization?
(b) What is your desired reputation?
(c) What differentiates you from your competitors?

If you cannot answer these three questions quickly and in simple terms, then there is a good chance that your primary stakeholders (customers and employees) and other important groups such as journalists and stock market analysts cannot answer them either. It is also prima-facie evidence that your desired corporate reputation lacks the power of a corporate super brand—like ABB, AT&T, Body Shop, BMW, Canon, Disney, Ford, General Motors, IBM, Intel, Microsoft, Mobil, NTT, Philips, Qantas, 3M, Shell, Sony, Toshiba, Virgin, Volvo, Wal-Mart, and Xerox.

Another way to think about the McGraw-Hill ad is to ask yourself whether the *raison d'être* of your organization passes the IDUS test. Is what your organization does *important* to employees and customers? Can the organization really *deliver* a valuable product and/or service to customers and society? Is this *unique*? And is it *sustainable* over time? If your organization fails any aspect of the IDUS test, then the task of attracting good employees and marketing products and services is harder than it should be.

This book is designed to help managers build and sustain their organization's most valuable strategic marketing asset, namely, the images and reputations of the organization held by various groups of stakeholders. Since starting to write, research, and consult in this area, I have seen a number of companies use the blueprint outlined in the following chapters to enhance the respect in which they are held by their employees, customers, and the communities in which they operate. I have also seen many companies caught by the traps discussed in Chapter 13.

A good corporate reputation enhances the value of everything an organization does and says. A bad reputation devalues products and services, and it acts as a magnet that attracts further scorn. As the American essayist and poet Ralph Waldo Emerson once said:

> What you are speaks so loud,
> I can't hear what you say.

The management of an organization's desired image and reputation is too important to be outsourced to an ad agency, public relations group, or corporate design firm, although each of these groups may play a crucial role in helping to build this strategic asset. It is also too important to be captured by the chief executive officer (CEO)—although he or she must champion the cause. Reputation management is the responsibility of senior management, and its implementation is the responsibility of *every* employee. Why? Because employees have the most to gain from a good corporate reputation, and the most to lose if they and other people hold the organization in poor repute.

Four things differentiate this book from others with the title *Corporate Image* or *Corporate Reputations*. First, it draws its insight from a wide range of research (cited at the end of each chapter) and the experience of managers and consultants who have shared their ideas with me over the last twenty years. Second, it provides a more balanced approach to corporate image and reputation management than books written by consultants, advertising agencies, corporate designers, and public relations firms. Each of these tends to see reputation building predominantly from the perspective of a consulting service that can be offered. Third, it differentiates among the terms corporate identity, corporate image, and corporate reputation. These are not the same concepts. In fact, separating identity, image, and reputation is the key to understanding what to measure and what can be changed. Finally, building a better corporate reputation is not a task that can be outsourced to a consultant—senior management *must* take primary responsibility. The reason for this is that the major drivers of good images and reputations are inside the organization, namely, its vision, strategy, and formal policies. It is a mistake to entrust to a spin doctor the task of trying to build a better reputation.

Finally, I would like to thank my academic colleagues who provided valuable comments on the research papers that underpin the theory embedded in this book. Also, thanks are expressed to all those CEOs, managers, and consultants who talked so openly about how they manage the images of their organizations.

Monetary amounts expressed in dollars are US dollars unless otherwise specified.

CONTENTS

Part 3   Managing Corporate Images and Reputations

LIST OF EXHIBITS

LIST OF FIGURES

LIST OF TABLES

LIST OF ABBREVIATIONS

ABCD	accuse, bluster, conceal, deny
CEO	chief executive officer
CFO	chief financial officer
CPA	certified practising accountant (Australia)
	certified public accountant (USA)
CRM	cause-related marketing
CRUDD	credible, relevant, unique, deliverable, and durable
FAX	facsimile (machine)
HOG	Harley [Davidson] owners group
HOT	human, organizational, and technological
IDUS test	important, deliverable, unique, and sustainable
IMC	integrated marketing communication
IMT	image management team
IT	information technology
JIT	just in time
MBA	Master of Business Administration (degree)
OEM	original equipment manufacturer
PAC	Public Affairs Council [of General Motors]
PBS	public broadcasting system
PDA	personal digital assistant
PC	personal computer
PIMS	profit impact of market strategy
PR	public relations
R&D	research and development
RIP	regulatory, infrastructure, and preparedness
ROA	return on assets
SBU	strategic business unit
SEC	Securities and Exchange Commission (USA)
TQM	total quality management

TV	television
USP	unique selling proposition
VALS	values and lifestyles
WII-FM	what's in it for me
WOM	word-of-mouth (communication)

AUTHOR BIOGRAPHY

Dr Dowling is a Professor of Marketing at the Australian Graduate School of Management in the University of New South Wales. Originally trained as an accountant, he retrained as a marketer and for the last twenty years has been actively studying how companies create and capture the value that customers see in their products and services. Grahame's consulting, teaching, and research focuses on implementing the philosophy that there is nothing as practical as a good theory.

Over the past twenty years Grahame's research has concentrated on two main areas—the adoption and diffusion of new products, and the development of corporate reputations. Research on both these topics has been published in the world's leading academic journals such as the *Journal of Marketing* and the *Journal of Consumer Research*, and in a book entitled *Corporate Reputations: Strategies for Developing the Corporate Brand* (London: Kogan Page, 1994). In 1997 Grahame was named The Distinguished Marketing Researcher in Australia and New Zealand for his work on the adoption and diffusion of new products. Grahame's research has also been made more easily accessible to businesspeople by presenting it in management seminars and through numerous articles in business magazines and newspapers. Grahame is a frequent speaker at academic, industry, and in-company conferences both in Australia and overseas on these and other marketing topics.

Most of Grahame's teaching at the Australian Graduate School of Management is to businesspeople. This interaction with managers is a good source of research topics and necessitates a continued search for the practical applications of abstract theories. One outcome of this approach to knowledge development, is that some of marketing's 'sacred cows' have been questioned, e.g. customer loyalty programs, the shortening of product life cycles, and the traps involved in changing corporate identity symbols. Because of this willingness to challenge conventional marketing wisdom, Grahame is often invited to help companies think about their marketing problems.

Dr Dowling's degrees are: BCom and Dip Bus Stud in accounting (University of Newcastle); MCom and PhD in marketing (University of New South Wales).

grahamed@agsm.edu.au

Introduction

The central argument of this book is that if your company has a good image and reputation, then it can always be used to support the organization's business activities. If your company has a poor reputation, then it *pays* to improve it. Many senior managers (especially chief executive officers—CEOs and chief financial officers—CFOs) ask whether there is any hard evidence to support a relationship between a better corporate reputation and enhanced financial performance. The less polite managers just say: 'prove it!' Until recently, the answer involved relying more on anecdotal than on scientific evidence. However, because *Fortune* business magazine has conducted corporate reputation surveys now for more than a decade, there are sufficient data to conduct some scientific studies.

Starting in 1984, *Fortune* published the results of a 'beauty contest' among the Fortune 500 companies. Each year executives and corporate analysts rate the companies in their economic sector on eight attributes: management quality, product quality, ability to develop and keep key people, financial soundness, asset use, investment value, degree of innovativeness, and community and environmental friendliness. From these ratings *Fortune* derives an overall corporate reputation score and nominates 'America's Most Admired Companies' (visit *www.fortune.com* for more data). Table I.1 shows the top- and bottom-rated companies for 1999.

The data from these surveys have been analysed by academic researchers to see whether or not an above-average corporate reputation in the firm's industry sector has any relationship to the level of the firm's financial performance. While no single scientific study can be conclusive, the good news is we are accumulating reliable evidence that such a relationship does exist. In short, firms with an above-average *Fortune* reputation score exhibit either (a) a greater ability to *sustain* an above-average

Table I.1. America's most admired companies, 1999

The most admired	The least admired
1. General Electric	495. Humana
2. Microsoft	496. Revlon
3. Dell Computer	497. Trans World Airlines
4. Cisco Systems	498. CKE Restaurants
5. Wal-Mart	499. CHS Electronics
6. Southwest Airlines	500. Rite Aid
7. Berkshire Hathaway	501. Trump Resorts
8. Intel	502. Fruit of the Loom
9. Home Depot	503. Amerco
10. Lucent Technologies	504. Caremark Rx

Source: *Fortune* (21 Feb. 2000).

return on assets (ROA), or (b) a greater ability to *attain* an above-average ROA.[1] These findings support the 'comparative advantage theory' of corporate strategy, which says that firms can gain a sustainable competitive advantage by developing their intangible and inimitable assets—such as their corporate reputations.[2]

Hence, it does seem to pay to proactively enhance the reputations people hold of an organization. In Chapter 1 I outline some of the ways in which good reputations pay off. The list presented there also suggests that public sector and not-for-profit organizations can benefit from a better reputation.

The challenge to build a great reputation, and thus a corporate super-brand, starts at the top of the organization. The company's top team establishes a vision and strategy, and moulds the overall culture of the organization. This provides the leadership and direction for employees to create an organization that is meaningful and authentic for those stake-holders who control its destiny. Corporate reputation building requires a long-term commitment to the ideas outlined in this book. However, the potential rewards to both the architects of change and the organization itself can be substantial.

On a personal level, our reputation is one our most valuable assets. The same is true for any organization. The early chapters of this book outline just how valuable these reputations are. To enhance this value, it is necessary to manage the factors that combine to create these reputations. As we look into the different types of information stakeholders use to form their images and reputations of an organization, it becomes clear that some of the most widely used strategies, namely, advertising, name changes, and corporate signage, are by themselves insufficient to create a good corporate reputation. The reputations people hold of an organization are the net result of *all* its activities. In essence, reputation reflects a firm's culture and performance much more than its packaging.

Typically reputations take a long time to form, and once developed, they work like a flywheel—delivering a sustained stream of power to whatever they are attached to. If they become strong and unique they can be quite difficult to change. Reputations can be an asset to an organization if they are good, but a crushing liability if they are bad. For example, government bureaucracies around the world tend to have poor reputations. These are then perpetuated in television shows such as the *Yes Minister* and *Yes Prime Minister* series (both from the UK), and in sayings such as 'you should be glad that you don't get all the government that you pay for'. Thus, the reputations of organizations are a long-term strategic asset or a liability. In a highly competitive market it is better to be well armed with respect and status, than to have to rely solely on tactical manœuvres.

This is not a book based on a group of in-depth studies of excellent or 'winning' organizations. This was the approach adopted by Tom Peters and Robert Waterman in their best-selling business book *In Search of Excellence*. However, the companies they chose to study soon lost their lustre, and many of the corporate success factors they identified did not distinguish between good and bad performers.[3]

Rather than try to pick a series of winners, the approach adopted here is to look at a wide variety of companies that have managed their corporate images and reputations well or poorly. While these come mainly from the USA, some reside in Australia, Asia, and Europe. Introducing some cultural diversity provides insights which are sometimes more vivid and can help provide a better understanding of the process of image and reputation management. When these anecdotal corporate histories are combined with scientific research evidence, we have a rich database from which to develop a practical and robust framework to enhance corporate status and in some cases, create a corporate super-brand.

In effect, this framework is a descriptive theory of the development of corporate brands. I am a firm believer in the saying that 'there is nothing so practical as a good theory'. Every day most organizations rely on such theories to guide their operations: they are called strategic, corporate, and marketing plans. These plans are created in exactly the same way that scientists create many of their theories, namely, by developing a series of hypotheses about what will work in a particular circumstance. The plan is then 'tested' by implementing it in the real world.

After reading this book you will know about the key factors that drive good and bad corporate identities, images, and reputations. Also, you will understand the two strategies for achieving corporate super-brand status. The first is to have excellent operational performance, as do the top ten companies listed in Table I.1. A second strategy is to link the values in the corporate vision to the values of employees and target customers. This shared-values strategy has been used very successfully by companies like Apple Computer, Body Shop, Harley-Davidson, Playboy Enterprises, Porsche, Qantas, and Virgin—firms whose status far exceeds their operational performance.

An organization intent on becoming a corporate super-brand starts by identifying the factors that it can use to enhance its status. These factors include a vision and the leadership to guide business decisions and employee behaviour. The organization's strategy, culture, and workplace incentives also must be aligned with this vision. Then it is important to communicate to outside stakeholders that this has been done. The product/service offering and its publicity are important in communicating this message. In essence, the approach starts inside the organization and only moves to the outside when there is a strong internal foundation. The following chapters outline this process.

This book is organized into three broad sections. Part 1 discusses what corporate identities, images, and reputations really are. In both the academic and management literatures there is some confusion about these concepts. In the 'real world', managers tend to have a good feel for what is meant by the image or reputation of their organization, but they often confuse corporate identity with corporate image. This confusion can result in the wasting of millions of dollars, as we will see later. By defining our terms in Chapter 1 we can build a strong foundation for the second section of the book, which focuses on the factors that combine to shape an organization's various images and reputations.

Part 2 of the book identifies the key factors that must be changed, in order to achieve the image an organization wants to project. This is a task that many management teams struggle to come to grips with. I see many companies that hope to change their image by telling (or yelling at) people about their virtues and aspirations, when what they should be doing is changing some of the fundamental aspects of their behaviour. Also, many companies neglect the crucial role that employees play in the process of forming image and reputation. By identifying the core set of factors that drive a corporation's desired image, it is possible to reduce substantially the risk of wasting a considerable amount of time and money for little or no effect.

Part 3 describes how to measure corporate images and reputations, how to use these findings to guide the refurbishment of the organization's desired image, and notes some 'traps' that may ensnare managers who embark on a programme of corporate image change. If the desired image is to be used as a competitive weapon, it is necessary to know what different groups of stakeholders think about the company and its competitors. It is also useful to know how stakeholders think an ideal company in a particular industry should behave. With this information, and the blueprint from Parts 1 and 2 of the book, the task of outlining the stages in the process of image enhancement and reputation change is straightforward. From here, it is just a matter of time to becoming a corporate super-brand.

NOTES

1. P. W. Roberts and G. R. Dowling, 'The Value of a Firm's Corporate Reputation: How Reputation Helps Attain and Sustain Superior Profitability', *Corporate Reputation Review* (Summer 1997), 72–6.
2. S. D. Hunt and R. M. Morgan, 'The Comparative Advantage Theory of Competition', *Journal of Marketing*, 59, 2 (1995), 1–15.
3. T. Peters and R. Waterman, *In Search of Excellence* (New York: Random House, 1982). D. T. Carroll, 'A Disappointing Search for Excellence', *Harvard Business Review*, 83, 6 (Nov.–Dec. 1983), 78–88; 'Who's Excellent Now?', *Business Week* (5 Nov. 1984), 76–88.

CORPORATE REPUTATIONS

1

Corporate Reputation Value: Good Really Is Better Than Bad

While I was writing this chapter I visited a large retail bank which posed the following dilemma:

We would like to have the best corporate reputation among our competitors BUT we would prefer to have a better bottom line profit.

This dilemma was illustrated in the bank's pricing policy. Every time the cost of funds changed in the wholesale market the bank and its three major competitors passed on the change to their retail customers. When the cost of funds fell, the bank lagged behind the others by a few days, and when it rose this bank was one of the first to pass on the extra charge. Thus it gained as much as it dared relative to its competitors. There are two problems with this strategy. First, the bank's customers were not fooled. Existing (loyal) customers felt a little cheated and new, price-sensitive customers went to a competitor until the rates equalized. Second, many employees felt that the bank should follow the customer-focused sentiment expressed in its Vision Statement and pass on any saving as soon as possible. The net result of this strategy was that short-term profits were up, customer satisfaction fell slightly, and some employees were concerned about the balance between profit and customer welfare.

There were two reasons why the bank could get away with this strategy. First, for existing customers, switching costs were high and there was a general perception, backed by extensive research, that all four banks in this market 'were bastards'. Hence, the irritation was not sufficient to cause mass customer defection, but it did reconfirm the bank's poor reputation. The second reason was that there were strong internal incentives to pursue this strategy. Senior managers were under heavy pressure from institutional investors and the board of directors to improve financial performance. And the CEO and top management team were financially rewarded for achieving better results. Middle-level managers and customer service staff, however, were somewhat embarrassed by the bank's strategy.

This is a classic example of the trade-off between short-term gain and potential long-term pain. A technical description is that management was discounting future earnings at a higher rate than was optimal for the bank to establish the best reputation among its competitors. It also highlights how appeasing one group of corporate stakeholders may be done at the expense of the reputations held by other groups—in this case many employees and customers. There is no simple solution to this type of dilemma. Also, as we will see in the next section, many companies face the challenge of surviving in the short term at the expense of investing for the longer term. However, it pays to be aware of the long-term effects of diluting an organization's desired reputation.

THE REPUTATION CRISIS

Whom the gods would destroy, they first ridicule

During the last two decades thousands of enterprises have suffered a loss of reputation. Often it was the result of a lack of perceived social responsibility such as Nike's use (many people said exploitation) of cheap Asian labour, or AT&T increasing its executives' compensation packages after announcing the lay-off of many workers, or British Airways spending millions of pounds painting new designs on the tail-fins of its aircraft while bargaining with employees for cost reductions. In other cases, reputation loss was the result of a specific event such as the 1989 grounding in Alaska of the Exxon corporation's oil tanker, the *Exxon Valdez*. Sometimes it was caused by a lapse of ethical standards by managers who became greedy to make huge short-term profits for themselves and their companies. The aftermath of the October 1987 collapse of world stock markets highlighted many such cases. Another cause was the deregulation of markets. This revealed that many companies were not able to compete effectively in the new market conditions. Classic examples of this were the banking industry in Australia and the domestic airline industry in the USA.

As often as not, loss of reputation was caused by poor marketing. Many once-great companies lost the ability to develop new products and services that provided real or perceived value to customers. This is a type of reputation crisis that creeps up on many companies and is difficult for managers to detect. Sometimes loss of reputation was the result of failure of a new product (such as New Coke, the IBM PC Jr., the Apple Newton PDA, the Body Shop's launch of a range of hemp-based products in Asia where many governments are vehemently opposed to anything related to the drug culture). In other instances it was caused by a company's own short-sighted marketing tactics. For example, the manipulative and hard-sell sales tactics still employed in some car dealerships reflect poorly on the car manufacturers whose cars are being sold. In any event, the result is the dilution of equity in the company's reputation.

These crises assume that reputations are something to be protected—they are! The corporate strategy researchers argue that they are among the most important intangible, inimitable strategic assets for the firm. Hence, firms face an opportunity cost if they do not continually reinvest in enhancing the images and reputations of their key stakeholders.

Given the financial value of an above-average reputation (mentioned in the Introduction), and the various case studies and research findings that suggest that good corporate reputations are more valuable than bad ones, one would expect every organization to have a programme to actively manage its corporate reputations. Some big companies do have a formal programmes. Others assign *de facto* responsibility to the corporate affairs department. For many others, however, there is no person or programme or budget to oversee this crucial strategic asset.

When corporate reputation management disappears from the formal management agenda, the company leaves itself open to the types of crisis mentioned earlier. There seem to be four reasons for this state of affairs. First, many managers do not fully appreciate the value of a good corporate reputation. (This is the topic of the next section.)

Second, most managers have only a fuzzy understanding of how reputations are formed and what people currently think about their company. While they may feel that business in general, and their company in particular, does not receive the social status that it deserves, it is not clear what can be done to rectify this situation. The lack of a conceptual framework leads to a third problem—how to measure what various groups think of the company. Unless a clear picture can be drawn showing the current situation then it becomes almost impossible to agree about whether or not the organization has a reputation problem. A wise old management guru once said that 'If you can't measure it, you can't manage it'. If it is difficult to pin down the quality of the reputations people hold of your company, then it becomes doubly difficult to manage this strategic asset. This is the fourth problem that feeds the continuing crisis. Research has shown that like most management tasks, this one is multifaceted. Hence, if you pull the wrong levers, or pull them in the wrong sequence, you can cause more harm than good.

THE VALUE OF A GOOD CORPORATE REPUTATION

When people think highly of a company, it can pursue more opportunities and be more efficient and effective in its current operations. A poor reputation can have the opposite effect—people don't trust the company, its market offerings, or what it says about itself. It seems that good reputations pay off in both operational and financial ways.

Operational value

Here are some of the ways in which a good reputation helps a firm:

(1) It adds extra psychological value to your products (e.g., trust) and service (e.g., when it is difficult to evaluate the quality of a service, then it will be rated slightly higher from a company with a good as opposed to a poor reputation).

(2) It helps reduce the risk customers perceive when buying products or services (e.g., managers seldom get fired for buying the market leader).

(3) It helps customers choose between products (e.g., televisions) and services (e.g., education, legal services, consulting advice) that they perceive as functionally similar.

(4) It increases employee job satisfaction (good companies seem to exert a halo effect on employee job satisfaction ratings).

(5) It provides access to better quality employees when recruiting (most people would rather work for a highly respected company).

(6) It increases advertising and sales-force effectiveness (e.g., a favourable reputation can boost the credibility of the firm's advertising).

(7) It supports new product introductions (e.g., the launch of Windows 95 from *Microsoft* was delayed several times—but customers waited for it).

(8) It acts as a powerful signal to your competitors (e.g., Procter & Gamble have a reputation for a quick and sometimes savage reaction to competitors' price cuts and new product introductions).

(9) It provides access to the best professional service providers (e.g., the best advertising agencies want to work for the best clients—so they can 'rent' the clients' good reputations).

(10) It provides a second chance in the event of a crisis (e.g., after the two Tylenol product-tampering crises, Johnson & Johnson's market share bounced back, in large part because of the good reputation of the company).

(11) It helps raise capital on the equity market (e.g., the year before the Australian airline Qantas became a public company it made an after-tax profit of $A156 million on revenues of $6.6 billion—not enough to buy one new jumbo jet! Yet the float was fully subscribed).[1]

(12) It enhances bargaining power in trade channels (e.g., when IBM entered the PC market its good reputation assured it of distribution support).

(13) It acts as a performance bond when the firm contracts with other business enterprises such as suppliers and advertising agencies.[2]

A poor reputation can endanger a corporation's health:

(1) Many CEOs say that share market analysts do not like their company and undervalue its share price.

(2) Journalists seem to pay particular attention to companies with poor reputations, and even when these companies do something good, the journalists may remind their audience that this company has a bad history.

(3) Customers seem more concerned and price sensitive about products and services from less well-respected companies.

(4) Poor (external) reputations tend to 'feed' poor employee morale. (See the Air-India case study at the end of Chapter 2.)

Most of the benefits of good reputations relate to an organization's external activities. However, it is arguable that a good corporate reputation is more valuable on the inside of the organization. Managing the reputation of the enterprise held by employees has particular poignancy for organizations experiencing dramatic changes such as downsizing or facing a deregulated market. Well managed, the employees' reputations can help create a sense of trust, belonging, and commitment. Companies like 3M (known for its innovation), Disney, and Singapore Airlines (with reputations for good service), which rely heavily on their employees to support the external positioning of the company, have been practising this philosophy for years.

Corporate reputation-building activities can also pay off for a firm when it operates in a market where competitors have incomplete information about its strategy. Here, the company can use its reputation to credibly signal information about its future plans to these competitors. For example, companies may think that Procter & Gamble has a reputation for aggressive price competition, and hence, this enables P&G to 'lead' the pricing behaviour of other market participants.

A good corporate reputation can also have strategic value if it is used to add an extra element to the company's marketing mix, or to complement existing elements of the mix. A company's marketing mix is often referred to as the '4 Ps'—product, price, place (of distribution), and promotion (now commonly referred to as integrated marketing communications). For example, the IBM case history in Exhibit 1.1 illustrates the power of a corporate reputation to enhance a new product marketing campaign.

Financial value

While any one of these operational and strategic reasons seems to be justification enough for investing in building a better reputation, there is now some empirical evidence that good reputations pay off in a financial sense. An example of this, valued at $128 million, is illustrated in Exhibit 1.2. In the next couple of paragraphs I elaborate on the expected financial returns from a better corporate reputation.[3]

An above-average corporate reputation can have two effects on a firm's financial performance. It can help the company to attain superior profits or, once the company reaches this position, it can help it to sustain such superior profits. In the study Peter Roberts and I conducted, reputation was measured in terms of the perceptions of executives and corporate analysts across the eight attributes of: management quality, product quality, ability to develop and keep key people, financial soundness, asset use, investment value, degree of innovativeness, and community and environmental friendliness. Financial performance was measured in terms of the after-tax return on total assets (ROA). An above- or below-average measure of both corporate reputation and ROA for each firm is defined relative to other firms in that firm's economic sector (to remove the industry effects on the level of these variables).

The data were collected as part of *Fortune*'s 'Most Admired Corporations' study between 1984 and 1995. Each year during this time, approximately 4,000 managers rated the Fortune 500 companies in their

Exhibit 1.1. Introduction of the IBM personal computer

When IBM entered the US personal computer market in 1981, it seemed to be courting catastrophe. The original IBM PC offered no exciting technology and almost no proprietary features—most of the system's components came straight off the shelves of outside suppliers. Also, compared with other machines, the PIC looked overpriced. To sell it IBM also needed to use retail channels that viewed Big Blue as a threatening stranger. Apple Computer, the market leader at the time, was so far from being frightened that it ran cocky advertisements welcoming IBM to the world of personal computing.

However, by 1983 the IBM PC had become a smash hit, outselling Apple's computers, raking in nearly $2 billion in revenue for IBM, and entrenching itself as the industry standard. By launching a 'plain vanilla' machine, IBM made it easy for outsiders to design hardware and software to work with the PC. Thousands of companies did this, which vastly enhanced the IBM PC's value to users.

But the biggest reason for IBM's early success was its name. Decades of superior service had convinced business buyers, who were wary of personal computers and the upstart companies that made them, that IBM was the safe choice. They knew that if the machines failed to perform as advertised, IBM would stand behind them. Thus Apple and others ruefully discovered what mainframe computer companies had known all along: IBM often wins because of the 'FUD' factor—the fear, uncertainty and doubt that assail corporate customers when they think of buying any computer gear that isn't blue. As those customers had been saying for nearly a quarter of a century: 'Nobody ever got fired for buying IBM'.

In fact, many people who bought IBM PCs from a retailer later complained that they couldn't get good service and support because IBM had shuffled off those burdens on to dealers who sold the machines. Thus IBM started to use up the equity in a very important part of its corporate reputation. But by this time, the 'damage' had been done—IBM's sales were booming.

Source: Derived from W. H. Davidow and B. Uttal, *Total Customer Service: The Ultimate Weapon* (New York: Harper & Row, 1989). See also R. Cringely, *Accidental Empires* (Reading, MA: Addison-Wesley, 1992).

economic sector. These data were then matched with financial data. Our study involved testing the relationship between a firm's reputation being rated as above or below average in a particular year and the firm's movement (if any) between above- and below-average ROA. We found support for the following two relationships:

Exhibit 1.2. What's the value of a name?

In 1983 Toyota and General Motors formed a joint venture known as the New United Motor Manufacturing Inc. Since 1989 this joint venture has made two almost identical cars on the same production line—the Toyota Corolla and GM's Geo Prizm. The Toyota-badged car sold in 1989 for just over $9,000, or 10 per cent more than its twin. The Corolla then depreciated more slowly than the Geo Prizm, so that its second-hand value was almost 18 per cent higher than that of the American model after five years. Why the difference in price?

The answer is the stronger Toyota brand name. That is, buyers trusted Toyota more than GM. They thought that the same car from Toyota would be of better quality than one from GM. After purchase, the good service from the Toyota dealers sustained and amplified the Japanese car's initial edge.

The effect of brand and reputation strength on sales and profits was dramatic. For example during the years 1990–4 the two cars cost the same to produce—$10,300. Toyota sales were approximately 200,000, priced to dealers at $11,100 each. GM sold only 80,000 to its dealers at $10,700. The result was that Toyota made $128 million more than GM in operating profits from the joint venture on the same car—and its dealers made $107 million more than GM's dealers.

Source: Based on 'What's in a name?', *The Economist* (6 Jan. 1996), 65.

(1) Good corporate reputations increase the length of time that firms spend earning superior financial returns (a carry-over effect).

(2) Good corporate reputations may reduce the length of time that firms spend earning below-average financial returns (a lead-indicator effect).

The practical significance of these results for Fortune 500 firms is important. It *pays* to invest in building a better corporate reputation. Research reported in the corporate strategy literature also supports the contention that a good corporate reputation can lead to a firm's achieving higher profits than other industry participants. The mechanisms by which this occurs are: inhibiting the mobility of rival firms, acting as a barrier to entry into markets, issuing signals to consumers about the quality of the firm's products and possibly enabling the firm to charge higher prices (as illustrated in Exhibit 1.1), attracting better job applicants, enhancing access to capital markets, and attracting investors.[4] These are a potent set of strategic benefits which may be derived from a good reputation.

Common sense, business case studies, and scientific research all suggest that there is both operational and financial value in a good reputation. Given this, it is time to focus on the main aim of this book, namely, to provide a framework to help proactively enhance the reputations stake-holders hold of an organization. The first step on this journey is a short trip into the history of advertising to discover the power of what became known as 'brand image' and is now referred to as 'brand attitude'. This topic is important because people also create images and attitudes of organizations. And what is more important is that images are different from reputations. The acceptance of this idea is one of the keys to success-ful reputation enhancement.

WHAT ARE BRAND AND CORPORATE IMAGES?

David Ogilvy, one of the founding fathers of modern advertising, hit upon the idea that consumers do not buy products, rather they buy products with a personality, namely 'brands'.[5] What he did was to use advertising to give products a 'personality'. This 'brand image', as it became known, was designed to fit the 'self-image' of the target consumer.[6] David Ogilvy's suc-cessful brands were those where there was a tight fit between the brand image and the target consumer's desired self-image.

Ogilvy's idea that brands can have a personality or image reflects the fact that people buy many products and services not only for what such products or services can do, but also for what they mean to the person and his or her reference group. In marketing terminology, products and ser-vices offer the user both functional and psychological benefits. For ex-ample, some middle-aged men are thought to buy sports cars to provide transportation, and to reflect a desired self-image of youth and virility—'the young at heart'. Many clothing styles are bought as visual signals to identify the wearer with a particular reference group, or to reflect the wearer's mood and emotions. Products given symbolic meaning help consumers choose among functionally similar offerings. Some advertisers are legendary in their ability to create brand images in their advertising which tap into people's desired lifestyle and self-image (e.g., the Marlboro cowboy).

The notion of brand image is easily generalized to companies and other types of organizations. One of the earliest demonstrations of this outside the field of advertising was by Pierre Martineau, who, while doing research for the *Chicago Tribune* newspaper in the late 1950s, discovered that cer-tain types of customers felt uncomfortable in particular retail stores.[7] What Martineau had stumbled across was the fact that sometimes the image of a retailer was not compatible with the perceived social status (or self-image) of the shopper. Since this time there has been much research on the impact of retailers' images on the patronage habits of consumers.[8]

If shoppers can form a distinct image of a retail store, then they can (and do) form images of other types of organizations like schools, hospitals, advertising agencies, and companies. People also form images of countries. Often when the overall image of a country is favourable (e.g., Switzerland) marketers rent the image by using the words 'made in (country)' on their products or in their advertising. In the 1950s, the label 'made in Japan' signalled inferior quality relative to products made in Western Europe, the United Kingdom, and the United States. In the 1990s, however, the image of Japan was an asset rather than a liability for products such as cameras, cars, consumer electronics, and watches. Such country-of-origin effects can have an important influence on corporate images, as we will see in Chapter 9.

The key idea here is that images of things (countries, industries, companies, and brands) reside in the heads of people—they are not a fixed attribute of an organization. The reason for this is that we all have different information about, and sometimes different experiences with, these things. It is for this simple reason that an organization does not have a single image—it has *many images*. Henceforth, I will use the plural images—and later reputations—to remind us that different people hold different images of the same organization.

To proceed, we now need a set of working definitions of corporate identity, corporate image, and corporate reputation.

WORKING DEFINITIONS

Consultants, managers, and many academics use the terms corporate identity, corporate image, and corporate reputation interchangeably. It is important, however, to make a distinction between these three concepts. One of the most common mistakes that managers make is to change their organization's identity symbols (and nothing else) in the hope that this will automatically improve the images and/or reputations people hold. Such an outcome seldom happens. The definitions given in Exhibit 1.3 and the relationships between them, illustrated in Figure 1.1, suggest why.

These working definitions differ somewhat from the more formal definitions found in some recent academic papers. However, they reflect the traditional origins of these concepts and they are all that is needed for this

Exhibit 1.3. Working definitions

Corporate identity: the symbols and nomenclature an organization uses to identify itself to people (such as the corporate name, logo, advertising slogan, livery, etc.).

Corporate image: the global evaluation (comprised of a set of beliefs and feelings) a person has about an organization.

Corporate reputation: the attributed values (such as authenticity, honesty, responsibility, and integrity) evoked from the person's corporate image.

Corporate super-brand: the trust, confidence, and support that flow from the person's corporate reputation.

book.[9] In short, corporate identity helps people find or recognize a company. This is extremely important when 'high-street visibility' (to use the UK expression) is necessary. Corporate image is a set of beliefs and feelings about an organization.

Corporate reputation is a value-based construct. In effect, the individual's corporate image is compared to his or her free-standing values about appropriate behaviour for this type of organization. Values are enduring beliefs that a specific mode of conduct or end-state of existence is personally or socially preferable to some other conduct or end-state.[10] In the context of corporate behaviour, values such as accomplishment, authenticity, integrity, honesty, responsibility, and stewardship (of the environment, employees, the economy, etc.) are relevant. These are long-term concerns (i.e., they have a low discount rate for most people). Other values such as enjoyment and excitement (associated with, say, a corporate sponsorship) tend to be of shorter-term relevance.

In the Chinese culture, reputation is similar to the concept of face—of which there are two types: *lien* and *mien-tsu*. *Lien* represents the confidence of society in the integrity of the organization's (or person's) moral character, the loss of which makes it impossible to function properly within the community. *Mien-tsu* refers to the kind of prestige that is gained by getting on in life through success and ostentation.[11] This in turn is similar to the Western concepts of respect, esteem, and status.[12] As we will see when we focus on measuring corporate reputations in Chapter 10, it is the shared values of the company by its stakeholders that drive the trust, confidence, and support an organization can expect from the reputation held by a person. High levels of these factors define a powerful corporate brand—hereafter called a super-brand.

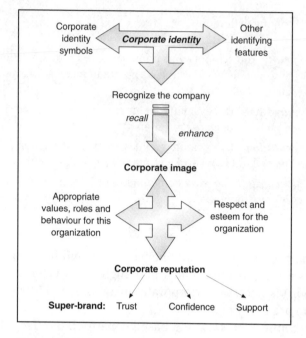

Figure 1.1. Corporate identity, image, and reputation

To see how the three concepts of identity, image, and reputation are interrelated consider Figure 1.1.

The top portion of Figure 1.1 shows that a good corporate identity can have two possible effects on corporate image. First, people can make the correct association between the company and its identity symbols—'Ah, yes, that's the golden arches of McDonald's'. Then hopefully these identity symbols help people recall their image of the company—which may include a mental picture (of a McDonald's outlet) and/or sensory feelings about it (we had a good time there when we last visited). However, much of this image may be the result of rote learning. For example, through years of advertising and widespread availability, most people now recognize McDonald's and associate it with fast food and a family restaurant atmosphere. Some corporate identity symbols may also automatically enhance the organization's image. For example, the bull symbol used by Merrill Lynch, which signifies a rising (or bull) stock market, may help (potential) investors associate positive feelings with this investment (brokerage) company.

The definition of corporate image above suggests that this construct has two components: a 'logical' (cognitive belief) component and an emotional (feeling) component. Both of these are necessary and both are usually experienced simultaneously in the person's mind. They fit together to form an overall corporate image. The role of the emotional component is to energize the individual to respond to the company—such as a customer buying a product or an employee working harder. Beliefs without emotions are not effective—someone or something else has to stimulate action. Likewise, emotions without beliefs may excite you, but leave you not knowing which company is 'logically' best.

If some beliefs and feelings about a company (i.e., its image) fit with a person's values about the appropriate corporate behaviour, then the individual will form a good reputation of that company. This applies for both internal stakeholders (e.g., employees) and external stakeholders (e.g., customers). In effect, a good corporate reputation represents a tight 'fit' between the image of the company and the individual's free-standing value system. To illustrate this notion of fit, consider the case of the Wal-Mart discount department store. Sam Walton, the founder of Wal-Mart, made his company one of America's most respected by giving rural Americans, people of modest means, more choice and quality for less cost than ever before. Did customers value this?—*Yes*. Were employees proud to deliver this service?—*Yes*. Did the community value it?—*Yes*. Is Wal-Mart successful and does it have a good reputation?—*Yes* (except among many of the local merchants that were forced out of business by its success).

Another good example of how people's values influence their corporate reputations and their behaviour is the positioning of Body Shop cosmetics. Anita Roddick has firmly positioned Body Shop to appeal to employees and customers who value taking care of the environment. As CEO she promotes this cause through the corporate philosophy (profits with principle—environmental stewardship, fair trade, community development, and activism), her shops are painted green, products are made from natural ingredients, and they are developed without recourse to animal testing. For many Body Shop customers, these products have a tight fit to their social values. They also stand as a 'protest' against the excesses of the mainstream beauty industry.

Many other companies have made the link between stakeholder values and corporate image. For example, for the Walt Disney company, the core value that its products (films, theme parks, etc.) touch is good, clean, family entertainment. (Its subsidiary Touchstone Pictures handles the adult and R-rated products.) The British retailer Marks and Spencer built its reputation by operating a no-questions-asked product return policy. What a great way to demonstrate, as opposed to talk about, trust. For the Virgin group of companies, the quirky Richard Branson and his well-publicized antics sell a corporate character as the 'challenger brand' in airlines, cola drinks, financial services, and music. For Johnson & Johnson, the company practises the human values codified in its credo—which is outlined in Chapter 4.

It is important to note that values are culture dependent. For example, in Japanese companies like Canon, Kao, and Sharp, being perceived as innovative is an important value for employees and many customers. In the mid-1990s, the giant Japanese advertising agency, Densu, conducted a research study that indicated that many Japanese were shifting their values from 'what to own' to 'how to live'. This transformation was being expressed in six value themes, namely:

- value for money;
- simple innovation (simple to use, manageable technology);
- relevant function (to personal lifestyle);
- clean and natural products;
- spiritual well-being;
- contribution to society.

Advertising agencies and social commentators frequently report on these values and how they evolve from generation to generation.

While some professional readers (academics, consultants, and researchers) may consider that the concepts of corporate image and corporate reputation overlap, it is important to keep them separate. Operationally, the route to a good reputation is through designing a desired image (set of beliefs and feelings) and then linking it to one or more values important to stakeholder groups. While you cannot change a person's values, you can change their perceptions and sometimes the emotional attachment they have to an organization. For example, in the case of America's 'Most admired companies' (Table I.1 in the Introduction), much of their corporate status is driven by operational and financial performance, and the leadership of the CEO. These are the attributes that are valued highly by the managers and company analysts who rate the Fortune 500 companies. In order to achieve a good ranking in this poll, a company must have superior financial performance and an exceptional CEO to trumpet the company's activities. (The CEOs of the top ten companies were: Jack Welch—General Electric; Bill Gates—Microsoft; Michael Dell—Dell Computer; John Chambers—Cisco Systems; David Glass (previously Sam Walton)—Wal-Mart; Herb Kelleher—Southwest Airlines; Warren Buffett—Berkshire Hathaway; Craig Barrett (previously Andy Grove)—Intel; Arthur Blank—Home Depot; Richard

McGinn—Lucent Technologies.) As we will see in the next two chapters, to achieve a high rating from either employees or customers, these companies would need to emphasize other corporate attributes.

Where many corporate reputation enhancement programmes fail is in their lack of understanding of the key emotions that different groups of stakeholders want from an organization, for example, the excitement of investing (with Merrill Lynch, for example). Others fail to make the explicit linkage between image and personal values. In this case, the attributed characteristics of authenticity, honesty, stewardship, and so on, fail to be linked to the organization. When there is a good fit between stakeholder values and the corporate image, the organization's good reputation may become a super-brand. The company is now respected and held in high esteem. This in turn leads to high levels of confidence, trust, and support among stakeholders.

INVESTING IN REPUTATION CAPITAL

The value of a good reputation to a company is a function of the number of times and the number of ways in which it can be used. The greater the number of these situations, the more incentive there is to establish a good reputation. Of particular interest to marketing managers is how corporate reputations might help a company gain and maintain customers. From the consumer's perspective, a good reputation reduces the perceived risk of buying a company's products and services, because the reputation is posted as a performance bond by the company. This will be more important in situations where (a) the consumer is buying the product for the first time, (b) the product is difficult to evaluate after it is consumed and the customer wants psychological assurance that a good job has been performed, such as with dental treatment, and (c) the person buys the company as well as the product because they have to trust that the company is offering a reliable product or service, such as with airlines, financial services, and pharmaceutical products.

The distinction between 'search', 'experience', and 'credence' products and services is also relevant here. Customers can determine the quality of search products prior to purchase, while they can only determine the quality of experience products and services after use. It may never be possible accurately to judge the quality of credence products and services, such as consulting advice. It has been argued that producers of high-quality products can credibly signal such quality through the amount of money spent on advertising. Also, if consumers are more likely to repeat the purchase, producers should be willing to spend more money to attract first-time customers. Producers of low-quality goods should not invest as heavily in advertising because they will not capture the profits from repeat purchases.[13]

These arguments suggest that firms selling experience and credence products and services should invest more than those selling search products in developing their corporate images and reputations. Activities like corporate advertising, publicity, sponsorships, and the use of stand-out corporate identity symbols represent an investment in non-salvageable goodwill.

For target audiences where traditional communication activities are thought to be ineffective ways to enhance the company's desired image, a company needs other strategies to enhance its perceived standing. For example, Philips and Lucent Technologies (the old Bell Laboratories) rented each other's reputations for expertise in design and consumer electronics (Philips) and innovation (Lucent) when they formed a joint venture to make consumer communications products. Participation in and donations to community service programmes are tactics thought to enhance community and government respect for companies.

The use of corporate communication and other activities such as community support programmes to enhance corporate images and reputations leads to the question of cheating. That is, under what conditions are advertising and other signals of reputation likely to be cost-effective ways to misrepresent corporate status?

INCENTIVES TO CHEAT

Cheating in this context refers to a company intentionally signalling a characteristic that would cause another party to incorrectly forecast its behaviour. For example, a professional service firm that falsely advertises that it has international affiliations, or that it has worked for prestigious clients, is misrepresenting its standing, usually in the hope of attracting bigger clients. A more subtle form of cheating occurs when a company is accused of using devices such as sponsorships to enhance its desired corporate images and reputations in the wider community and at the same time it is exploiting other stakeholder groups (e.g., Nike has been accused of exploiting the Asian workers who make its products and, while Shell advertises its concern for the environment, its critics accuse it of environmental degradation in Nigeria).

There is often a fine line between reputational cheating and corporate boasting. It is a personal judgement whether a company that advertises its aspirations as if they are its capabilities has overstepped this line. For example, some years ago when the Ford motor company began using the advertising slogan, 'Quality is Job 1', it was really advertising its aspirations rather than certifying that it could actually deliver Japanese-level quality. A more blatant example was the 1998 television commercial run by Saab in Australia for the launch of its 9-5 model luxury car. These ads made an explicit link between Saab's design and manufacture of military aircraft and the new car. They did not mention that Saab's automotive division had been owned by General Motors since 1990.

A company that tries to mislead people about search products will find this a costly exercise because potential customers will notice any false claims before their purchase decision, and not purchase the product. Also, when customers are frequent users of these products and services, strategies to mislead will be ineffective. They might purchase once, but use of the product/service will inform them of its true worth. There are three circumstances, however, where we would expect companies to try to overclaim their status.

One is often referred to as the end-game situation. That is, when a company is about to leave a market or end a relationship with another company there is an incentive to use up all the goodwill embedded in the corporate reputation. Another circumstance is where there will be only one encounter with the other party, such as a once-only service encounter, or when a company goes public.[14] The third circumstance concerns credence products and services. When customers cannot judge quality and repeat purchase is important, there is an incentive to overstate corporate and/or product quality. This can enhance the psychological value of the product/service, and may also have a dissonance reduction effect.

CONCLUSIONS

This chapter poses a dilemma. On the one hand, good corporate images and reputations are operationally and financially valuable to a company. On the other hand, the actions of many organizations put their corporate reputations at risk. Also, we find relatively few organizations that have formal programmes to protect and enhance the set of reputations held by their internal and external stakeholders. To provide full strategic value, an organization's desired image and reputation needs to be designed to add value to employees' working lives, and to the consumption experience of products and services. This is only possible if the major elements that combine to form the images in the minds of people can be identified. Chapter 2 provides just such a blueprint.

Two crucial points are made in this chapter. The first is that an organization has many images and reputations. Different types of stakeholders will form their own distinct evaluations of an organization. This is an important insight because it suggests that the factors identified in Chapter 2 will differ in their influence on the formation of organizational images and organizational reputations among different groups of people. The second point is that it is essential to be clear about whether it is corporate identity, corporate image, or corporate reputation that is the focus of attention. Corporate identities are relatively easy to change, but their effect on corporate reputations is likely to be limited. Figure 1.1 shows that corporate identities work through corporate image, an issue that is discussed at length in Chapter 8. Corporate images are the focal point for change. Part 2 of this book outlines the factors that drive good images. Good corporate reputations, and thus super-brand status, are the Holy Grail for most organizations. The path to this treasure is achieved by designing a desirable corporate image and then ensuring that it is linked to important stakeholder values.

The gods are well pleased when they see great men and women contending with adversity.

NOTES

1. Institutional investors know that, when floating public assets the Australian government (like other governments) has a policy of slightly undervaluing, and thus underpricing the assets it places on the market. It does so to win voter loyalty and to create a market for other privatizations. Small, private investors do not know about this policy and thus rely on their reputation of the company.
2. T. Devinney and G. Dowling, 'Getting the Piper to Play a Better Tune: Understanding and Resolving Advertiser–Agency Conflicts', *Journal of Business-to-Business Marketing*, 6, 1 (1999), 19–58.
3. See the following papers in the Summer 1997 edition of the journal *Corporate Reputation Review*: P. Roberts and G. Dowling, 'The Value of a Firm's Corporate Reputation', 72–6; L. Gaines-Ross, 'Leveraging Corporate Equity',

51–6; J. Gregory, 'ROI: Calculating Advertising's Impact on Stock Price', 56–60; R. Srivastava, T. McInish, R. Wood, and A. Capraro, 'The Value of Corporate Reputation: Evidence from the Equity Markets', 62–8; D. Deephouse, 'The Effect of Financial and Media Reputations on Performance', 68–72; B. Brown, 'Stock Market Valuation of Reputation for Corporate Social Performance', 76–80; G. McMillan and M. Joshi, 'Sustainable Competitive Advantage and Firm Performance: The Role of Intangible Resources', 81–5.

4. C. Fombrun and M. Shanley, 'What's in a Name? Reputation Building and Corporate Strategy', *Academy of Management Journal*, 33, 2 (1990), 233–58; R. Beatty and J. Ritter, 'Investment Banking, Reputation and the Underpricing of Initial Public Offerings', *Journal of Financial Economics*, 54 (1986), 213–32; J. McGurie, T. Schneeweis, and B. Branch, 'Perceptions of Firm Quality: A Cause or Result of Firm Performance?', *Journal of Management*, 16, 1 (1990), 167–80; B. Brown and S. Perry, 'Removing the Financial Performance Halo from Fortune's Most Admired Companies', *Academy of Management Journal*, 37, 5 (1994), 1347–59.

5. David Ogilvy's book on his approach to advertising is worth reading: D. Ogilvy, *Ogilvy on Advertising* (London: Pan Books, 1983).

6. The term self-image has a long history in psychology. The definition that I favour is pertinent to consumer behaviour, namely, 'our self-image is what we think of ourselves'. In fact, we have two types of self-image: our actual self-image—what we truly think of ourselves, and our ideal self-image—what we would like to be.

7. P. Martineau, 'The Personality of the Retail Store', *Harvard Business Review*, 36 (Jan.–Feb. 1958), 47–55.

8. See various issues of *Journal of Retailing*.

9. For the academic sleuth who reads this note, the advertising, psychology, and corporate strategy literatures sometimes distinguish between corporate identity, corporate image (a mental picture or sensory representation), corporate attitude (what I call here corporate image), corporate reputation, and corporate status (namely, the transfer of reputation that results from an exchange between two parties). Some of the original writings in this area are: S. Kennedy, 'Nurturing Corporate Images', *European Journal of Marketing*, 11, 3 (1977), 120–64; R. Worcester, 'Corporate Image Research', in R. Worcester (ed.), *Consumer Research Handbook* (London: McGraw-Hill, 1972).

10. M. Rokeach, *The Nature of Human Values* (New York: The Free Press, 1973); L. Kahle, *Social Values and Social Change: Adaptation to Life in America* (New York: Praeger, 1983); S. Schwartz and W. Bilsky, 'Toward a Universial Psychological Structure of Human Values', *Journal of Personality and Social Psychology*, 53, 3 (1987), 550–62.

11. H. Hu, 'The Chinese Concepts of Face', *American Anthropologist*, 46 (1944), 45–64.

12. See, for example, J. Podolny and D. Phillips, 'The Dynamics of Organizational Status', *Industrial and Corporate Change*, 5, 2 (1996), 453–71.

13. P. Nelson, 'Information and Consumer Behavior', *Journal of Political Economy*, 78, 2 (1970), 311–29; and 'Advertising as Information', *Journal of Political Economy*, 82, 4 (1974), 729–54.

14. When a company goes public, the short-term incentive to misrepresent is generally offset by the long-term reputational incentive of the investment bank to attract investors for its future offerings.

2

Stakeholders: Each Group Holds a Different Image and Reputation

Chapter 1 emphasized that an organization does not have a single image or reputation—it has many of them. In fact, each person will form a (slightly) different evaluation of an organization! This diversity presents a daunting task only if you try to manage all these separate evaluations. What is needed is a way of clustering people into groups who are likely to hold similar evaluations of the organization, dissimilar from those of other groups. Chapter 1 referred to these people as stakeholders. Here the task is to split these stakeholders into a manageable number of groups. This grouping is based on one of the fundamental organizing principles of modern marketing, namely, market segmentation.

Psychologists have been studying how and why people differ for as long as there have been psychologists. We have different experiences, needs, and wants. These combine to cause us to see things slightly differently from other people around us. A simple piece of research that you can undertake to illustrate this is to talk to some people who have just come from the same event, whether it be a meeting, football match, movie, dinner party, or other interesting 'occasion'. Ask them to give you their personal impressions of what happened at this event, and how they felt about the overall experience. You will not need to talk to many people to discover that there were some quite different meetings, dinner parties, and so on going on!

The problem with so much individual diversity is that it means that there is no single, sensible description of the organization's image and reputation. This in turn, can make it difficult to convince other managers that it is possible to manage and shape these evaluations. What we need is a simple approach to segmenting stakeholders into groups, and understanding the basis for their different impressions of an organization. It turns out that researchers who have been studying differences in consumer behaviour have uncovered the key to this problem.

BENEFITS AND SOLUTIONS TO PROBLEMS

Marketing researchers have known for some time that consumers only ever buy two types of things from any organization. These are:

- benefits; and/or
- solutions to their problems.

That is, customers, and most employees for that matter, tune into the same radio station with the call sign: WII-FM—'What's in it for me?'

This simple assertion is true whether you are selling to (or serving) business organizations or individuals. It is an easily illustrated principle. For example, people do not buy drills and drill bits—they buy the ability to create holes of various diameters. Men and women do not buy cosmetics—they buy self-confidence. Charles Revson, the founder of the Revlon cosmetics company, once made the classic comment that: 'In the factory we make cosmetics; and in the store we sell hope.' He also quickly realized that people are not especially price sensitive when buying hope. Exhibit 2.1 lists a few more examples.

While managers need not worry too much about whether customers are buying benefits or solutions to their problems, their advertising agencies should, because the creative tactics needed to communicate the two situations may well be different.[1] The only fine-tuning we need here is to understand that benefits and solutions to problems can be of the *functional*, *psychological*, and/or *economic* variety. A good example of the relative importance of functional and psychological benefits is illustrated by what is often referred to as the great cola war in the USA.

Pepsi often stated in their advertising that more people preferred the taste of Pepsi to that of Coke. That is, on one of the primary functional benefits of a soft drink, Pepsi was the winner. Yet for years Coke outsold Pepsi all over the world.[2] In the legends surrounding these blind taste tests, it was once claimed (probably by a Pepsi executive) that a senior Coke executive had mistaken a Pepsi for a Coke! What gave Coke the sales edge? The emotional connection to customer values (i.e., the psychological benefit) that their advertising developed over the years. Remember their famous slogan 'It's the real thing'. What a fantastic positioning statement. If Coke was 'the real thing' then Pepsi, or any other cola must be

Exhibit 2.1. What do your customers buy?

Apple, Compaq, and the other PC makers sell personal computers, but Apple's old corporate slogan summed up what customers were really buying, namely, 'The power to be your best'.

Xerox sells photocopiers, but Xerox customers buy office productivity and the ability to communicate with other people.

Banks sell financial products and services, but most (business and individual) customers really want to buy wealth creation, wealth management, and wealth protection.

Management consultants often come into an organization to solve a specific problem, but they often also act as a catalyst for change. From the CEO's viewpoint he or she is often also buying peace of mind: an 'insurance policy' if a poor decision is made, and someone to blame for insisting that changes are necessary.

The National Geographic Society sells its *National Geographic* magazine, and what is the reader buying? Cheap educational travel.

Polaroid sells instant cameras, but young people buy them for entertainment, a professional portrait photographer buys risk avoidance (getting the set-up correct before changing cameras and shooting a reel of film), and a maintenance engineer buys an instant picture record.

inferior. In fact, this statement became so well established in the market that 7-UP used it as a reference point to differentiate their soft drink. They called 7-UP 'The Uncola'.[3]

In consumer and industrial markets, astute managers use the benefits and/or solutions to problems desired by their customers as the basis for segmenting their markets. This is often referred to as 'needs' or 'benefit' or 'value' segmentation. Precision over terminology is not crucial here. What is important is that a person's needs and values will shape the benefits that person wants from an organization, or the problems the organization may help that person to solve. If there is mutual benefit to be gained, then the person and the organization can exchange something of value, for example, money for products and services, or employment for a salary.

Over time the exchanges a person has with an organization will result in the formation of different types of relationship with the organization. For example, a weak transaction-based relationship may be reflected in a bank customer's use of an ATM, while a stronger loyalty relationship may be evident if the person has an investment and/or loan product. Similarly, employees may be loyal to their company and may exhibit this by wearing the corporate logo on their (casual) clothing. In extreme cases some employees, like those of Harley-Davidson and Nike, get tattooed with the corporate logo!

In a broader sense, stakeholder relationships can be characterized into various emotional types. For example, Harley-Davidson is thought of as a best friend by many of its customers and employees (intense, socio-emotional, equal, informal), while McDonald's often feels like a childhood buddy to many people (friendly, fun, and informal). Many Japanese companies have a parental relationship with their employees, while South Korean companies like Samsung are militaristic (rigid, hierarchical).[4] Other common types of relationship are: compartmental friendship, master–slave, partnership, fling, and casual acquaintance.[5]

The type of (desired) relationship a company has with its stakeholders is important because it can have a big impact on the beliefs and feelings (i.e., images) people hold of the organization, and on the fit between these and the free-standing values of the person (and thus their reputation). For example, the biggest ready-to-eat breakfast cereal in Australia is Weet-Bix made by the Sanitarium Health Food Company. The company has a very conservative heritage, and is owned and run by the Seventh-day Adventist Church. Sanitarium has a somewhat righteous parental attitude towards its customers, which is reflected in what is left out of their products, namely, sugar to make Weet-Bix taste good to young people. (It has only 3 per cent sugar, as opposed to 30 per cent in some of the other major cereal brands.) Research shows that when consumers link the Sanitarium name with the brand name Weet-Bix, their perceptions of the company were clearly more positive than of competitors such as the giant Kellogg corporation.[6]

The different functional relationships people have with an organization will also influence the amount and types of information they want about its activities. For example, shareholders and financial analysts are typically interested in indicators of financial and management performance. Other types of information such as that about the sponsorship of a sporting team, and the training and development of staff is of interest only to the extent that the effects of these factors can be linked (however tenuously) to financial performance. On the other hand, employees and customers are typically interested in a broader spectrum of information.

Managers need to understand which groups of stakeholders are important to the organization, what type of relationship they have with it, and how these relationships affect their beliefs and feelings about the organization. Research can also be used to profile the different mix of free-standing values each group holds. An example of such value profiling for different customer groups is provided in the Chevron case history reported at the end of Chapter 7.

GROUPS OF STAKEHOLDERS

Stakeholders are linked to an organization in different ways. They may have different needs that the organization can help fulfil, or the organization may be subject to their surveillance. Some of these linkages will be much more important to operational success than others. In order to define which groups will be most pertinent to an organization, the divisions shown in Figure 2.1 can be a useful starting point.[7]

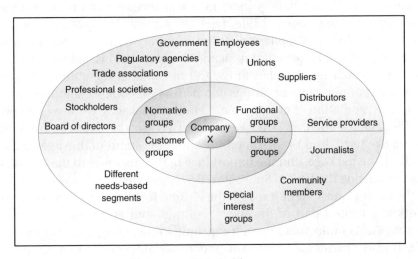

Figure 2.1. Stakeholder groups

Normative groups provide the authority for an organization to function and they set the general rules and regulations by which activities are carried out. They may also provide a report card on performance. Government departments, local councils, regulatory agencies (and laws such as those on trade practices), and consumer and environmental groups may set limits on an organization's scope and conduct of operations. Good examples of two very powerful normative organizations are the international credit rating agencies Standard & Poors and Moody's. The treasury operations of international borrowers, and even governments can be significantly affected by the risk ratings issued by these two organizations. A good example of a normative person is Elaine Prior— bushwalker, mountain climber, and, in 1997, the number one equity analyst of the world's largest diversified resource company, BHP. After one of her profit-downgrade reports, BHP's market capitalization fell by $A1.56 billion![8]

Normative groups also exist within organizations. For example, the activities of the board of directors sanction many of an organization's activities. Other normative groups such as trade and industry associations and professional societies have less direct links with organizations. They do however set normative guidelines for the activities of their members and they disseminate information to employees. For example, many of these groups do an annual salary survey of their members which is often used as an internal benchmark for salary negotiations.

Functional groups directly affect many of the day-to-day activities of an organization. They facilitate operations and serving customers, and they are generally the most visible type of stakeholder group. Examples include: employees, suppliers, distributors, retailers, and service providers such as postal and telecommunications organizations, advertising and market research agencies, law firms, and consultants. Sometimes the good reputation of one of these groups can be used to enhance another organization's reputation. For example, sending packages by a well-known courier service such as DHL, FedEx, or UPS (so the courier companies would like us to think) says something about the status of the organization sending the package, and the importance of the customer to the organization, that using the United States Postal Service does not.

By far the most important of these functional groups is employees. Work is a central part of the social, cultural, and economic life of most people. Paid employment provides income to sustain a person's quality of life. It also provides a significant part of an individual's identity that is important for self-esteem and social confidence.[9] Being 'in work' and doing a particular type of job for a respected organization can be extremely important for many people. Many employers forget the importance of these psychological aspects of work, despite the fact that they can affect the culture of the organization—a topic discussed in Chapter 6.

When employees hold their organization in poor regard, it can poison the atmosphere at work and demoralize staff at the point of service delivery. When they hold it in high regard, many are prepared to promote their company. Employees' perceptions can have a direct impact on how outsiders perceive an organization. For example, surveys have shown that people who know (and like) someone who works for an organization tend to regard that organization more highly than similar people who do not know anyone working there.

To foster employees promoting their organization some companies sponsor them in sporting events and community activities. For example, under CEO Joseph Wilson, Xerox was one of the first US companies to give employees paid leave to do voluntary work. Another tactic is to get employees to run the organization's customer (loyalty) club. For example, Harley-Davidson employees run the Harley Owners Group (HOG).

Diffused groups are particular types of stakeholders that take an interest in an organization when they are concerned about protecting the rights of other people. Issues which may attract the attention of these groups include: freedom of information, privacy of information, the environment, interests of minority groups, equal employment opportunities, childcare in the workplace, and so on. Generally the most important of these groups is journalists. Their impact on shaping the public agenda and publicizing specific issues is well known. Journalists can become a friend or foe depending on how well the corporate affairs department understands the media, and the skills various people have acquired for dealing with journalists. Organizations are particularly vulnerable in their dealings with the media during a crisis. Poor handling of journalists can result in an incident developing into a crisis and the degradation of the images and often the reputations which people hold of the organization. This area is so important that Chapter 12 is devoted to it.

Customers are an extremely important set of stakeholder groups. Non-marketers may wonder why customers are not referred to as a single group. A moment's reflection on the discussion in the previous section of this chapter provides the answer. Different types of customers will want different sets of benefits and/or solutions to their problems from an organization. (Recall the Polaroid example in Exhibit 2.1.) This means that to service these needs, the organization will have to offer a tailored marketing mix (product, price, promotion, distribution, service level, etc.) to each different segment of customers. Professional marketers call this strategy 'target marketing'. In the context of corporate reputation management, it means that if you serve distinctly different types of customers, then they are likely to have different images and reputations of the organization.

We have now progressed from the position where everyone holds a different reputation of an organization to being able to classify stakeholders into four broad types. Within each type it is easy to identify particular groups of people whose functional and emotional relationships with the organization may cause them to form different images and/or reputations of it. This is a substantial improvement over much current thinking about corporate reputations. To illustrate this point, recall that the outer circle of Figure 2.1 lists more than 15 different stakeholder groups. In a review of corporate advertising in the USA, it was found that most of the corporate image-building advertising was directed at only two of these groups, namely, the business and financial community, and customers.[10] While corporate advertising may not be the best way to communicate with all the groups in Figure 2.1, it should be applicable to more than just two of them.

In Chapter 3 I outline how different sets of factors combine to create the images held by different stakeholder groups. Before I do this, however, it is instructive to discuss two more important aspects of stakeholder groups. One is the topic of opinion leadership. Within each group some people will act as catalysts in the image-formation process for other people. These are the key people to target to maximize the efficiency and effectiveness of change. The second topic is potential conflict among the needs of different stakeholder groups.

OPINION LEADERS

Within each stakeholder group the question arises as to who really matters with respect to shaping the organization's images. A related question is how these people transmit and evaluate the different types of information they receive about an organization. Answers to these questions can be found in academic research on personal influence. Because theories abound, I will focus on the role of opinion leaders and draw from research in sociology and marketing (most notably advertising and the diffusion of innovations).[11]

The idea that some people can amplify the credibility of information and speed up its diffusion within their communication network is a fascinating one. Because these opinion leaders can boost the effectiveness of both positive and negative information (such as a rumour) it is particularly important that they be identified. Also, it suggests that corporate advertising and publicity will be most effective if organizations explicitly consider the roles of these opinion leaders in their social networks. These roles can be to (a) act as an extra channel of communication for the information, and/or (b) boost the credibility of (new) information. Exhibit 2.2 illustrates how Nestlé tried to use opinion leaders to increase the effectiveness of a corporate advertising campaign.

It is useful to understand that opinion leaders are not 'leaders' as we commonly know them. Leadership in this context is a much more subtle process. In many social networks it will be almost invisible. Often it will occur simply as the result of a person's becoming aware of other people's beliefs, feelings, and behaviour. This is particularly true for many consumer groups. For example, for companies that design and sell fashion clothing, the opinion leaders tend to 'lead' other customers' fashion opin-

Exhibit 2.2. Using opinion leaders

In the early 1990s, the Swiss food company Nestlé conducted a research study which indicated that Americans considered that it made the best chocolate and coffee. They were largely unaware that the company made many more products than these two (e.g., Quik, Carnation, and Contadina pasta). In November 1992 Nestlé USA started an $8 million corporate advertising campaign to reposition the world's largest food company as warm, approachable, and friendly. In 1993, the same ad campaign was rolled out to countries like Australia.

The ad campaign was targeted directly to opinion leaders in the grocery trade, in business, the family grocery decision maker, and key members of the community. It was hoped that these people would like the advertising and generate positive word-of-mouth (WOM) communication and thus support the advertising message. In theory it was a good idea.

My assessment is that the opinion leaders largely ignored the ad campaign. There are two reasons for this conjecture. First, the message that a very large overseas company is warm, approachable, and friendly does not fit most people's beliefs. Second, these are not well-known characteristics of the Swiss. As we will see in Chapters 7 and 9, using advertising to try to counter people's beliefs is unlikely to be effective.

A better strategy would have been to talk to opinion leaders to find out what positive things they believed about: (a) large multinational food companies, (b) Swiss companies, and (c) Nestlé. From this information Nestlé could have selected factors that it could use to promote its corporate and product values—such as attention to detail, quality, and so on. Then it could have used the leaders' beliefs as the basis for the ad campaign targeted at opinion leaders and others. In this way, the ad campaign would have been more likely to support any opinion leader's WOM communications.

ions by talking about fashion and 'being seen' in various garments. In a professional field like advertising, the leading ad agencies influence opinion through their clients' advertising as much as by their own formally stated opinions about good/bad advertising and the awards they receive.

There are some occasions, however, where the influence of opinion leaders may be much more transparent. The leaders (and spokespeople) of lobby groups, political parties, unions, professional societies, and regulatory authorities can at times be quite open and blatant in their opinion forming activities. In these cases it is relatively easy to monitor the position of these groups and their potential impact on the reputations of an organization.

A theory called 'the strength of weak ties' helps with the understanding of the role of opinion leaders in communication networks.[12] The insight of this theory is that while the relationship between the opinion leader and other people is stronger within a particular network than between networks, it is often less important than the relationship between networks. For example, consider an organization's employees as a social system. Co-workers in the same work unit would tend to have stronger relationships with each other (strong ties) and weaker ties with people in different units of the organization. These strong (within-networks) and weak (between-networks) interpersonal relationships play different roles in the way information is diffused throughout a social system. Research indicates that weak ties transmit much of the (informal) new information from one social network to another, while strong ties facilitate the flows of information and influence within a particular group.[13] Hence, opinion leaders can be used to help or inhibit the spread of information from group to group. They can also be used to help influence their group members' beliefs and feelings (i.e., their image of the organization).

Another important question is whether opinion leaders react differently to (mass media) information about an organization than other people. There is some indirect empirical evidence to suggest that they use mass media information in a different way than other people do. My academic research on the adoption and diffusion of innovations suggests that a segment of customers called 'innovative communicators' often play the role of opinion leaders. We have found that these people are more confident than others about evaluating a new product without seeking the social support of other people. They also tend to rely more on mass media sources of information to keep their product knowledge up to date than do other groups of adopters.[14] In short, these innovative communicators are likely to form their image about an organization on the basis of their own personal experience and through various media sources. This positive or negative image will then influence what they say about the organization to other people.

The degree of influence of an opinion leader's WOM communications will depend on a number of factors. One is the strength of ties within and across social groups. That is, how many people opinion leaders contact and how frequently they talk with them. A second factor that can modify the impact of this source of influence is the credibility of the opinion leader, as compared with the credibility of the organization's media communications. Psychologists have demonstrated that in general, WOM communication is more influential than media communication.[15] Also, the personal characteristics and the fact of being the opinion leader in their group will influence the credibility of this person's opinions. For example, physically attractive people are generally more persuasive, as are people with more power and prestige.[16] These factors combine to provide the opinion leader with a certain amount of source credibility.

Another factor that shapes the personal influence an opinion leader has on another person is the strength of the image (beliefs and feelings) and reputation (how well the image fits with their values) they currently hold. Well-formed images are less likely to be changed than weak images. Strong images (and reputations) tend to be based on better information, and sometimes a wider variety of factors, than weak images. For example, employees typically know more about the organization they work for than customers do. Because their base of information and experience is extensive, their overall image will be a composite of many factors. It is therefore more difficult to change this image (or web of information) than one based on fewer or less well-connected pieces of information.

Finally, a recurring question about opinion leaders is how you identify them. Researchers have made some generalizations about this. For example, when compared to 'followers', they (a) have greater exposure to mass media, (b) are more cosmopolitan, (c) display greater social participation, (d) have higher socio-economic status, and (e) are more innovative when the social norms favour change.[17] Exhibit 2.3 describes some of the common research approaches that are used to help identify opinion leaders.

Given the crucial role that opinion leaders may play in shaping other people's images and reputations, it is a good policy to identify who these people are in each stakeholder group. It can then be quite cost effective to monitor what they think and say about an organization. Reputation formation among stakeholder groups resembles the 80–20 rule, namely, that 80 per cent of the talk about an organization will be done by 20 per cent of the stakeholders (in a particular group).

STAKEHOLDER CONFLICT

Whenever an organization has distinct groups of stakeholders who make different demands on management the potential exists for conflict between their demands. While surveys of the American public often show that the primary obligation of US companies should be to employees, top executives see themselves as representatives of three separate constituencies, namely, investors, customers and suppliers, and employees.[18] Also, there are now some strong financial incentives in many public companies

Exhibit 2.3. Identifying opinion leaders

Researchers have tended to use one, or a combination, of the following approaches:

(a) The *sociometric method* asks people to nominate who they turn to for information and advice about particular issues. By asking a group of people in a social network, it is possible to identify the people whose opinion is sought most often (i.e., the ones with the strong ties). Also, by asking people if they seek advice from people in other networks, it is possible to locate opinion leaders who have weak ties to other groups. This method of identifying opinion leaders is quite good for small groups.

(b) The *key-informant method* asks a set of judges (or informed experts) to identify the opinion leaders in a group. The validity of this method rests on the knowledge of the judges about the social characteristics of the group in question.

(c) The *self-designating method* asks individuals in the group to assess whether they see themselves as an opinion leader. An alternative approach is to ask them about the quantity and types of information they share with other people. The validity of either of these approaches may, however, be biased because of the tendency for people to mis-state their influence.

(d) The *observation method* measures opinion leadership by recording information exchanges and influence as it occurs. Such an approach often requires that the observer be a part of the group. If the group is aware of the observer's role then this can bias the group's behaviour.

that suggest that shareholders will become the dominant group over the next few years. The evidence for this prediction comes from the field of financial economics.

Over the last two decades, a small but influential group of researchers has focused on the issue of corporate governance. They have been seeking answers to questions like the following: Whom do managers think they represent? What factors influence managerial incentives? How can the incentives offered to management hurt shareholder value? Why can't shareholders really control managers? What is the effect of management shareholding on stock prices? What happens when executive pay is tied closely to firm performance?[19]

While much more research needs to be done to answer these questions, it seems that two changes to the rules of the Security Commission in the

1990s have made managers more responsive to the interests of their share-holders. One change was the requirement to make full disclosure of exec-utive compensation packages. The other change made it easier than it had been for shareholders to obtain information about the other shareholders of a company. The first change made it easier for shareholders to assess the value added by managers. The second change reduced the costs of staging a proxy fight against managers who were thought to be under-performing. In addition to these two changes, there was a more active takeover market, and there were more active institutional shareholders. The conditions were ripe for focusing the minds of top executives on the needs of shareholders.

When top executive compensation is tied directly to the specific inter-ests of a particular stakeholder group, it should not be a surprise to dis-cover that the balance of power tips towards this group. For example, when the CEO's compensation is based on the financial performance of his or her firm, that person can make millions of dollars each year in cash, stock, and options.[20] Here we see a classic example of the (potential) con-flict induced by people having to juggle 'what is *expected*' of a company, namely, serving all stakeholder groups, versus 'what is *inspected*', namely, bottom-line performance. To offset the potential bias that such large com-pensation packages can induce, other stakeholder groups would do well to consider having top executives evaluated by a more balanced score-card.

An underlying theme in this chapter is the need to achieve harmony among the competing interests of stakeholders. The Singapore govern-ment proclaims that *wa* (or harmony) is one of the country's secret weapons underpinning their country's success. Reputation problems start to emerge when the interests of one group of stakeholders start to domi-nate the rest, as alluded to in the example which introduced Chapter 1, and which is dramatically illustrated in case study 2.1, Air-India. In the 1970s, the most powerful organized labour groups gained such an advan-tage that stakeholder harmony was shattered for many organizations. In the twenty-first century, the financial interests of powerful shareholders have the potential to create similar disharmony for many organizations.

CONCLUSIONS

This chapter identifies the major groups of stakeholders that an organiza-tion should monitor. It describes these without using research to confirm that each group does hold a different reputation of the organization.

Hence, it breaks one of my fundamental rules, namely, that 'the most dangerous place to look at your stakeholders is from behind your desk'. At this stage of our discussion however, using the taxonomy of stakeholder groups presented in Figure 2.1 is an acceptable compromise. Chapter 10 describes various research techniques that can be used to check the number of stakeholder groups to monitor.

While employees and customers are often the two most important stakeholder groups, other stakeholders should not be ignored. Most people form their links with an organization on the basis of how it can help fulfil their needs. It is important to understand these needs because they influence the set of factors that shape the images and reputations of the organization among stakeholders. Other people have links to an organization because their job requires them to monitor its activities (e.g., journalists and regulators). The adversarial nature of many of these relationships requires special care and attention—especially during a crisis, as we will see in Chapter 12.

Managers also need to understand the social dynamics of how people interact with each other and communicate information about an organization. It is crucial to identiy opinion leaders, and it is important to monitor their strong and weak ties. It is also important to understand how to stimulate favourable word-of-mouth (WOM) communication among stakeholders—especially the opinion leaders. Jerry Wilson has written a book on this topic.[21] While it focuses on customers, many of its ideas can be used to shape communications with other groups of stakeholders.

Increasingly, organizations are being confronted with conflicting demands from different stakeholders. To paraphrase Charles Wilson, the president of GM in 1953, it is no longer true that 'what is good for General Motors is good for the United States, and vice versa'. More and more, companies have to explain their value to a wide range of stakeholder groups. They need to communicate the win–win value of a relationship with the organization. This is summarized in the question: 'What resources and support do we need from our stakeholders, and what do we need to give them in return?'

NOTES

1. J. Rossiter and L. Percy, *Advertising Communications & Promotion Management* (New York: McGraw-Hill, 1997), chs. 8 and 9.
2. In fact, in blind taste tests many people if not most, will make errors of identi-

fiction when nominating whether they have just sampled a Coke or a Pepsi. The same outcome is likely when people taste similar alcoholic beverages.

3. 7-UP is a lemonade and the uncola positioning was later changed (in Australia) to 'it's cool to be clear'. This is another (vague) reference to the colour of cola.

4. S. Brull and J. Lim, 'Samsung's $8 billion Gamble on Upscale Chips', *Business Week* (2 June 1997), 18–19.

5. S. Fournier, 'A Consumer-Brand Relationship Perspective on Brand Equity', in S. Sood (ed.), *Brand Equity and the Marketing Mix: Creating Customer Value*, Marketing Science Institute Conference Summary, Report No. 95-111 (Sept. 1995), 13–15.

6. P. McIntyre, 'Sanitarium Against Rivals' Grain', *Australian Financial Review* (6 August 1996), 33.

7. This scheme is a modification of the one presented in: D. ten Berge, *The First 24 Hours* (Oxford: Basil Blackwell, 1988). Another scheme can be found in G. Savage, T. Nix, C. Whitehead, and J. Blair, 'Strategies for Assessing and Managing Organizational Stakeholders', *The Executive*, 5, 2 (1991), 61–75.

8. M. James, 'Intimacy Key to Analyst's Success', *Australian Financial Review* (21 April 1997).

9. J. Dutton, J. Dukerich, and C. Harquail, 'Organizational Images and Member Identification', *Administrative Science Quarterly*, 39, 2 (1994), 239–63.

10. D. Schumann, J. Hathcote, and S. West, 'Corporate Advertising in America: A Review of Published Studies on Use, Measurement, and Effectiveness', *Journal of Advertising*, 20 (Sept. 1991), 35–56.

11. E. M. Rogers, *Diffusion of Innovations* (New York: The Free Press, 1995), chs. 8 and 9.

12. M. S. Granovetter, 'The Strength of Weak Ties', *American Journal of Sociology*, 78 (May 1973), 1360–80.

13. J. J. Brown and P. H. Reingen, 'Social Ties and Word-of-Mouth Referral Behavior', *Journal of Consumer Research*, 14 (Dec. 1987), 350–62.

14. D. F. Midgley and G. R. Dowling, 'A Longitudinal Study of Product Form Innovation Using a Contingent Factor Approach', *Journal of Consumer Research*, 19, 4 (1993), 611–25.

15. W. J. McGuire, 'Attitudes and Attitude Change', in G. Lindzey and E. Aronson (eds.), *The Handbook of Social Psychology*, Vol. II (New York: Random House, 1985), 233–346.

16. D. Aaker and J. Myers, *Advertising Management* (New York: McGraw-Hill, 1987), ch. 11.

17. E. Rogers, *Diffusion of Innovations* (New York: The Free Press, 1995).

18. A poll taken by Yankelovich in 1996 showed that 51 per cent of Americans believed that a company's primary obligation was to its employees while 17 per cent suggested that it was to shareholders (*Wall Street Journal*, 21 May 1996). The views of top executives were reported in G. Donaldson and J. Lorsch, *Decision Making at the Top: The Shaping of Strategic Direction* (New York: Basic Books, 1983).

19. M. Grinblatt and S. Titman, *Financial Markets and Corporate Strategy* (New York: McGraw-Hill, 1998).

20. For example, *Forbes* business magazine (22 May 1995) listed the compensation packages of the USA's top CEOs: Michael Eisner, Walt Disney: $235m.; Stanford Weill, Travelers': $152m.; Tony O'Reilly, H. J. Heinz: $120m.; Stephen Hilbert, Conseco: $89m.; and Bernard Schwartz, L'Oreal: $66m.

21. J. R. Wilson, *Word-of-Mouth Marketing* (New York: John Wiley & Sons, 1991).

2.1

Air-India: War on the Ground: Too Many Stakeholders with Competing Interests

In 1996 Air-India was a company whose major stakeholders were at war with each other. The result was a disgruntled chairman, stressed managers, striking employees, unreliable services, unhappy customers, and a general feeling that the politicians were really to blame for most of the airline's problems. In 1995, the 76-year-old chairman of the board of Air-India, Russi Mody, was quoted as saying that 'even God cannot save Air-India'.

In the 1970s Air-India was the proud national airline of India. It had a 50 per cent market share of India's international air traffic. During the 1980s and early 1990s India experienced a rapid growth in international air travel. However, in the 1980s Air-India's market share was 40 per cent, and by 1995 this had fallen to 20 per cent. These falls in market share were accompanied by a fall in total passenger numbers, a fall in the utilization of the aircraft (the passenger load factor), an increase in costs, a decrease in ticket prices, an increase in late aircraft departures, and a deterioration of the airline's reputation among all groups of stakeholders. New competitors such as British Airways, Cathay Pacific, Lufthansa, SAS, Singapore Airlines, and United Airlines established more reliable air-bridges into India.

Politicians, bureaucrats, senior management, and unions all played a role in the demise of Air-India. For example, past CEOs would not buy new aircraft, with the result that, by 1995, the airline had a very old and unreliable fleet. They also reported profits when in fact the airline was making operational losses. For example, in 1993–4 the royalties from other airlines flying into India, ground handling charges to foreign airlines, interest from investments, and currency exchange rate profits offset the airline's operational losses.

These 'paper profits' helped inflate the demands of employees for higher salaries. Rolling strikes became a frequent occurrence. Because Air-India is closely controlled by the government, and in order to maintain industrial harmony, management and the politicians repeatedly gave in to union demands. For example, senior pilots were paid allowances for the 'extra' hours that junior pilots were flying on their behalf. All this saw total employee costs rise dramatically.

Politics was never far away from Air-India. Despite the dire state of the airline, it started 1995 with a part-time chief executive who spent half his time in his permanent job as joint secretary in the ministry of civil aviation. In the previous ten years Air-India had eight such operational chiefs. Also, while the headquarters of the airline was in Bombay, the chairman of the board sat in Calcutta, and the CEO was located in Delhi—the seat of government. So heavy was the interference of the government that some politicians were known to have tried to get involved in the selection of the air-crew uniforms and the buying of on-board crockery.

Airline analysts suggested that Air-India faced a tough future—privatize or perish. The privatization option had widespread support among airline management and the general public. It had little support, however, within unions and the government. So in 1995, Air-India embarked on two strategies to fix the company. First, it hired the Denmark-based firm of Time Manager International (TMI) to train 10,000 (out of 18,000) employees about the human side of quality. Second, it asked the government to (let it) fund the purchase of 23 new aircraft over the next seven years. (In 1995 it had 26 aircraft in its fleet.)

At the beginning of 1996, Air-India was a company at war with itself. Managers were fighting employees via their unions who knew that strike action would always influence the politicians to force management to accede to their demands. Management morale was also at an all-time low, with many people saying that they were victims of the politicians and the bureaucracy. In 1995, 44 per cent of airline travellers voted Air-India as the worst airline flying out of India—eight times more travellers condemned Air-India than any other airline! The only stakeholders who were enjoying the demise of Air-India were the journalists. The airline could always be relied on to produce a story.

A FAILED RESURRECTION STRATEGY

Given the above situation, what did Air-India do? In short, just about everything wrong! Their overall strategy was to try to increase both passenger numbers and market share. This strategy was implemented by:

- A new advertising campaign stressing the three factors of which passengers were most critical, namely, performance, convenience of schedules, and on-board amenities. (However, little was done to actually improve these!)
- Price discounting on most routes.
- Introducing a 'Win the World' lottery game for people buying airline tickets.
- Boosting their frequent-flyer scheme.
- Closing half their offices.

Let us examine some of the effects of each of these tactics on Air-India's corporate reputation—in reverse order:

- Closing half of the airline's offices reconfirmed that Air-India was in severe financial difficulty. It also made it harder for travellers to use the airline. Not much positive impact on Air-India's corporate image and reputation here.
- Frequent-flyer schemes offer a set of golden handcuffs to customers. The rewards are travel upgrades, free flights, and so on. However, there are many conditions placed on claiming the rewards, and surveys indicate that members often become frustrated with the airlines when trying to claim a reward. Frequent-flyer schemes can therefore be a two-edged sword for a company's image—people feel good about the airline when they join but frustrated when they make a claim.
- A good signal that the quality and value to customers of a company's product and service is weak is the offering of some form of gambling incentive to customers to entice them to buy. Gamblers may respond to such an offer, but the 'thinking' customer (often the business frequent-flyer) knows that this is a sign of desperation. Again this was not a strategy to enhance Air-India's desired corporate image.
- A widespread strategy of price discounting can help reposition a company at the cheap end of the market. In the United States, this market positioning has been successfully exploited by Southwest Airlines. My personal discussions with the top management team of Air-India, however, suggested that this was not the desired long-term position for the airline. Hence, their new advertising campaign.
- Air-India's customer feedback, which I confirmed with my own flying experience, clearly demonstrated that the airline was below world standards in terms of customer performance. Running an advertising campaign to suggest otherwise *before* service had actually improved was a flawed strategy. The reason for this is that people who see the advertisements and experience poor service lose confidence and trust in the airline's communications. They will then start to argue against all the airline's external communications. One of the constant themes of this book is that you fix problems inside the organization before you advertise to employees and customers that you have improved.

POSTSCRIPT

The net result of Air-India's new strategy was more operational losses, no improvement in corporate image and/or reputation, and, at his third attempt, Russi Mody, the chairman, finally had his resignation accepted by the government. If we move the clock forward to 1999, we find that Air-India was still thinking about buying new aircraft, over-manning was still prevalent, and the interference of politicians in operational matters continued. While the Indian government tries to make up its mind whether or not to privatize the airline, high levels of protection keep the airline aloft.

NOTES

This case study is based on the following sources: N. Radhakrishnan and S. Verma, 'Can Air-India be Saved?', *Business India* (18–31 Dec. 1995), 62–73; M. Maqbool and A. Khan, 'Air-India Shifting to Prayer from Jokes', *Ad Age International* (Nov. 1996), I4; personal conversations with the directors of Air-India (Bombay: Jan. 1996); and J. Elliott, 'Passage to India? No, Thanks', *Fortune* (1 March 1999), 30–1.

3

How Corporate Images Are Formed: Identifying the Pieces of the Jigsaw Puzzle

Chapter 2 left us with the problem that different stakeholders form different corporate images and reputations. The Air-India case study illustrated what happens when the harmony among some of these stakeholder groups is broken. Fortunately, such severe conflict is rare. What this discussion suggests is that different sets of factors will drive the images that each group forms.[1] The aim of this chapter is to identify these factors.

I first identify the set of factors that influence the images held by most stakeholder groups. When integrated into a loose causal network, they form the map for Part 2 of the book (viz., Figure 3.1). With this as our overall framework, we can see how managers need to focus on different sets of factors when considering how to change the desired images held by the different stakeholder groups.

As a way to organize the following discussion, I start by focusing on the question of how to improve an organization's desired corporate image. The definition of corporate image in Chapter 1 states that this is the set of beliefs and feelings you want stakeholders to evoke when they think about your organization. For example, in the USA many companies adopt the attributes used in *Fortune* magazine's poll of 'America's Most Admired Companies' as the key super-brand attributes of their desired corporate image, namely:

- quality management;
- quality products;
- the development and retention of key people;
- financial soundness;
- efficient use of corporate assets;

- long-term investment value;
- innovativeness;
- community and environmental responsibility.

In Asia, many companies adopt the attributes used by the *Far Eastern Economic Review*'s *Review 200* in its poll of respected companies, namely:

- quality products and services;
- management with a long-term vision;
- innovative responses to customer needs;
- financial soundness;
- being a company that others try to emulate.

While these sets of attributes are a useful way to *begin* to think about an organization's desired corporate image, a moment's reflection suggests that they are really the minimum conditions that most companies need in order to be successful in the modern business environment. Also, they ignore one crucial aspect of corporate image, namely, how the company is positioned relative to its competitors. We return to this issue in Chapter 10, when we focus on measuring corporate images and corporate reputations.

IMPROVING CORPORATE IMAGES

The first step in improving a company's images is to profile the images people currently hold of the organization. Often there is no common understanding and agreement among managers and employees about:

(a) what beliefs and emotions different groups use to describe the organization; and
(b) how an ideal organization in the industry is characterized by each stakeholder group.

One of the key questions that research can answer is whether the organization has an awareness problem or an image problem. For example, when customers, potential employees, and other people think about your industry do they recall your company name? Do they recognize your organization's identity symbols (e.g., logo, corporate colours, etc.)? Can they recall (seeing) your advertising? Do they confuse your organization with another organization? Can they answer the questions posed in the McGraw-Hill advertisement reproduced in Exhibit P.1 in the Preface to this book?

Negative answers to any of these questions signal an awareness problem. This may be a deliberate strategy if the company has decided to keep a low profile. For example, the cigarette company Philip Morris is happy that most food buyers do not know that Kraft and General Foods are divisions of the world's largest manufacturer and seller of tobacco products.

However, many companies that keep a low corporate profile pay a price. For example, if a consumer needs to trust the company that manufactures a product, such as a pharmaceutical product, which must comply with purity standards, the risk that a consumer perceives when buying the product will be reduced if the image of the manufacturer (e.g., Johnson & Johnson) held by the consumer is good.

A low corporate profile can also make staff recruitment more difficult. For example, the giant US packaged goods manufacturer Procter & Gamble has a policy of promoting its brands rather than the company. While brands such as Pert, Pringles, Pantene, Pampers, Tide, Folgers, Oil of Ulan, and Crest have been very successful with consumers, outside the United States P&G has not found it as easy to recruit top managers as many other high-profile leaders that use the corporate name as part of the brand name. For example, the company's late entry into the Australian market (1985), and its lack of corporate advertising (in the business press) meant that P&G was, and still is, largely unknown among many potential employees.

The second step in improving corporate images is to identify the major factors that combine to influence how people perceive an organization. In essence, these image drivers are the set of activities that influence every aspect of how a typical organization communicates with both its internal and external stakeholders. Having identified these factors, it is possible to specify how they interact with each other to form the overall image a person holds of the organization. Figure 3.1 is a diagram of this overall process.

Figure 3.1 shows the main factors (or sources of information) that employees and external groups typically use to form their images of organizations. This diagram provides critical insight into the management of corporate images because it shows both the logic and the complexity of the image formation process. For example, research on employee behaviour suggests that a strong determinant of how employees behave—both inside and outside their organizations—is driven by whether or not they believe that the images of their organization held by outsiders are favourable.[2] When they believe that outsiders see their organization in a positive light, they bask in its glory. This in turn can translate into greater self-confidence, co-operation, and citizenship behaviours. This relationship is depicted by the dashed feedback arrow in Figure 3.1.

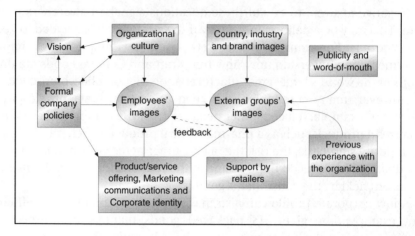

Figure 3.1. Creating corporate images

Figure 3.1 also suggests a number of managerial guidelines. For example, it is unlikely that simply changing the organization's corporate identity symbols will have a major impact on the images held by employees or external groups. To achieve significant change in the way people think about an organization usually requires changes to some very basic organizational activities, such as the work practices of front-line employees, product/service quality, the organization's culture, et cetera. Quick-fix solutions like changing the corporate slogan or introducing a customer loyalty programme are seldom effective by themselves. If other things an organization does are not integrated to achieve a particular desired image, then external stakeholders will become cynical. Figure 3.2 illustrates how the German sports car manufacturer Porsche integrates the three major internal factors in Figure 3.1 to achieve its desired image, and a (substantial) price premium for its cars.

Chapters 4 to 9 of this book elaborate the major elements of Figure 3.1. By examining each factor individually, it is possible to avoid being overwhelmed by the complexity of the overall image management process. It is also possible to identify the specific factors that are responsible for the strengths and weaknesses in an organization's current images. The strengths can be used to gain more leverage for marketing and public relations activities, while the weak areas can be isolated for immediate attention. This type of analysis can lead to some quick improvements. For example, most organizations have one or more practices which routinely upset their stakeholders. Exhibit 3.1 lists some of these. Once identified, they can be easily changed.

Having identified the major factors that people use to form images of organizations, we can now focus on how the base model presented in Figure 3.1 needs to be modified in order to reflect the different relationships that different stakeholders typically have with an organization. To illustrate this, let us focus on three important groups, namely, employees, customers, and company analysts.

FORMING EMPLOYEE'S CORPORATE IMAGES

Figure 3.3 outlines the set of factors that influence the formation of employees' images of their organization. The shading, darker lettering, and heavier arrows are used to indicate the more significant factors. Three new factors have been added to Figure 3.3 that are not in Figure 3.1. These are CEO leadership, Professional values, and Competitors' activities. Each of the major image drivers is now briefly discussed.

The upper left portion of Figure 3.3 suggests that CEO leadership is an important determinant of Vision, Formal policies, and Organizational culture. During the turnaround years of Chrysler, Lee Iacocca was a high-profile leader who embedded his vision into the company's formal policies. During the 1980s, Lee Iacocca, Victor Kiam of Remington, and Dave Thomas of Wendy's starred in their company's television advertising in an

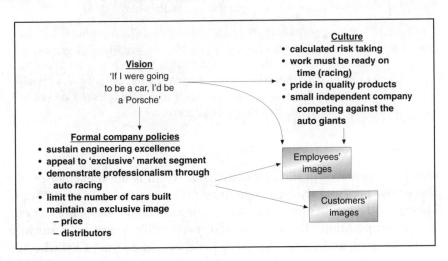

Figure 3.2. Porsche

Source: Derived from P. Schultz and J. Cook, 'Porsche on Nichemanship', *Harvard Business Review* (March 1986), 98–106.

Exhibit 3.1. How to upset people

Many organizations have a number of annoying practices that routinely upset people. Here are some classics:

(1) Use your lawyers to talk to your most valued customers. For example, the frequent-flyer application forms from the two Australian airlines Ansett and Qantas contain some very heavy-handed terms and conditions (one being that the airline can terminate the customer loyalty scheme at any time). Is this a good way to start a relationship with the people who will most frequently support the airline? Does it begin to build trust?

(2) In their search to attract new staff and customers, many organizations offer the new recruits a better deal than existing employees and customers. The rationale they give is that 'the market' has changed. If so, why isn't everyone offered the new deal? It seldom happens.

(3) During holiday periods, some companies put up the price of their products (e.g., petrol companies in Australia).

(4) McDonald's strategy of opening more and more restaurants in the USA to achieve sales growth has made many existing restaurants less profitable for their existing franchisees. This strategy has created some angry franchisees and generated some negative publicity (see *Business Week*, 2 June 1997, 30–2).

(5) During the 1990s the Italian clothing company Benetton used a very dramatic advertising campaign featuring socially controversial issues, which upset many of its customers and retailers in the USA.

The point about practices of this type is that people lose confidence in an organization when they think that it, or its employees, are wasteful, greedy, or stupid, or when they think that it discriminates between similar types of people, has power over them, or does not trust them. The only way for an organization to identify these practices is for it to periodically ask its stakeholders what the organization is doing that annoys them.

attempt to personalize the company. Jack Welsh is another high-profile CEO whose personal style and operating philosophy (simplicity, self-confidence, and speed) drives the top management of the giant General Electric corporation. During the first twenty-five years of Southwest Airlines' growth and prosperity, Herb Kelleher was another CEO who significantly influenced the airline's vision, culture, and the images held by employees. In fact, in 1998 Southwest Airlines was voted by its employees as the best company to work for in America.[3]

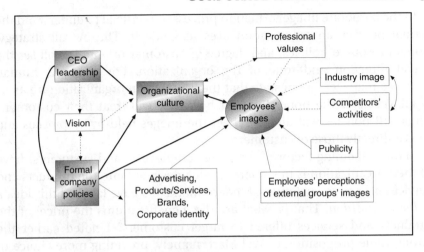

Figure 3.3. Factors affecting employees' corporate images

Promoting the CEO as a major attribute of the organization may, however, be a high-risk strategy, especially at the time of succession to the leadership. The problems that may arise are illustrated by what occurred when, in 1983, John Sculley from PepsiCo took over the Apple Computer company from its co-founder Steve Jobs. Sculley's corporate personality was so different from that of the sometimes exasperatingly eccentric Steve Jobs, that it was not long before Jobs left the company he had once dominated. In 1997, long after Sculley's departure, a more chastened Jobs returned to guide Apple's future. A year later, he had refocused the company back to the core image attributes that made Apple into an early PC super-brand, namely, design brilliance. The new corporate slogan, 'Think Different', was designed to reflect this new/old image.

To avoid the problem of the CEO's style and values dominating the organization, many organizations create a Vision Statement (or Mission or Credo) which is independent of any individual. This set of values is to act as a more objective touchstone than the sometimes erratic beliefs of a high-profile CEO. For example, the exuberant personality of Richard Branson has to date defined the Virgin brand. However, he and his colleagues are establishing a set of 'super-brand values' (namely, quality, innovation, value for money, and fun) in an attempt to distinguish the company's strengths from those of its CEO. At Hewlett-Packard, the company's corporate values are expressed in a document called 'the HP way'. Chapter 4 reviews the role of these statements in helping to form an organization's internal and external corporate images.

In the corporate image formation process, it is crucial to understand the formal policies an organization uses to guide it. The overall strategy, human resource policies, and degree of customer orientation all set the broad direction and tone of the organization. For example, human resource managers often state that the way that an organization treats its employees sets the upper limit for how they will treat their customers. Thus, HR policies will directly affect the images held by employees and thus indirectly those of customers.

Another defining factor of the image employees (and customers) have of their organization is the inherent value designed into the products and services offered to customers. Modern marketers have labelled this idea a *value proposition*. That is, what are the 'benefits minus the price' of the products and services offered to target customers? I noted earlier the strong value proposition of Wal-Mart, namely, providing more choice of quality, branded merchandise, at less cost. The Southwest Airlines value proposition is built around short-haul discount air travel delivered with 'a sense of warmth, friendliness, individual pride and Company Spirit' (words in the Mission Statement) that has opened up the skies to millions of people who otherwise could not have considered flying. It is not surprising that employees of Wal-Mart and Southwest Airlines feel good about offering great customer value.

Research in sociology has shown that the values and ethical principles that people develop during their professional training can have a significant impact on their workplace attitudes and behaviour. Also, professional affiliations often provide people with enhanced authority in organizations; for example, accountants, and in particular the in-house auditor and corporate lawyer, seem to be members of a special 'ruling class'. This professional authority, and the codes of behaviour sanctioned by various professions, can be particularly strong for groups such as accountants, engineers, in-house advertising, market researchers, health workers, and lawyers.[4] Their professional values can affect the overall organizational culture and their image of the organization. It has been suggested that identification with the company is a distinguishing characteristic of the Japanese, as opposed to many employees of Australian, European, and US organizations, who often identify more with their job, profession, or union.

Another factor that can affect employees' perceptions of their organization and the industry in which they work is the actions of competitors. For example, when the oil tanker *Exxon Valdez* ran aground in Alaska and created one of the biggest environmental disasters of our time, every oil company's image and reputation probably suffered. In a similar way, every airplane crash degrades the images and reputations of the airline industry. Management of the overall image of an industry is often delegated to an industry association which only gets to speak on behalf of its members during a crisis or when the government is threatening more regulation. It is the actions of individual organizations, however, which are likely to be a more powerful determinant of industry image than statements from the industry's mouthpiece.

FORMING CUSTOMER'S CORPORATE IMAGES

Figure 3.4 outlines the major factors that influence the formation of images held by customers. In short, what customers think and feel about an organization is driven primarily by the relative perceived value of its product and services. Offer better value and your image and reputation will improve (because good value is a widely held personal value). The new factors that appear in this model, and not yet discussed, are Service quality (which, given the previous discussion, also includes images held by employees), Brand and retailer image, and Advertising. All of these factors can add to the perceived value of your offer to customers.

There is now a considerable amount of research that shows that service quality leads to satisfied customers, and satisfied customers think more highly of the organization that provided the quality service.[5] As the organization's image improves, we also find that it is easier to create satisfied

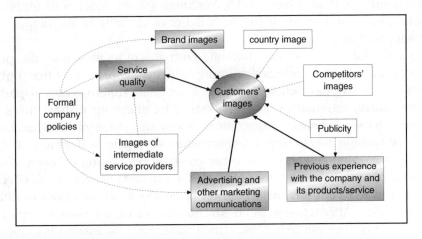

Figure 3.4. Factors affecting customers' corporate images

customers. That is, a positive feedback effect operates whereby people expect good service from an organization with a good image, and if they cannot judge whether the service is good or bad (e.g., a visit to a dentist, doctor, lawyer, accountant) they will tend to think that it is good, if for no other reason than to confirm their own expectations. For example, one US study found that firms which had developed an image based on high perceived quality had fewer dissatisfied customers, and that these customers were more likely to provide positive word-of-mouth recommendations about the firm.[6]

The final factors to discuss in Figure 3.4 are the marketing tools of advertising, brand image, and the selection of retailers. While Chapter 7 provides an extensive discussion of advertising (both corporate and brand), it is worth mentioning here that much corporate advertising is not a very cost-effective way to improve the organization's desired image. The reason for this is that many corporate advertisements focus on the organization's aspirations rather than its deeds. Such aspirational advertising is often appreciated by employees but ignored by customers. The corporate advertising that seems to work best is that which directly supports the value proposition of the products and services offered to customers.

For many companies, advertising is the primary device used to build the image of a brand. In the cases of Procter & Gamble and Philip Morris, mentioned earlier in this chapter, there is no direct connection between their brands and the parent company. Other companies, especially in industrial (or business-to-business) markets, are known by the brands they make. Or in the case of retailers, 'the brands they keep' in stock. As we will see in Chapter 9, when a company owns a very powerful (or icon) brand such as Post-It Notes (3M), Walkman (Sony), Macintosh (Apple), Coke, Levi's, and so on, it can be a defining attribute of the corporate images held by customers.

Many studies have shown that different types of retailers have distinct images in customers' minds. For example, many people expect that 'duty free' stores will have cheaper prices. Boutiques, supermarkets, department stores, warehouses, and 'markets' all conjure up distinct images which shape customers' expectations about the range of merchandise offered and the overall price level. Sometimes a retailer will try to shift its image from one category to another category by altering its name. For example, a furniture store that calls itself a 'furniture warehouse' is effectively trying to rent the image of lower price which people associate with warehouses. Alternatively, when McDonald's call their outlets (family) 'restaurants' they are trying to upgrade their image by associating themselves with restaurants rather than other fast-food outlets.

Research indicates that when a brand or corporate image is linked with a retailer image, then an averaging process occurs in consumers' minds. For example, if the Apple Computer company sells its PCs through the ComputerLand chain of stores, then some of Apple's reputation will 'rub off' on to ComputerLand's image and vise versa. ComputerLand gains a little prestige and Apple loses a little prestige (assuming that Apple starts off with a better image than ComputerLand). A more formal explanation of this phenomenon is provided in Chapter 9.

FORMING CORPORATE ANALYSTS' CORPORATE IMAGES

Financial markets theory suggests that the value of a company is driven by a combination of realized value and market expectations. CEOs often feel that the public perceptions of both these factors are driven by a small group of market analysts and institutional shareholders. In Chapter 2 Elaine Prior was identified as such a market opinion leader for the resources company BHP. So were the credit rating agencies of Standard & Poors and Moody's. Market analysts are generally well trained and subscribe to one of the various theories of corporate valuation taught in business schools around the world. Hence, knowledge of these theories can provide an understanding of the types of information they use to form their image and valuation of a company.[7] Figure 3.5 identifies some of the factors that seem to drive the corporate images held by this group of stakeholders.

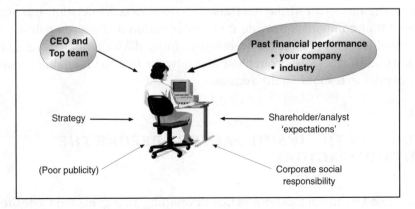

Figure 3.5. Factors affecting analysts' and shareholders' corporate images

The appearance of the factor *corporate social responsibility* in Figure 3.5 rather than in both Figures 3.3 and 3.4 may seem strange. Most employees and customers (and other stakeholders, for that matter) would agree that a company that is known for its corporate social responsibility would have a better image and reputation than one that is not. However, the academics have been arguing for decades about whether or not a good rating on social responsibility translates into better financial performance. Two theories labelled the 'stakeholder theory' and the 'slack resources' theory, assert a positive relationship between corporate social responsibility and the firm's financial performance. On the other hand, neo-classical economics can mount an equally compelling argument that the relationship should be negative.[8] A 2000 paper, as yet unpublished, reviewed fifty empirical studies and concluded that the economists are likely to be wrong.[9] This represents good news for organizations that are investing in society and the environment, and a plea to the hard-nosed analysts to take another look at this issue.

The factor *poor publicity* in Figure 3.5 is enclosed in parentheses because there is conflicting evidence about whether this factor will change the evaluations of analysts and shareholders—notwithstanding the claims of the various public relations consulting firms. I provide a more extensive discussion of this issue in Chapter 12 where I deal with crises.

The other factors in Figure 3.5 (CEO, top management, strategy, and financial performance) are included to emphasize the importance of how companies manage the 'expectations' of analysts and shareholders. Often, the primary vehicle for managing analysts' expectations is a series of private briefings, and that for shareholders is an annual report that contains a great deal of sterile accounting information, glossy pictures, and glib statements rationalizing past poor performance and making rosy forecasts. The chairman of the Australian Shareholders Association has suggested that companies provide more information and more analysis for shareholders.[10] A look at the websites of Intel, IBM, Compaq, Microsoft, 3Com and Northern Telecom illustrates how the Internet is enabling some companies to respond to this request.

WORK ON THE INSIDE FACTORS BEFORE THE OUTSIDE FACTORS

The overall theme of this book is that developing an organization's desired image into a strategic asset starts on the inside of the organization. The left-to-right 'logic' of Figures 3.1 to 3.5 illustrates this process. This idea is now gaining widespread support. For example, at the 1998 Asia Pacific Corporate Image conference in Hong Kong every speaker at the two-day programme had the same basic message—*Behaviour* before *Branding*.

When an organization builds its desired image from the inside out, that is, on its values, policies, capabilities, commitments to stakeholders, and culture, it has an opportunity to present itself as authentic, concerned, unique, reliable, honest, and trustworthy. Because these values are also widely held personal values, an image designed on these foundations can be easily built up into a good corporate reputation or super-brand. Also, this is the only option for many organizations. Consider China Light & Power. They cannot really base their desired image on their product—it is not easy to tell customers that your electrons are customer focused, better than others, reliable, friendly, safe, or caring. It is more meaningful to make a corporate commitment to customers.

Good super-brands are strategic assets that allow organizations to grow and enter new markets. Poor super-brands are liabilities. For example, during the 1970s and 1980s the General Motors super-brand lost much of its gloss among the car-buying public. In the early 1980s GM conceived the Saturn company to compete with small, economical imports from Japan. The company was designed as one that would break away from the mould of a traditional (outdated) GM division. Its employees, work practices, cars, and then its advertising reinforced this new position. (The corporate advertising slogan is 'A different kind *of* company. A different kind *of* car.') By all accounts, Saturn has been a marketing success. So successful, in fact, that in 1998 40 per cent of people still did not know that it was a division of GM, and as its customers aged and moved up to larger vehicles, many of them turned to Honda and Toyota rather than another GM division. However, in 1998 there were clouds on the horizon as the United Auto Workers Union clashed with management and Saturn cars were no longer demonstrably superior in terms of styling, performance, reliability, and service.[11]

CONCLUSIONS

Given the potential complexity of the task of image management, it is worth pausing to assess whether trying to actively manage this strategic asset is really worth the effort. The answer to this question comes in two parts. First, it depends on how bad your current images and reputations really are. Chapter 10 outlines how to answer this question in a quantitative (and scientific) way. At this point, however, if no market research is available, then the personal assessment of the management team is a good place to start. The second issue concerns the importance of your reputations for achieving operational and financial success. While it is difficult to think of cases where a good reputation will not help, the critical issue is cost versus benefit. Here the answer is less clear, as was illustrated in the bank example used to introduce Chapter 1.

To calculate the potential gains from embarking on a major corporate image redesign project follow these steps:

(1) Define the role of corporate reputation for your organization. For example, for Procter & Gamble and Philip Morris it is not as extensive as for 3M or Levi's.

(2) Assess the images and reputations of your organization relative to those of competitors. Research can tell if your organization is at a disadvantage.

(3) Review your portfolio of potential image building factors, namely, the corporate attributes where you excel (e.g., the very committed employees of Southwest Airlines, the icon brands of Procter & Gamble, the innovation capability of 3M, the service of Ritz Carlton hotels, the dominant product design standard of Intel and Microsoft, etc.)

(4) Determine which image attributes connect with the values of important stakeholder groups (e.g., in Japan being seen to be innovative is important for managers, employees, customers, and the government).

(5) Do a cost–benefit calculation, namely, what would be the benefits (across various stakeholder groups) of X per cent improvement and what would need to be changed to achieve this?

(6) If appropriate—invest.

As the first three chapters outline, the task of crafting a new desired image and then linking it to one or more key values of stakeholders is not an easy job. Many CEOs have known this for some time. Relatively few, however, have been willing to implement all the changes necessary to create an organization of distinction. It can be done—by proactive CEOs and management teams. The rest of this book outlines how.

NOTES

1. In this chapter the focus is on corporate image, not reputation. The reason for this, as established in Chapter 1, is that managers can try to change the beliefs and feelings that people have about their organization but not the personal values that people have developed over their lifetime.

2. J. Dutton, J. Dukerich, and C. Harquail, 'Organizational Images and Member Identification', *Administrative Science Quarterly*, 39, 2 (1994), 239–62.

3. In *Fortune* (12 Jan. 1998) see: A. Fisher, 'The 100 Best Companies to Work for in America', 33–4; and R. Levering and M. Moskowitz, 'The 100 Best Companies to Work for in America', 38–47.

4. P. M. Blau and M. W. Meyer, *Bureaucracy in Modern Society* (New York: Random House, 1987).

5. W. H. Davidow and B. Utal, *Total Customer Service* (New York: Harper & Row, 1989).

6. W. P. Rogerson, 'Reputation and Product Quality', *Bell Journal of Economics*, 14 (1983), 508–16.

7. T. Copeland, T. Koller, and J. Murrin, *Valuation: Measuring and Managing the Value of Companies* (New York: Wiley, 1994).

8. The faint-hearted reader might like to refer to two articles from *The Economist*: 'Civics 101' (11 May 1996), 73 and 'The Cecil Rhodes of Chocolate-Chip Cookies' (25 May 1996), 86. The first article provides an overview of the theoretical debate while the second article provides a case study of the Sara Lee company. The more adventurous reader might like to tackle the following: S. A. Waddock and S. B. Graves, 'The Corporate Social Performance–Financial Performance Link', *Strategic Management Journal*, 18 (1997), 303–19; D. J. Wood and R. E. Jones, 'Stakeholder Mismatching: A Theoretical Problem in Empirical Research on Corporate Social Performance', *International Journal of Organizational Analysis*, 3 (1995), 229–67; D. B. Turban and D. W. Greening, 'Corporate Social Performance and Organizational Attractiveness to Prospective Employees', *Academy of Management Journal*, 40 (1997), 658–72.

9. M. Orlitzky, F. L. Schmidt, and S. L. Rynes, 'The Positive-sum Game of Modern Capitalism: a Meta-analysis of Corporate Social/Environmental Performance and Financial Performance', unpublished paper, Australian Graduate School of Management (2000).

10. A.-M. Moodie, 'Taking the Gloss off Annual Reports', *Australian Financial Review* (15 May 1998), 55.

11. H. L. Murphy, 'Saturn's Orbit Still High with Consumers', *Marketing News* (31 Aug. 1998), 2 and 6.

FACTORS THAT AFFECT CORPORATE IMAGES

4

Vision and Mission: The Soul of Corporate Reputation

This and the next two chapters focus on the internal foundations of a good corporate reputation. Here, I discuss *vision* and *mission*—or as the subtitle suggests, the soul that guides what an organization does.

In some organizations managers articulate a clear vision that is noticeable even to an outsider. In others, the visitor may see a copy of a vision statement but struggle to find any evidence that employees believe in its sentiments or have even read it. Vision statements *per se* are unimportant. A core component of leadership style is having a clear sense of vision that the leader can communicate throughout the organization.[1] A sense of vision is also a vital factor in creating a strong image among managers and employees. Organizations that have vision can inspire a high level of commitment among their employees that can spill over to affect external stakeholders. It may also have a financial pay-off, as Exhibit 4.1 suggests.

An enduring idea from the management consulting firm McKinsey & Company is that organizations need to understand the interrelationship of seven key factors which are critical to their success. This scheme is known as the McKinsey 7-S framework.[2] Three factors are considered to be the 'hardware' of success—strategy, structure, and systems. (These are discussed in Chapter 5.) The remaining four are the 'software' of success—style, staff, skills, and shared values. Here, and in Chapter 6, I explore how the soft side of an organization helps shape its images and reputations. This builds on McKinsey's research, which has shown that companies differ in the relative emphasis placed on the hardware and the software elements of the organization. For example, in the USA many managers concentrate on the hardware elements, while in Japan there is a better balance between the importance of hardware and software factors.[3]

In order to communicate the important role of the software factors, the

Exhibit 4.1. We should invest in visionary companies

Two Stanford Graduate School of Business professors, James Collins and Jerry Porras, conducted a study to see if there is a financial pay-off for visionary companies. They asked 170 American top managers to identify the 20 companies they thought were the most visionary. A notional dollar was then invested in each company in the mid-1920s. If any of the companies did not exist at that time, the dollar was left in an interest-bearing account until the firm was born; it was then invested.

On average, over the period, the visionary companies outperformed Wall Street by a factor of 50. Interesting—but not conclusive because 'visionary' could just be a synonym for successful.

Source: Derived from 'The Vision Thing', *The Economist* (9 Nov. 1991), 89.

Two more American researchers, John Pearce and Fred David, set out to examine the proposition that a comprehensive mission statement is linked to making better strategic decisions, which, in turn, should contribute to improved organizational performance. They found that a sample of Fortune 500 companies that performed better financially (in terms of profit margin) had more extensively developed mission statements than low performers. In effect, these mission statements were used as a surrogate measure of the comprehensiveness of the firm's strategic plans. (Other research has also shown that firms that engage in strategic planning tend to outperform firms that do not.)

Source: Based on J. Pearce and F. David, 'Corporate Mission Statements: The Bottom Line', *Academy of Management Executive*, 1, 2 (1987), 109–16.

In the entrepreneurship and business strategy literatures, the importance of vision and its effects on organizational-level performance has been stressed in various theories. A study of 183 companies in the US architectural woodwork industry found that a clear, well-communicated vision directly affected the subsequent growth of these firms. This study suggests that CEOs with no vision performed significantly worse than those with visions.

Source: Based on J. Baum, E. Locke, and S. Kirkpatrick, 'A Longitudinal Study of the Relation of Vision and Vision Communication to Venture Growth in Entrepreneurial Firms', *Journal of Applied Psychology*, 83, 1 (1998), 43–54.

McKinsey consultants would present their 7-S framework as a set of six factors interconnected by the shared values factor. This is shown in Figure 4.1. Having shared values as the hub of the set of key success factors was not meant to indicate that it was more important than the other factors. Rather, it suggested that the role of this factor was to act as a 'compass' to guide the activities of all employees. At IBM these shared values once dictated that no employee should ever sacrifice customer service, while at the giant Japanese firm of Matsushita they meant that nobody would ever cheat a customer by knowingly producing or selling defective merchandise.[4] If they are constructed thoughtfully, and 'sold' well within the organization, these shared values, or super-ordinate goals as they are sometimes known, can play a very pragmatic role by influencing the day-to-day activities of employees. Vision statements are a frequently used internal selling device for the soft side of a business.

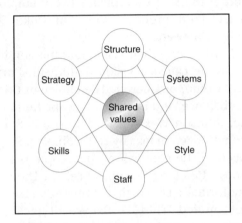

Figure 4.1. The McKinsey 7-S framework

Source: Thomas J. Peters, *In Search of Excellence*. Copyright ©1982 by Thomas J. Peters and Robert H. Waterman, Jr. Reprinted by permission of HarperCollins Publishers, Inc.

VISION AND MISSION

In every organization people have a vision, that is, an ideal that represents or reflects the shared values to which the organization should aspire.[5] In this context, vision resembles McKinsey's shared values. It has no set time limit or use-by date, and it should have broad appeal to both internal and external stakeholders. Vision should also have a 'feel-good' tone and purpose. For example, Merck, the big American health-care company, summarizes its vision this way: 'We are in the business of preserving and improving human life. All our actions must be measured by our success in achieving this.' The Walt Disney company's vision is simply: 'To make people happy'.[6] In Fujitsu (in 1991) the vision was expressed as: 'What mankind can dream, technology can achieve'.

Mission, on the other hand, is more specific. James Collins and Jerry Porras suggest that a good corporate mission has three elements: (a) it should have a finishing line so that you know when you have achieved the goal, (b) it should be risky—attainable, but only with effort, and (c) it helps to have a time limit, which should be short enough to be within the reach of present employees.[7] A mission's goals are often externally focused, sometimes on a competitor. As a way of communicating an important theme in the mission, some companies develop an internal slogan. For example, PepsiCo's mission has long been simply to 'beat Coke'. Sony sums up one of its mission goals with its internal slogan: 'BMW—Beat Matsushita Whatsoever'. The Japanese earthmoving equipment company Komatsu's mission is to 'Beat Caterpillar'. Every employee in PepsiCo, Sony, and Komatsu (and probably those of Coke, Matsushita, and Caterpillar) knows why they come to work each day.

Some organizations capture their vision and mission in a single formal document. This may be called a Vision Statement, Purpose Statement, Mission Statement, Credo, or Charter. The choice of title does not really matter—it is the substance, and in some cases the heritage, that is important. For example, Johnson Wax's (S. C. Johnson & Sons) guiding principles were first summarized in 1927 by H. F. Johnson, Sr., in his Christmas Profit Sharing speech: 'The goodwill of the people is the only enduring thing in any business. It is the sole substance. . . . The rest is shadow!' In 1976 the company formally stated their founder's sentiments in a fairly lengthy document entitled 'This We Believe'. Typically these visionary documents are only a page or two in length and contain a statement of 'what the organization stands for' as this relates to the major stakeholders. A collection of 301 such statements from American companies (including the full Johnson Wax document) can be found in *The Mission Statement Book* by Jeffrey Abrahams.[8]

The value of a visionary statement to an organization can derive both from the process used to create it, and the general guidance it provides to employees in the workplace—especially when they are scattered around the world. To write such a statement, management must consciously contemplate, debate, and articulate the nature of their business, the reasons for the organization's existence, and the customers and markets to be served. Creating the statement entails some risk because it can lead to disagreement and dissent among managers—especially when different groups of employees believe that different factors are key to their organization's success (e.g., teaching versus research in a university). Many managers, however, believe that the benefits far outweigh the effort involved. These benefits relate to the role that the formal vision/mission statement can play in strategy formation and evaluation, performance evaluation, and setting the expectations of internal and external stakeholders.[9]

Exhibit 4.2 shows one of the most famous of these statements, the Johnson & Johnson Credo that the company has used since 1948 to guide its business decisions. The 1997 version reproduced here has hardly been changed from the original—it is just 'politically correct' for its time.

Exhibit 4.2. Our Credo

We believe our first responsibility is to the doctors, nurses and patients,
to mothers and fathers and all others who use our products and services.
In meeting their needs everything we do must be of high quality.
We must constantly strive to reduce our costs
in order to maintain reasonable prices.
Customers' orders must be serviced promptly and accurately.
Our suppliers and distributors must have an opportunity
to make a fair profit.

We are responsible to our employees,
the men and women who work with us throughout the world.
Everyone must be considered as an individual.
We must respect their dignity and recognize their merit.
They must have a sense of security in their jobs.
Compensation must be fair and adequate,
and working conditions clean, orderly and safe.
We must be mindful of ways to help our employees fulfill
their family responsibilities.

Employees must feel free to make suggestions and complaints.
There must be equal opportunity for employment, development
and advancement for those qualified.
We must provide competent management,
and their actions must be just and ethical.

We are responsible to the communities in which we live and work
and to the world community as well.
We must be good citizens—support good works and charities
and bear our fair share of taxes.
We must encourage civic improvements and better health and education.
We must maintain in good order
the property we are privileged to use,
protecting the environment and natural resources.

Our final responsibility is to our stockholders.
Business must make a sound profit.
We must experiment with new ideas.   *cont.*

Exhibit 4.2. *cont.*

Research must be carried on, innovative programs developed
and mistakes paid for.
New equipment must be purchased, new facilities provided
and new products launched.
Reserves must be created to provide for adverse times.
When we operate according to these principles,
the stockholders should realize a fair return.

Source: Johnson & Johnson.

What is interesting about Johnson & Johnson's Credo, and other such statements, is that they reflect many of the elements of the organization's ideal corporate image and reputation. For example, for Johnson & Johnson (J&J):

- Important stakeholder groups are: doctors, nurses, patients, parents, suppliers, distributors, employees, communities, stockholders, and so on.
- Key corporate image attributes are: high-quality products, safe working conditions, ethical practices, environmental protection, paying one's fair share of taxes, etc.
- The community values that are at the heart of good corporate reputation are: better health by responding to the needs of doctors, nurses, and patients.

While considerable time and effort is devoted by senior management to articulating their company's values, the way they are broadcast throughout the organization sometimes causes disquiet. The result is that many employees struggle to see the direct relevance of these general values to the organization's overall strategy, and/or to their specific day-to-day activities. They, and some business commentators, criticize these statements as being just motherhood and apple PR (or pie).

Organizations use different strategies in order to overcome employee resistance to 'internalizing' the message in the vision/mission statement. I once saw a CEO walk around his organization and ask *every* manager he met to recite The Vision. They all got it correct and they all looked embarrassed during their recital. (You can get away with this strategy when you own the company.) A slightly more subtle approach is to translate the vision into a company song—as is done by some Japanese organizations. Another version of this approach was adopted by Australia's international airline Qantas. They printed their vision/mission statement on a plastic 'credit' card so that each employee could carry it in his or her wallet.

Other companies feel that to get employee buy-in and the most benefit from their vision/mission statements they need to make them public. When an organization adopts this strategy it will print the statement on a poster or plaque to be exhibited throughout the organization. It is sometimes included in the annual report and in corporate advertising. Publicizing the company vision is one way to put employees and managers on notice that customers and other external stakeholders now fully understand what the organization stands for.

These concerns about the usefulness of vision/mission statements and how employees are sometimes browbeaten into accepting them can be well founded. However, they relate more to coming to grips with how such a statement can and should be used, rather than to the value of spending the time and effort to create a statement of values and purpose. The next few sections describe some different types of vision/mission statements and how to create them. Attention then switches to showing how these statements can be communicated to stakeholders.

STYLES OF VISION AND MISSION STATEMENTS

As Exhibit 4.3 shows, in the world of vision and mission statements one size and style does not fit every company. Collecting some of these statements from organizations you respect, and from some of your competitors, can provide information that is useful for creating or reviewing your own statement(s). When reviewing these statements, I use the following four criteria, namely, how they:

- motivate and focus all employees on a guiding philosophy or set of corporate values;
- define the boundaries of the business (in terms of the enabling technology, business processes, and markets);
- provide an overall unifying theme for the key stakeholder groups; and
- help differentiate the organization from its competitors.

This is a difficult set of objectives for a short document to fulfil. However, it is important to list criteria such as these before setting out to design a statement of corporate philosophy. In fact, to achieve these objectives it may be necessary to design more than one vision/mission statement.

Exhibit 4.3. Vision and mission statements

American Marketing Association

The American Marketing Association is an international professional society of individual members with an interest in the practice, study, and teaching of marketing. Our principal roles are, first, to urge and assist the personal and professional development of our members, and second, to advance the science and ethical practice of the marketing discipline.

Source: www.ama.org/about/ama/mission.asp

Burnett (Leo Burnett Advertising)

The mission of the Leo Burnett Company is to create superior advertising.

In Leo's words: Our primary function in life is to produce the best advertising in the world, bar none.

This is to be advertising so interrupting, so daring, so fresh, so engaging, so human, so believable and so well focused as to themes and ideas that, at one and the same time, it builds a quality reputation for the long haul as it produces sales for the immediate present.

Source: J. Abrahams, *The Mission Statement Book* (Berkeley, CA: Ten Speed Press, 1995).

Microsoft

A computer on every desk and in every home. (1975–1993)

To create software for the personal computer that empowers and enriches people in the workplace, at school and at home. (1999)

Source: www.microsoft.com/mscorp/

The Walt Disney Company

Disney's overriding objective is to create shareholder value by continuing to be the world's premier entertainment company from a creative, strategic, and financial standpoint.

Source: wysiwyg://9/http://disney.go.com/investors/index.html

Nike

To maximize profits to shareholders through products and services that enrich people's lives. (1993)

Source: J. Abraham, *The Mission Statement Book* (Berkeley, CA: Ten Speed Press, 1995). See also: http://www.nike.biz.com/story

Southwest Airlines (1988–present)

The mission of Southwest Airlines is dedication to the highest quality of Customer Service delivered with a sense of warmth, friendliness, individual pride, and Company Spirit.

We are committed to provide our employees a stable work environment with equal opportunity for learning and personal growth. Creativity and innovation are encouraged for improving the effectiveness of Southwest Airlines. Above all, Employees will be provided the same concern, respect, and caring attitude within the organization that they are expected to share externally with every Southwest Customer.

Source: http://www.iflyswa.com/info/mission.html

Before moving on, the Disney mission is worthy of a brief comment. Recall that in Chapter 2 I mentioned that some CEOs are compensated on the basis of the financial performance of their companies. In 1993 Michael Eisner, Disney's CEO, was reportedly paid $235 million for his services (see Chapter 2, n. 20). While Disney's vision might be to make people happy, the company's mission (and senior management compensation) is to create shareholder value.

Some organizations develop separate versions of their vision/mission statement for internal use and external stakeholders. The external version is sanitized to ensure that competitors are not notified of any confidential information. Other organizations feel the need to develop a single vision statement but different mission statements for different strategic business units, national operations, or functional groups. For example, the operations of some big diversified companies are so vastly different from one another that a single mission statement written for everybody is irrelevant to many.

The potential problem that arises from having a number of different mission statements is that they may have only a tenuous relationship to one another. A good way to avoid this situation is to link the individual missions to the activities of the parent organization. This can be done by including a short paragraph at the beginning of each mission statement that expresses the overall role and goal(s) of the organization. For example, the various schools and faculties of the academic institution of which I am a member could use the following paragraph from the university's mission statement:

Together with other universities of the western tradition, the University of New South Wales shares a responsibility to support scholarly activity in the humanities and the natural and social sciences, and to express this activity in undergraduate teaching, postgraduate teaching, continuing education, and research.

CONTENTS OF VISION AND MISSION STATEMENTS

As Exhibit 4.3 illustrates, the contents of vision/mission statements are as varied as the companies that develop them. A comprehensive review of the theories of leadership, business strategy, and entrepreneurship has identified seven attributes that make a vision effective—that is, significantly affect organizational performance.[10] Vision statements should be:

- brief;
- clear;
- abstract;
- challenging;
- stable;
- desirable;
- future oriented.

To this list I would add that they should be expressed in a creative way. For example, compare the Porsche vision in Figure 3.2, 'If I were going to be a car, I'd be a Porsche', with the uninspiring 1993 Microsoft vision in Exhibit 4.3.

Many consultants will help organizations to develop vision and/or mission statements. One particularly good framework for developing a mission statement is the following:[11]

Strategy sections
  (1) Context
  (2) Business definition
  (3) Competencies and capabilities
  (4) Future directions

Stakeholder sections
  (5) Employee value systems
  (6) Employee development and work practices
  (7) Stakeholder commitment

(1) *Context.* This paragraph sets the context for the other six paragraphs and 'introduces' the organization. It should outline the broad area of operations in a way that does not inhibit the future directions of the organization (which are outlined in paragraph (4)). For example, a person unfamiliar with Johnson & Johnson who read their Credo in Exhibit 4.2 for the first time would not get a clear picture of what the company actually does. Reference to doctors, nurses, and patients indicates that J&J has

interests in the health care industry. However, exactly what the field of operations is, or the company's relative expertise in this industry, is somewhat unclear. By contrast, the first sentence of the American Marketing Association's mission statement (in Exhibit 4.3) provides a clear indication of the AMA's field of activities.

(2) *Business definition.* This paragraph describes the organization's current business activities. It is important to define the scope or boundary of the business in terms of its customers' needs, and the (business) technology and people used to satisfy these needs. In his classic *Harvard Business Review* article entitled 'Marketing Myopia', Professor Ted Levitt vividly illustrated the consequences of a poor business definition.[12] The American railroads thought they were in the railroad business rather than the transportation business and as the demand for passenger and freight transportation grew their share of this market steadily declined. Companies operating fleets of cars, trucks, and aircraft realized that customer needs varied, and that they could be better served by companies not in the railroad business. The list of organizations that have lost touch with their customers is long—very long indeed! The film industry took years to adapt their products for television; the postal monopolies failed to update their products and services and provided the opportunity for courier companies to enter the market; telephone companies were fixated with their phone networks and allowed the electronics companies to develop telecommunications equipment such as fax machines and mobile phones. The list goes on and on. Chapter 5 looks further at how to define a business.

(3) *Competencies and capabilities.* The competencies and capabilities of an organization are the underlying skills, technologies, and resources that underpin that organization's success. They define how the organization competes, and will often reflect its historic development. Because competencies and capabilities define the backbone of the organization, it is not easy for competitors to emulate them in the short term. (If they can be copied they are really just a differential advantage.) For example, while a bigger advertising budget than a competitor offers a potential advantage, it can be quickly emulated. On the other hand, it is difficult and time consuming to develop a strong set of corporate images and reputations.

The Southwest Airlines mission statement (see Exhibit 4.3) suggests that customer service is one of the airline's capabilities, and that this is driven by the spirit of creativity and innovation of their employees. This is, however, only half of what makes Southwest such a successful airline. One of the core competencies that underlies its low-cost service is the productivity of its workforce and operating systems. Of the US carriers, Southwest carries more passengers per employee, and runs at the lowest cost per available seat mile. It seems that cost control is not an exciting enough topic for their mission statement!

(4) *Future directions.* This paragraph provides the dynamics of the mission statement. It signals the future direction(s) likely to be pursued. These will, however, be restrained by the organization's past activities, and should be contingent on the business definition and competencies built up by the organization. Hence, this paragraph should be a logical extension of the first three paragraphs. It should rarely signal that the firm is about to embark on a programme of discontinuous change.

What pursuit has fixated Corporate America more than any other? In a word, *growth*. The demand for growth drives companies to offer more varieties of products, branch out into new markets, create new strategic business units, buy companies which are often in unrelated industries, and form joint ventures with other companies. Japanese and European companies suffer a similar affliction. What it has also done, according to Al Ries, is to cause companies to become unfocused.[13] Ries, and many others, argue that, to compete, a company has to focus on particular products and markets and establish both a reputation and a market presence.[14] Philips Electronics of the Netherlands is a classic example of an unfocused company (medical equipment, multimedia, music production, mobile phones, public telecommunications, defence systems, consumer electronics, light bulbs and lighting systems, personal computers, traffic control systems, special projects, etc.). On a $40-billion turnover, it struggles to be profitable. More important for our purposes, it has a very diffuse image because it is good at some things and marginal at many others.

(5) *Employee value systems.* For many employees this and the next paragraph are regarded as the essence of the organization's mission statement. They tune into Radio Station WII-FM or 'What's In It For Me?' Hence, this paragraph must clearly reflect the value system of management and employees, or, as discussed in the next chapter, the organization's internal culture. It has to communicate how the basic values and attitudes an employee brings to the workplace can help the organization achieve its goals and further develop its distinctive competencies. For organizations like Southwest Airlines where face-to-face service is crucial for success, this section of the Vision/Mission statement is particularly important.

When an organization employs many professionally trained staff, the way the organization's culture is expressed in this paragraph can have a big impact on the behaviour and priorities of these employees. For example, accountants, engineers, lawyers, and scientists often need direction to balance the values developed during their professional training with the values needed to make their organization competitive and successful in the marketplace. This tension between professional and corporate values can be addressed in the mission statement. For example, in many professional service firms partners only want to do work associated with their vocation. The important tasks of 'finding' (new business development) and 'minding' (account service) may take second place to 'grinding' (doing the work) and are often delegated to specialists like a marketing manager.

(6) *Employee development and work practices.* This part of the statement makes a commitment to ongoing staff development, the renewal of the organization's value system, and desired work practices. To be taken seriously by employees, these activities must be linked to the organization's formal policies. This link is extremely important because it creates a 'contract' between the organization and its employees concerning acceptable behaviour and rewards. There is an old saying that 'people do what is inspected, rather than what is expected'. Because much of the statement focuses on what is expected, an explicit statement of how these expectations will be formally rewarded is important for gaining commitment to the organization's vision and mission. Most statements ignore this issue, as reflected in Exhibits 4.2 and 4.3. One interesting exception is a small Australian (merchant) bank, Macquarie Bank, which stated in its 1997 Annual Report that 'employees absorb much of any volatility of the bank's financial performance'. (Real merchant bankers don't write vision and mission statements!)

(7) *Stakeholder commitment.* Chapter 2 outlined how an organization might go about identifying various key groups of stakeholders. The last paragraph of the statement should make explicit mention of any groups that have not been identified in the previous six paragraphs and should state how the organization relates to them. For example, manufacturing companies may want to state their preferred type of relationship when dealing with suppliers and distributors (e.g., a strategic partnership versus an 'arm's length' relationship). In the case of companies listed on a stock exchange this is the place where a commitment is made to a balance between shareholder wealth creation, the payment of taxes, protection of the environment, and service to the community. Also, for organizations that aspire to something more inspirational than shareholder value, this is the section in which to state these aspirations. In effect, this paragraph is a statement of the organization's ethical position. The Johnson & Johnson Credo in Exhibit 4.2 focuses predominantly on these issues.

WRITING A VISION OR MISSION STATEMENT

While the process of writing a vision or mission statement has been mentioned earlier in this chapter, it is now time to outline briefly how an organization can commit its vision and mission to writing. Mark Lawley from New Zealand Post (now the world's most efficient postal service) summed up the options:

Either this can take a month with a consultant, or we can do it in half an hour.

They opted for the half-hour option and ten years later the mission statement was still hanging on the wall.[15]

Many other organizations take a longer route to formalizing their vision/mission. Generally, the first task is to gain the commitment of the senior management committee. As noted earlier, there is often scepticism about the idea of writing such a formal statement. Familiar criticisms are: 'We know what we are doing and where we want to go, so there is no point in wasting time writing this down', or 'They are just motherhood statements and the staff will not take any notice of them', or 'Is this the latest gimmick from the management consultants?' Without commitment at the top of the organization then there is no point in proceeding further.

The second task is to agree on a set of objectives for the vision/mission statement(s). The Johnson & Johnson Credo is used to outline the company's responsibilities to stakeholders. The Hewlett-Packard statement explains the 'H-P Way' that ties the behaviour standards of employees together. Whatever the objectives, they should be agreed to before a single word is written because they will guide the type(s) of statement to be developed—its content, tone, and the appropriate channels for communicating the message. For example, a 'motherhood statement' for inclusion in the annual report may contain only the information normally found in paragraphs (3), (4), and (7).

Once there is commitment to create a formal statement and a set of objectives to be achieved, one of three approaches is often adopted:

(1) The founder, CEO, and/or Corporate Management Committee drafts and circulates the statement for comment (preferably favourable) and approval (preferably fast).

(2) The senior management committee produces a first draft, circulates it widely for comment and input, then redrafts (often repeatedly).

(3) The statement is democratically produced by a representative group of employees.

With options (2) and (3), the services of an external facilitator are often used to guide the process and to ensure that the job titles and seniority of the participants are not permitted to influence the discussion.

A good example of how not to implement option (1) is the way the chief of the London Metropolitan Police created a sense of mission for his men and women.[16] After the Brixton race riots in 1982 he decided that the force had lost sight of the old 'bobby on the beat' values that made the British police so special. In an 80-page book entitled *The Principles of Policing*, he set down the behaviour standards and values that his police were to follow in their work. The book was circulated to all police personnel, and discussion groups were organized to 'sell' the message about changing some of the current policing practices. Individual police had two options: either change their behaviour or ridicule the book as an example of how their leaders had lost touch with the problems of policing. Not surprisingly, they chose the latter option. In the corporate world, visions 'from above' are only enthusiastically endorsed by employees when they hold the CEO in high regard.

When either of the democratic options ((2) or (3)) is used to write the vision/mission statement, phase two involves internally marketing the document to (representatives of) all groups who will be affected by the statement. To many people the contents of this first draft will come as a surprise. This should not be too disconcerting because the perceptions of the drafting team will seldom be exactly the same as those of people in other parts of the organization. In fact, the revelation of these different perceptions (or realities) can be one of the benefits of the process of creating such a statement.

Comment and discussion about the draft vision/mission should be collected and tabled at the next drafting meeting, at which a second version is produced. This can be shown to key opinion leaders within the organization for their feedback and hopefully their acceptance. When a final set of words is agreed upon the statement can be printed and circulated throughout the organization. At this stage the CEO needs to personally 'sell' the statement to target stakeholders. He or she needs to explain the statement's objectives, how it was created, and how individuals within the organization can use it. A key part of this sales pitch is to demonstrate (not just communicate) that the CEO and top managers are committed to the philosophy contained in the document.

COMMUNICATING THE VISION OR MISSION

One of the most difficult 'sales' for a vision or mission statement is to employees—especially those not involved in its creation. In many cases, these statements, especially long-winded ones, can seem intimidating because: (a) they may set higher standards than people practise in their everyday lives, and/or (b) it may be difficult to see how one element relates to the others. What the world of advertising has taught us is that the more ideas one puts into a piece of communication, the fewer the reader is likely to take out! This creates a problem for the sort of seven-paragraph statement outlined above.

The 1993 Microsoft mission statement in Exhibit 4.3 takes the opposite perspective—one idea stated in nine words. However, the problem with this statement was that it left a crucial question unstated and unanswered, namely, 'Why put a computer on every desk and in every home?' (The 1999 mission statement rectified this problem.) Apple Computer knew the answer and advertised it for years in their corporate slogan: 'The power to be your best'. That is, PCs are only wanted because they allow people to enhance their skills, or productivity, or learning, or whatever.

It is possible to build a link between a long vision/mission statement and a very short one, and thus have the best of both. Again it is advertising which suggests how this might be achieved. Have you ever noticed that about half of the advertisements in business magazines such as *Business Week*, *Forbes*, *Fortune*, *The Economist*, and *Review 200* include a corporate slogan? These slogans or tag-lines are generally three to eight words in length, and together with the organization's name they are used to 'sign off' many advertisements. This type of corporate slogan can be used to capture a core element of the vision/mission statement. It can be designed solely for internal use such as the one used by Komatsu—'Beat Caterpillar', or it can be designed to talk to both internal and external audiences. For example

- Qantas airlines—'the spirit of Australia'. This tells customers what to expect and staff how to deliver their service.
- SAS—'the business airline of Europe'. Only business people need to fly with us, and staff should deliver 'business standard' service.
- Mercedes-Benz cars were 'engineered like no other car'. This is the focus for design and manufacture, and, for customers, a reason to buy.
- US Army—'be all you can be'. Speaks to new recruits, instructors, and current personnel.

- AT&T—'the right choice'. Reinforces the customer's choice, and tells staff to deliver the best products and service.

If such a slogan is to be used, it is critical to ensure that employees know how the slogan relates to the vision or mission of the organization. Also, if a slogan is to be used for both internal and external audiences, it should avoid talking about the future directions of the organization. Slogans about the future often sound vacuous, especially when they are compared with a slogan which talks directly to (the emotions of) the target audience. For example, I think that AT&T's 'the right choice' and the US Army's 'be all you can be' are better than the old ICI chemical company's slogan, 'we're making the future'. (How is ICI making the future? My future or some other person's future? And so on.) Chapter 8 takes a longer, closer look at corporate slogans.

CONCLUSIONS

Many organizations do not have a formal vision/mission statement. However, many of those that do believe that the time and effort required to write such a formal statement is a worthwhile investment. Also, the evolution of vision/mission statements over time can serve as a partial record of the history of the organization. The downside of creating a vision statement, however, is that the CEO may use it as a substitute for leadership (as was the case with the London Police example discussed above). As a supplement to the CEO's leadership, however, the vision statement can play a valuable role in helping to shape and communicate an organization's values and operating philosophy. It can also suggest some key performance indicators for employees' appraisal (e.g., customer service), corporate performance (e.g., innovation and new product development), and social responsibility (e.g., pollution control). In this way it can help to develop a balanced approach to corporate image and reputation development.

In conclusion, the best way to create a vision/mission statement is to do it *slowly*, and with the participation of as many people as practical. Over-eagerness on the part of the CEO and/or the executive management team can depreciate the value inherent in both the process of writing the statement, and its effect on employees. If it is done poorly, the process sends signals to employees that top management are not on top of their game.

What parts of the internal vision/mission statements to communicate to external stakeholders will depend on how much confidential information they contain, and whether or not they add to the store of information that people use to form their images and reputations of the organization. For many organizations, these statements provide the only concise public statement of the organization's ethical position. Given the definition of reputation outlined in Chapter 1 (and Figures 1.1 and 3.1) a vision statement can play an important role in the reputation formation process.

NOTES

1. J. R. Baum, E. A. Locke, and S. A. Kirkpatrick, 'A Longitudinal Study of the Relation of Vision and Vision Communication to Venture Growth in Entrepreneurial Firms', *Journal of Applied Psychology*, 83, 1 (1998), 43–54.
2. T. J. Peters and R. H. Waterman, Jr., *In Search of Excellence: Lessons from America's Best Run Companies* (New York: Harper & Row, 1982).
3. R. T. Pascale and A. G. Athos, *The Art of Japanese Management* (New York: Simon and Schuster, 1981).
4. Ibid.
5. R. J. House and B. Shamir, 'Toward the Integration of Transformational, Charismatic and Visionary Theories of Leadership', in M. Chemers and R. Ayman (eds.), *Leadership Theory and Research: Perspectives and Directions* (San Diego, CA: Academic Press, 1993), 81–107.
6. 'The Vision Thing', *The Economist* (9 Nov. 1991), 65.
7. J. C. Collins and J. I. Porras, *Built to Last: Successful Habits of Visionary Companies* (New York: Harper, 1994).
8. J. Abrahams, *The Mission Statement Book: 301 Corporate Mission Statements from America's Top Companies* (Berkeley, CA: Ten Speed Press, 1995).
9. R. Germain and M. Bixby Cooper, 'How a Customer Mission Statement Affects Company Performance', *Industrial Marketing Management*, 19 (1990), 47–54.
10. Baum, *et al.*, see n. 1.
11. Dr John Gattorna, currently a partner in Andersen Consulting in Sydney, Australia, first introduced me to this seven-paragraph framework for writing a mission statement. It is also embedded in the research of J. A. Pearce and F. David, 'Corporate Mission Statements: The Bottom Line', *Academy of Management Executive*, 1, 2 (1987), 109–16.
12. T. Levitt, 'Marketing Myopia', *Harvard Business Review* (July–Aug. 1960), 45 –56.

13. A. Ries, *Focus* (London: HarperCollins Business, 1996).

14. See, for example, W. Davidow and B. Uttal, 'Service Companies: Focus or Falter', *Harvard Business Review* (July–Aug. 1989), 77–85.

15. V. Smith, *Reining in the Dinosaur: The Story Behind the Remarkable Turnaround of New Zealand Post* (Wellington: New Zealand Post, 1997).

16. A. Campbell, 'The Power of Mission: Aligning Strategy and Culture', *Planning Review* (Sept./Oct. 1992), 10–12, 63.

5

Formal Company Policies: The Guiding Hands

In Chapter 4 I focused on the soul of corporate reputation. Here I discuss the role of strategy, structure, and business systems in shaping an organization's reputation. Simply stated, the development of a strong set of corporate images and reputations is driven in large part by the formal policies used to manage the organization. Much of what has recently been written about the management of complex organizations, however, is faddish. Concepts such as benchmarking, outsourcing, relationship marketing, strategic partnerships, and total quality management are just new names for what has always been a sound business practice. Other advice to managers to make radical changes to change their current operational procedures (such as by business process re-engineering) and structures (by flattening the organization structure) with new, untried alternatives is at best unproven and at worst dangerous to corporate health and wealth.[1]

Consequently, the material presented in this chapter stays with the basic ideas which (I think) have stood the test of time. While the way in which they are presented may be new to some readers, I seek to follow the advice of Sir Isaac Newton, namely that, to see further it is helpful to stand on the strong, broad shoulders of others.[2]

Reading about the most respected companies in the world suggests two things. First, they understand what makes them successful. These success factors are sometimes labelled their 'core competencies'. Second, these companies do not change their efforts to build these core competencies. Companies like General Electric, Motorola, Procter & Gamble, Rubbermaid, and 3M in the United States; ABB (Asea Brown Boveri), BMW, Ericsson, and Siemens in Europe, and Canon, Matsushita, Sony, and Toyota in Japan are focused around a few simple themes over an extended period of time. For example, Motorola has been preoccupied with quality for more than a decade, and 3M with innovation for an even longer period. Such a protracted investment pays off in numerous ways— the company learns this function better than competitors, and thus builds an inimitable asset. It also becomes known for this skill with business partners and customers. In the case of 3M, they advertise this core competence in their corporate slogan—'innovation'.

The business an organization chooses to participate in, and the way it seeks to create a competitive advantage, will have a profound impact on what people think about the company. Over the past two decades, managers have been under pressure to rethink some of the most fundamental aspects of their companies' business strategies. Many of the sources of this pressure have come from the environment in which the organization operates, and include factors such as the globalization of markets, deregulation, and breakthroughs in communication technology like the Internet. In other cases pressure has come from inside the company. For much of Corporate America this pressure is the relentless pursuit of *growth*. And if there is one thing that can degrade the images and then the reputations of companies among stakeholders (other than financial analysts), it is growth at any cost—see Exhibit 5.1.

In this chapter the term 'formal company policies' is used to refer to all the decisions that guide the strategy, structure, investments, business processes, and control systems of the organization. Figure 3.1 in Chapter 3 shows that these formal policies influence the organization's culture, employee images and reputations, product and service offerings to customers, and all forms of communication with stakeholders. The point of entry into an analysis of an organization's formal policies is via the strategic planning process.

STRATEGIC PLANNING

Big, complex organizations typically plan strategy at three levels—corporate, strategic business unit (SBU), and function (e.g., marketing). Research by the Strategic Planning Institute through its Profit Impact of Market Strategies (PIMS) database identified some key planning issues at these levels.[3] For example, to enable a company to compete effectively, it must define what business it is in, and it must build a set of core competencies which its SBUs can use to develop products and services.[4] At a functional level like marketing, the key concerns are to attain and retain customers. The problem with strategic planning at multiple levels is to get

Exhibit 5.1. Growth at any cost

Growth at the cost of becoming unfocused

The high-profile advertising and marketing consultant Al Ries argues that companies lose their focus, and thus their clear position in their stakeholders' minds for at least three growth-related reasons. One is that success creates the opportunity to branch out in new and different directions—General Motors in the 1960s, Sears in the 1970s, IBM in the 1980s, and Microsoft in the 1990s. The second is the now largely discredited strategy of unrelated diversification. IBM bought Rolm in 1984—and sold it in 1989; Coca-Cola bought Columbia Pictures in 1982—and sold it in 1989 (for a $1.5 billion profit); Eastman Kodak bought Sterling Drug in 1988—and sold it in 1994. And the list goes on and on. A third way to become unfocused is to operate in a market that shows no overall growth and be put under pressure to substantially increase sales and profits. What happens is that the company (a) offers more varieties and flavours of their current products, (b) branches out into new markets, (c) acquires other firms or products, and/or (d) sets up joint ventures.

Ries's point is that successful companies usually start out highly focused on a single product, service, or market, and then over time they become unfocused. The more broad-ranging they become, the more difficult they are to manage and the more likely it is that parts of them will be uncompetitive and unprofitable. Negative scores on these characteristics do not foster good corporate images and reputations. Thus, from a corporate image/reputation perspective, being in focus is better than being unfocused.

Source: Derived from: A. Ries, *Focus* (London: HarperCollins Business, 1996) and A. Ries and J. Trout, *Positioning: The Battle for Your Mind* (New York: McGraw-Hill, 1986).

Growth at the cost of your employees

Between 1985 and 1996 Rubbermaid consistently ranked in the top ten of the *Fortune* most admired companies. In 1997 it slipped to number 22. One of the attributes that kept Rubbermaid an all-star company for so long was its impressive growth. During the decade of the 1980s it had average, annual profit increases of 14 per cent and share price increases of 25 per cent.

Back in the 1950s Rubbermaid made a pledge to double in size every six years. This meant sales and earnings increases of 12.25 per cent each year. In the late 1970s, it raised the target to 15 per cent annual growth, or a doubling of size every five years. In the 1980s it achieved this target, in part because of the acquisition of some competitors and as the result of inflation. In the early 1990s, the company had to struggle much harder for growth and often fell short of its target. In the process it passed on cost increases to its customers and upset its biggest customer Wal-Mart. Wal-Mart's reputation is based on low prices to customers, so Rubbermaid's cost increase to help it achieve its growth target was an unwelcome move.

Inside the company the strain also showed. Schmitt, the CEO, did not hesitate to force out several upper-level managers who could not meet their ambitious sales goals. Also, the remaining managers know that to achieve the stated growth target, Rubbermaid had to grow by the size of a company like Dow Corning!

Sources: Derived from: A. Farnham, 'America's Most Admired Company', *Fortune* (7 Feb. 1994), 36–9; L. Smith, 'Rubbermaid goes thump', *Fortune* (2 Oct. 1995), 68–76.

co-ordination and alignment among the levels of planning. Figure 5.1 illustrates how the three levels of strategic planning can be focused around a theme that is important to various stakeholder groups, namely, that of creating value.

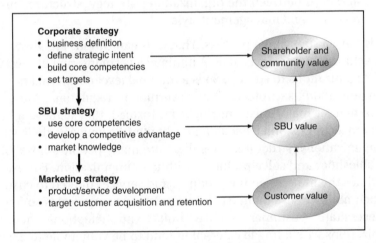

Figure 5.1. Strategic planning

Source: Derived from L. Brown, *Competitive Marketing Strategy* (Melbourne: Nelson, 1997), 22.

Figure 5.1 highlights the crucial planning decision that an organization must make which affects its desired image and reputation, namely, what its overarching goal will be. When Robert Haas took control of Levi's he made the overarching goal social value. When the company went public in 1971, its offering prospectus warned that profits might be affected by a commitment to social programmes.[5] For companies like Coca Cola, Gillette, Nike, and Disney the overarching goal is financial value.

To understand how an organization's strategic planning and other formal policies influence the images and reputations of that organization held by employees and outsiders, we start by looking at the concept of fit.

FIT, FAILURE, AND THE HALL OF FAME

A guiding principle in the process of strategic management is to ensure that each level of the organization's strategy, structure, and management processes complement each other. In a landmark strategic management paper, Raymond Miles and Charles Snow illustrated that successful companies are the ones that achieve a strategic 'fit' with their market environment, and support their strategies with appropriately designed structures and management control processes.[6] They identified two types of fit:

(a) *external fit* between the market environment and the organization's resources, competencies, and product/service offerings, and

(b) *internal fit* between the organization's strategy, structure, business processes, and management style.

Fit is both a state and a process. That is, organizations are always striving to achieve a tighter level of fit. A minimal level of internal fit is essential for all organizations to survive. So is a minimal level of external fit, unless the organization is protected by government regulation. Most firms achieve neither major misfit nor tight fit. Instead, they achieve a limited alignment with customer needs and a limited fit between their strategy and organizational structure. Thus there are many people whose job it is to troubleshoot and solve problems within an organization. For example, sometimes the fit between the products and services offered to customers and their ability to use them (such as a personal computer) is so fragile as to necessitate customer service units and telephone help-lines. Organizations with a fragile external fit tend to be vulnerable to changing market conditions and competitors that redefine the market—as we see happening with Internet commerce.

The dividing line between an acceptable level of fit, and misfit, is generally difficult to detect. Misfit tends to creep up on organizations and can come from internal sources, and/or environmental change. Exhibit 5.2 provides two examples.

Miles and Snow argue that finding the right strategy is not as important to success as achieving a tight fit. The primary reason for this is that many competitors will have a similar understanding of the forces driving the evolution of their market, and be considering similar market development or market penetration strategies. They argue that what differentiates the winners from the not so successful companies is the organization's ability to articulate a good strategy, and the ability to develop a structure to

Exhibit 5.2. Internal and external misfit

Miles and Snow offer the Chrysler Corporation as a classic example of internally generated misfit. From a strong position in the 1930s as the second largest US automotive manufacturer, Chrysler began its decline after the Second World War when it changed its strategy without significantly altering its organization structure or management processes. Chrysler decided to broaden its product line and compete with both Ford and General Motors world-wide. However, it did not support this new diversified product-market strategy with a modified organization structure. In fact, Chrysler tried (unsuccessfully) to use its centralized functional structure to support its new strategy. After many years of misfit, Lee Iacocca was appointed CEO to rescue the company and Chrysler needed Federal Government assistance to avoid bankruptcy.

A good example of externally generated misfit is the demise of the UK motorcycle industry. From the early 1900s until the 1960s, the United Kingdom was a major force in the manufacture and sale of motorbikes. By the 1980s, however, the famous names like BSA, Norton, and Triumph were out of the market. The early 1960s saw the entry of the Japanese into the UK market—Honda, Kawasaki, Yamaha, and Suzuki. The entry strategy of Honda was to avoid head-on competition with the established manufacturers. Instead, it targeted 'first time buyers' with lightweight, easy to handle, 125cc bikes, and a dealer network that provided good customer support to this 'beginner' market segment. From this base the Japanese moved up to the next engine size category (250cc), again with innovative design and strong marketing and dealer support. Many customers were their original first-time buyers who were trading up from smaller machines. This group was also a potential purchaser of British bikes. When the Japanese dominated this segment they moved up to the segment of the market which wanted big bikes. To demonstrate their capability to manufacture quality bikes, they went bike racing with great success.

The response of British manufacturers was very slow. They seemed to believe that they could rely on their established reputation to keep (attracting) customers. In fact, it was probably their reputation that helped to speed up their demise! At the time of the Japanese entry to the market, customers thought that the British manufacturers had a weak dealer network and poor product availability. Also, in contrast to the Japanese manufacturers, the British bike makers did not seem to have any type of long-term strategy. It took just ten years for a group of companies with good strategic insight, and the organization structure and management systems to back it up, to destroy the established market participants who had no sustainable competitive advantage.

Sources: Derived from: R. Miles and C. Snow, *Fit, Failure & the Hall of Fame* (New York: The Free Press, 1994) and M. Christopher, S. Majaro, and M. McDonald, *Strategy Search* (Aldershot: Gower, 1987).

support this before competitors. In essence, hall of fame companies achieve tight internal and external fit *before* their competitors.

The main factors that drive tight fit are shown in Figure 5.2. This is a contingency framework where corporate strategy is a determinant, while information technology, human resources, organizational structure, and culture enable and constrain what the firm can do. Competitive position and value creation are the measures of successful external fit.

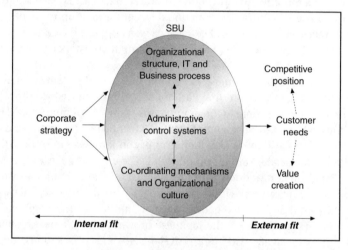

Figure 5.2. A model of strategic fit

Organizations with tight internal and external fits are usually associated with excellence—both operational and financial. Morale and confidence also tend to be high because people can see clearly how and why things work. Rewards can be structured around performance rather than hard work. When the internal and external aspects of tight fit are communicated and understood throughout the organization, this becomes a powerful driver of a good corporate image.

CORPORATE AND BUSINESS UNIT STRATEGY

When strategic planners talk about strategy they usually focus on decisions that involve major commitments of resources. This was nicely summed up by Robert Goizueta, until recently CEO of arguably the world's best-known brand—Coca-Cola: 'When you get right down to it, what I really do is allocate resources—capital, manpower'.[7] This perspective of irrevocable resource allocation manifests itself in the creation of assets (human, physical, information, perceptions) which a firm builds up over time. In the introduction of this book, I nominated good images and corporate reputations as one such asset. Overall, it is the differences in these assets, and how they are used to serve customers' real needs, that determine the competitive advantage that a company enjoys in its markets. This process of strategy formulation starts with the answer to a very difficult question.

Business definition

One of the most fundamental and difficult questions that managers must ask about their organization is, 'What business are we in?' How can such a simple question be so difficult to answer well? One reason is that many corporate chiefs are prone to get caught by the hype generated by the business gurus—especially those with a grand vision of the future. It is then easy for companies to aspire to be something that is beyond current capabilities. A good example was Xerox in the 1980s. In the 1960s and 1970s Xerox was *the* copier company. In 1970 it sold 95 per cent of all copiers. By 1982 however, Xerox's market share had fallen to 13 per cent of units. During this decline it suffered from visions of grandeur.

Xerox wanted to become an 'information company' and create the office of the future. A small step for customers, but a giant leap for Xerox. To achieve this mission it was forced into the computer business. To finance the expansion it moved into financial services, which it saw as a cash cow. For a variety of internal and external reasons, it could not make the transition.[8] A new Chairman (Paul Allaire) repositioned Xerox around its core competencies of printing and copying, within a world of digital products hooked together by networks. The 'document' was the customer product around which new product development was focused. Xerox became the Document Company, as illustrated in Figure 5.3. In effect, Xerox stepped back from the future and in the process became a much more focused and successful company.

An important problem for many organizations in a competitive market situation is that the business is defined in terms of what the organization does rather than what its customers want from it. That is, the concern of managers is for 'means' (products, production processes, R&D) rather than 'ends' (what customer benefits and/or solutions to problems to

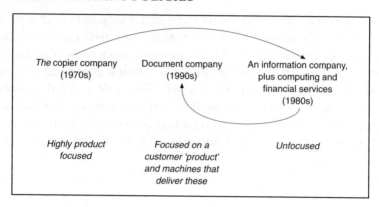

Figure 5.3. Xerox steps back from the future

offer). Professor Ted Levitt of the Harvard Business School (in 1960) and Kenichi Ohmae (in 1986) forcefully advanced the proposition that market definitions of a business are superior to product-based definitions.[9] They argued that products are transient, but that basic needs and types of customers endure. For example, new products that are often based on new technologies cannibalize the sales of existing products. Portable electronic calculators have replaced slide-rules, and audio tapes and compact discs have replaced gramophone records. The basic customer needs that these original products served have endured, but they are now serviced by completely different products.

Levitt and Ohmae have encouraged companies to define their businesses from a market, not a company perspective. In this way they can avoid the trap of being caught in the 'slide-rule' or the 'gramophone record' business. Instead, managers should focus on the underlying need for (portable) numerical calculation, or high-quality music reproduction. The business writer Derek Abell suggests using three criteria to create a market-oriented business definition.[10] These are:

(a) the customer groups to be served;
(b) the customer needs to be met; and
(c) the (business) technology used to satisfy these needs.

For example, the lighting division (SBU) of the Philips company serves a variety of customer groups (e.g., homes, factories, offices, outdoor stadiums), with incandescent and fluorescent lighting (technologies), to satisfy the needs of illumination, safety, and security. That is, the business definition of the Philips Lighting Division is defined by the intersection of these three factors. It is a relatively straightforward task for Philips' managers to survey the needs of different customer groups, identify competitors (and their strategies), and monitor the relevant technologies that will affect the production process for different types of lighting systems. Being a leader in this technology also allows Philips to reshape its markets. For example, in 1995 the company introduced its Alto fluorescent lamp (or bulb) in the USA. The traditional lamps contained toxic mercury and were costly for large-quantity users to dispose. The Alto lamps reduced customers' over-all costs and allowed them and Philips to promote environmental con-cern—enhancing the reputations of both parties.

Organizations and business units that define their business according to Abell's three criteria are in a good position to answer the question, 'How will we compete?' For example, some large pharmaceutical compa-nies have redefined their business as 'managed care' rather than drugs. While the motivation for this change was to capture a greater share of the health-care dollar, another motivation was that the images and reputa-tions of pharmaceutical companies was not as good as those of health maintenance organizations. Pharmaceutical companies often have low awareness among patients and they are mistrusted by politicians. In 1993, a group called Pharmaceutical Partners for Better Healthcare was formed by the heads of forty of the world's biggest drug firms to improve the image of the drug industry.[11]

Understanding where to compete in a market can have a major impact on an organization's images and reputations—especially when it reshapes a consumer market. Body Shop did this by distancing itself from the excessive glamour of the cosmetics industry. A corporate/brand image of low price; cheap, reusable packaging; little advertising; low-technology cosmetic science; natural ingredients; and community concern appealed to a group of consumers who valued healthy living, simplicity, and restraint more than glamour and glitz. The opposite strategy was adopted by Starbucks—the US coffee chain. They saw a market opportunity to add interest and emotion to coffee drinking after the marketing strategies of General Foods, Nestlé, and Procter & Gamble had trained consumers to buy on price and to regard coffee as a routine, commodity drink. Both these companies redefined a significant part of their market and in the process became small corporate super-brands.[12]

Core competencies and strategic intent

The work of C. K. Prahalad and Gary Hamel has helped many companies to identify the tangible link between the core competencies or collective learning of the organization and its ability to produce and successfully market certain products and services.[13] They argue that few companies will build leadership in more than five or six fundamental competencies. For example, Honda's core competence in engines and powertrains give it the ability to produce a range of world-class cars, outboard motorboat engines, generators, lawnmowers, motorcycles, and snow blowers. Canon's core competencies in the technologies of optics and micro-processor controls are imbedded in a range of products for the office—digital cameras, digital photocopiers, scanners, and laser beam printers.

By embedding the company's core competencies in its core products, a company can create a dominant market position to help it shape the evolution of applications and end markets. It is this portfolio of core products that builds what the advertising agencies call a company's share of mind, and thus its brand and corporate images. These products also allow the company to capture the benefits of economies of scale and scope. Elsewhere, I have labelled these companies as market driving as opposed to being market (i.e., customer or competitor) driven.[14]

The organization's core competencies should also shape its strategic intent, that is, how it competes. This aspect of corporate strategy is the firm's theory about success and failure. Typically, companies have adopted one or a combination of the generic strategies in Table 5.1. Core

Table 5.1. Generic strategies

Strategy	Characteristics	Example
Differentiation	Achieve superior performance in an important customer benefit area	Sony Walkman
Focus	On one or more market segments	Rolls-Royce cars
Overall cost leadership	Lowest delivered cost	Ikea
Playing the spread	Use process innovation to achieve low cost and high quality across a wide range of products for different market segments	Kellogg's, Toyota
Asset management	Unique access to resources	Argyle diamonds
	Flexible use of resources	Consulting
Innovation	Product	Intel's chips
	Process	Pilkington float glass
	Marketing	Body Shop, Nike

competencies can be thought of as shaping generic strategy by defining the DNA sequence of the company.

To illustrate how core competencies and a generic strategy help shape the image of a company consider Ikea (the Swedish furniture manufacturer), McDonald's, and Wal-Mart. They all practise a lowest delivered cost strategy. Wal-Mart has core competencies in IT and logistics to help it achieve its low costs. McDonald's has expertise in food processing and process innovation that allows it to achieve a consistent product worldwide. Ikea uses product innovation to design furniture that the consumer helps to assemble at home. Ikea calls their customers 'prosumers'—producer-consumers. Because cost leadership is a strategy that drives customer value through low prices, these three companies have been able to tap into widespread community support. This has helped them enhance their corporate images into corporate reputations.

MARKETING STRATEGY

Because marketing is often held responsible for the interface between the organization and the customer, this function can have a big impact on both external fit and the images and reputations held by customers. As some recent marketing initiatives indicate, this impact can be negative as well as positive. For example, in recent years, three marketing strategies have damaged the images of companies that aggressively implemented them, namely, price wars, price promotions, and customer loyalty schemes. Price wars often decrease the value of an industry—although customers like them; price promotions devalue brands and train customers to buy only when products are on special offer; and customer loyalty schemes (especially frequent-flyer programmes) often upset members when they try to claim their rewards.[15]

The key point about marketing's interface with customers is that good images and reputations are driven fundamentally by the offer of good, genuine customer value—not by trying to 'bribe' customers to be loyal to products and services. The path to offering such value starts with the appropriate segmentation of customers.

The concept of market segmentation can be an elusive phenomenon to pin down. To a sales-force manager it can mean geographically partitioning customers in order to allocate territories to the sales-force. To many advertising and brand managers, it means matching the characteristics of customers to the demographic audience profile of the media. To a business marketer, it may mean a single key account. Each of these examples, however, falls short of segmentation to *create* customer value.

Segmentation to create customer value starts with the allocation of (potential) customers to a group whose members have similar needs (needs that differ from those of other groups). Such needs-based segmentation is then used to set the specifications for product/service design and pricing. In this way, the functional and psychological benefits offered by the product/service are designed to fit the needs of customers. If the price can be set to fit the target customers' budget, then there is a good fit between what is offered and what is desired.[16] Such a good external fit will lead to a good corporate and/or brand image among target customers. If the customer value (benefits relative to price) can be linked to a free-standing cultural value held by customers, then a good corporate image may be upgraded to a good corporate reputation. Advertising is often used to make such a connection.

ORGANIZATION STRUCTURE

Figure 5.2 illustrated the important role of organizational structure and administrative control to the internal fit of a firm and thus the organizational images and reputations held by employees. In this section I briefly review the main generic structure and process configurations so that their impact on internal image formation can be gauged.

In 1979 Henry Mintzberg drew together much of the work on the structure of organizations. His ideas are widely used and are still appropriate for understanding the basic structural configurations of many SBUs.[17] He called the fundamental type of organization the *simple structure*. This organization is one with little or no formal structure. It typically consists of a boss (owner or manager) and the workers. Co-ordination of tasks is achieved by direct supervision, and strategy is formulated by the manager. Such organizations are flexible, but very limited in their capacity to cope with complexity. They tend to use simple technologies in simple operating environments. The image projected is often based heavily on the personality and style of the owner/manager.

As organizations grow they quickly become more formalized. Work is divided to facilitate specialization, and the organization strives to achieve reliability, predictability, and efficiency. Some of the key people are those who design work practices, and the formal and informal monitoring and control mechanisms. Institutionalized information systems are developed to monitor costs, throughput, and sales rather than customer needs. There is a tendency for decision making and power to be centralized. Mintzberg called the archetypal form of this type of organization a *machine bureaucracy*—a term that captures the mental image of these organizations. Such mechanistic organizations were suited to operating in a stable or predictable environment. The early Baton Rouge plant that made the Model-T Ford was a classic example. Its internal structure was reflected in its products. Customers could have any colour Model-T—as long as it was black.

Organizations that carry out complex tasks and operate in a stable or predictable environment are not restricted to being organized like a machine. Co-ordination of operations can be achieved by standardizing the skills and knowledge of workers (often through professional training), rather than their work practices. These organizations can be decentralized, in both the vertical and horizontal dimensions. Mintzberg called these *professional bureaucracies* and they are common in universities, research institutes, hospitals, schools, and public accounting firms. Strategy within a professional bureaucracy often has to blend the personal agendas of key people, with acceptable professional practice, and the desires of the organization. The CEOs of these firms often refer to their task as akin to trying to herd a group of cats. Needless to say, trying to project a coherent image can be difficult.

The *functional* organization arranges its resources into a set of quasi-autonomous functional entities (e.g., manufacturing, logistics, marketing, etc.). Co-ordination is via centrally devised plans, schedules, and control mechanisms. Many companies pursuing a strategy based on efficiency (e.g., lowest delivered cost) utilize some form of functional organization. For example, Wal-Mart integrates functional specialists with its state-of-the-art information system to produce huge logistical efficiencies. In organizations of this type the proactive management of the desired corporate image is usually the responsibility of the corporate affairs unit which reports directly to the CEO.

The *divisional* organization groups a collection of largely self-sufficient resources around a product or regional market. For example, in the mid-1990s, General Motors had six domestic and a host of overseas divisions. Each division had substantial operating authority that led to some corporate image problems. For example, Al Ries compared the base car prices for the US divisions: Buick ($13,700 to $33,084), Cadillac ($34,990 to $45,935), Chevrolet ($8,085 to $68,043), Oldsmobile ($13,500 to $31,370), Pontiac ($11,074 to $27,139), and Saturn ($9,995 to $31,370).[18] Two things emerge from this simple analysis—overlapping price ranges and sometimes a huge variation in prices within a division. From the customer's point of view it is legitimate to ask 'What is a GM car?' and 'What is a Chevrolet?' (The Chevrolet division had both the cheapest and the most expensive cars.)

Recently, a new form of organization structure has emerged that is based on networks of firms arranged along a value chain to produce products—component supplies, manufacturing, advertising, distribution, marketing, and service. For example, Nike focuses on its core competencies of athletic shoe design and marketing, and uses other firms for manufacturing, distribution, and retailing. Similarly, Dell Computer focuses on its core competencies of customized personal computer assembly, direct marketing, and customer support. All the PC components and accessories come from other firms and distribution to customers is via independent couriers. Both of these firms manage their desired corporate image by using quality suppliers (e.g., Intel chips for Dell) and/or through their creative advertising (e.g., Nike).

When an organization's environment tends to be turbulent (complex and/or dynamic), and when people must perform unusual or complex tasks which change each time they are performed, the various types of organization described above are generally unsuitable. Here, the organization must be designed for change. To compete under these conditions firms decentralize decision making, broadly define jobs, use as few rules and procedures as they can, and subjectively evaluate individual performance. IT systems are often distributed throughout the organization to provide specialized information processing capabilities to support the innovativeness of individuals.

Professional business consultants (management consultants, corporate lawyers, advertising agencies, etc.) are good examples of such organizations. People with different skills, goals, and time horizons must co-ordinate their work to satisfy the expectations of customers. Frequent meetings, often 'on the run', and proposals, briefing papers, and reports are used as co-ordinating mechanisms. Power and authority tend to be situational and based on expertise. Within work teams communication is open, and environmental (customer) monitoring is extensive. Mintzberg called this type of organization an *organic structure* or an *adhocracy*. In many of these organizations, the images and reputations of the firm are closely tied to those of its key individuals.

The diversity of ways that an organization can use to gain a competitive advantage means that there are no simple rules about what are, or are not appropriate strategy-structure configurations. Instead, managers must choose a generic strategy mix and then support this strategy with a suitable structure and complementary control activities. Major changes in business strategy are often triggered by some form of crisis (e.g., a fall in market share, the threat of a takeover, the entry of a new competitor, a change in technology, etc.). They also often involve a change of organizational structure. For example, when Xerox changed to become a Document Company, it changed from a functional structure (engineering, manufacturing, sales, service, etc.) to one organized into business units focused on end customers (e.g., desktop document systems and personal document products).

The key point about organizational structure is that its architecture, control systems, and co-ordinating mechanisms are powerful drivers of internal fit and employee perceptions. Structure can also help or hinder the amount of external fit achieved by organizations—especially in service industries (e.g., when administrative control systems inhibit the front-line people in delivering the standard of service illustrated in the advertising). When external fit is poor, the images held by external stakeholders are also likely to be poor.

EMPLOYEES DO WHAT IS INSPECTED MORE THAN WHAT IS EXPECTED

Managers often struggle to achieve a balance between what the organization expects its employees to do and how it actually measures their effort and achievements. In many cases there is little or no relationship between expectations and measures of performance. Consider the case of customer service—something that can have a big impact on the images that customers hold of an organization. One company measured the time taken to answer each inbound call from customers to the service centre as its index of responsiveness. It also measured the length of time the service centre person was in contact with the customer as its index of service. The employees were able to get good scores on these indices by answering the phone quickly and putting the customer on hold!

While this example can correctly be interpreted as a case of measuring the wrong things (an employee's activity rather than customer satisfaction), it also touches on the broader dilemma that introduced Chapter 1. Recall that managers were being directly rewarded for bottom-line financial performance in preference to building other aspects of corporate value such as a good image and reputation. The key issue in both cases is whether it is possible to design a performance monitoring system that enhances both customer satisfaction (and thus corporate image and reputation) and profitability. In theory, it seems that the answer is yes.

John Hauser and his colleagues at the Massachusetts Institute of Technology worked out the conditions when it makes financial sense for a firm to reward employees on the basis of customer satisfaction measures.[19] Briefly, what they found was that the less employees valued, or expected a long-term future with the firm, the more the firm needed to tie their rewards to measured customer satisfaction. The assumption here is that measured satisfaction is an indicator of employee efforts (or skill) which generate a better corporate image and thus future sales. When this condition holds, giving employees incentives based on customer satisfaction measures encourages them to make trade-offs that are in the best interests of themselves and the firm.

CONCLUSIONS

An organization's strategy defines how it wants to compete. The strategy is implemented by developing a supportive organizational structure and a set of appropriate business systems. An integral component of competitive strategy is the organization's positioning relative to its competitors. That is, how will an organization distinguish itself favourably from the other organizations that also seek to serve the same customers? Good competitive positioning is usually based on the functional and/or psychological benefits the organization offers to stakeholders. Chapter 11 elaborates the positioning element of competitive strategy, for this is another key attribute of an organization's desired image and reputation.

Successful organizations also learn how to read their environment and couple their strategy, business systems, and structure to deliver value to their employees and customers. In the case of Wal-Mart, Sam Walton once summarized this as giving rural Americans, people of modest means, more choice and quality, for less cost. Employees, customers, and the local communities all valued this—although existing competitors did not.

Tight (but not restrictive) levels of internal and external fit are a necessary but not sufficient condition for developing a strong set of images and reputations among various stakeholder groups. The consistent presentation of an organization to its stakeholders, based on a shared understanding of its business strategy, is essential to the formation of a distinctive image and a valued reputation. The next chapter focuses on a key driver of this process, namely, the culture of the organization.

NOTES

1. F. Hilmer and L. Donaldson, *Management Redeemed* (New York: The Free Press, 1996).
2. The full quotation is: 'If I have seen further it is by standing on the shoulders of giants' (1676).
3. R. Buzzel and B. Gale, *The PIMS Principles: Linking Strategy to Performance* (New York: The Free Press, 1987); B. Gale, *Managing Customer Value: Creating Quality and Service That Customers Can See* (New York: The Free Press, 1994).
4. C. K. Prahalad and G. Hamel, 'The Core Competence of the Corporation', *Harvard Business Review* (May–June 1990), 79–91.
5. N. Munk, 'How Levi's Trashed a Great American Brand', *Fortune* (12 April 1999), 32–42.
6. R. Miles and C. Snow, 'Fit, Failure and The Hall of Fame', *California Management Review*, 26, 3 (Spring 1984), 10–28; and R. Miles and C. Snow, *Fit, Failure & the Hall of Fame* (New York: The Free Press, 1994).
7. J. Huey, 'The World's Best Brand', *Fortune* (31 May 1993), 24–32.
8. S. Chakravarty, 'Back in Focus', *Forbes* (6 June 1994), 72–6.
9. T. Levitt, 'Marketing Myopia', *Harvard Business Review* (July–Aug. 1960), 45–56. For a more contemporary perspective, see K. Ohmae, 'Getting Back to Strategy', *Harvard Business Review* (Nov.–Dec. 1988), 149–56.
10. D. Abell, *Defining the Business: The Starting Point of Strategic Planning* (Englewood Cliffs, NJ: Prentice Hall, 1980), ch. 3.
11. 'Back to the Apothecary', *The Economist* (7 May 1994), 71–2.
12. W. C. Kim and R. Mauborgne, 'Creating New Market Space', *Harvard Business Review* (Jan.–Feb. 1999), 83–93.
13. C. K. Prahalad and G. Hamel, 'The Core Competence of the Corporation', *Harvard Business Review* (May–June 1990), 79–91; G. Hamel and C. K. Prahalad, *Competing for the Future* (Boston: Harvard Business School Press, 1994).
14. G. R. Dowling, 'Market Driving Companies: The Goal of Innovation is to Create a Dominant Design', Working Paper No. 95-013, Australian Graduate School of Management (1995).
15. G. R. Dowling and M. Uncles, 'Do Customer Loyalty Programs Really Work?', *Sloan Management Review*, 38, 4 (1997), 71–82.
16. Modern marketers talk about creating customer value—through the design of products and services; communicating value—through advertising; delivering value—through distribution arrangements; and capturing value—through pricing.
17. H. Mintzberg, *The Structure of Organizations* (Englewood Cliffs, NJ: Prentice Hall, 1979).
18. A. Reis, *Focus* (London: HarperCollins Business, 1996).
19. J. Hauser, D. Simester, and B. Wernerfelt, 'Customer Satisfaction Incentives', *Marketing Science*, 13, 4 (1994), 327–50.

6

Organizational Culture: The Invisible Web

Most people have a sense of their own culture and of differences in national cultures. These cultural differences are rooted in very basic beliefs about the origins of life, the role of time and nature in shaping people's lives, and how people should interact with each other. Such belief systems are a powerful force which shape our behaviour as a society, and our business dealings. With trade and commerce becoming more international, an appreciation of such differences is an important prerequisite to competing globally. This is despite the fact that the language used for much of the world's international business is English.

To an anthropologist a culture is revealed by its language, ritual, kinship structure, architecture, and symbols. History has often demonstrated how important a name (or other identity symbols such as a flag) is to helping people identify with a culture. An interesting example of this occurred with the last renaming of the city of St Petersburg. In 1703 the young Russian tsar, Peter I, began to build a city to project his self-image, and to be the new Russian capital. The name Peter gave to his new city was not Russian, but rather Germanic, in honour of his patron saint. St Petersburg was designed to be different from other Russian cities (especially Moscow), and in time it developed its own distinct cultural identity. To appease anti-German feelings arising during the First World War, the city was renamed Petrograd in 1914. A decade later, to commemorate Lenin's death, the city was given the new name of Leningrad. In 1991 the city's residents held a referendum and returned the city's original name—St Petersburg (Sankt-Peterburg). The power of the cultural identity symbolized by the city's original name somehow survived a generation of inhabitants, and powerful new identity-forming events such as 'the siege of Leningrad' during the Second World War.

It is not a big step from thinking about national cultures to thinking about the culture of work and organizational cultures. However it was only in the decade of the 1970s that researchers (in the business schools of Harvard, Stanford, and MIT) and consultants (most notably at McKinsey and MAC) began to realize that an organization's culture was a powerful force that shaped many aspects of its behaviour.[1] As more studies of the creation and functioning of organizations were conducted, it became clear that the cultures of individual organizations are also shaped by the general culture of work. For example, a 1996 study of 1,200 business students from thirty of the world's leading universities in ten countries indicated that the next generation of managers might well be described as the 'get-a-life' generation.[2] The overwhelming conclusion from this study was that these students had a strong desire to have a balanced lifestyle and a rewarding life outside work. Companies that can offer this environment to new managers might well get the pick of the next crop of university-trained managers.

In the context of the overall image formation process outlined in Chapter 3 (and Figure 3.1), the organization's culture plays a pivotal role in translating the values in the vision statement into employee behaviour. It also affects how many aspects of an organization's strategy, structure, and control systems are implemented (Chapter 5).[3] These interrelationships are graphically shown in the McKinsey 7-S framework outlined in Figure 4.1 of Chapter 4, where the factors Shared values and Style reflect an organization's culture. In fact, it is a lack of understanding of organization culture that causes many image rejuvenation programmes to fail to achieve their expected outcomes.

The following sections in this chapter describe the concept of organizational culture. A knowledge of this facilitates the task of assessing the culture of an organization. The focus then shifts to how this powerful force can enhance or hinder the development of the images and reputations of the organization among employees. We must deal with three issues about culture, however, before we proceed. First, culture is all about internal beliefs and values. Hence, it will influence the formation of both corporate images (beliefs) and reputations (values). Second, there is a relationship between organizational culture and long-term financial performance—see Exhibit 6.1. Third, while most executives have a natural desire for quick and decisive action, corporate culture is a slow, evolutionary force in the image and reputation formation process. They cannot adopt the attitude expressed in the following statement by a fictitious chief executive on discovering the importance of corporate culture: 'That sounds great! I want one by Friday afternoon.'

Exhibit 6.1. Corporate culture and financial performance

Two Harvard Business School professors, John Kotter and James Heskett, surveyed 207 US companies to describe their organizational cultures and to then assess the relationship between culture strength and financial performance over an eleven-year period. They found that highly profitable firms like PepsiCo, Wal-Mart, and Shell had what can be best described as an adaptive culture that emphasized the interests of employees, customers, and stockholders. Companies with this cultural trait had average revenue increases of 682 per cent and stock price increases of 901 per cent. Firms which did not focus on all three stakeholder groups had relatively poor financial performance, namely, average sales increases of 166 per cent and stock price increases of 74 per cent.

This research study provided some revealing and interesting insights about organizational culture:

(1) Strong organizational cultures help align the firm's goals, motivate employees, and provide needed structure and control.

However,

(2) They can blind an organization to changing market conditions and thus the need for internal change.
(3) 'Fit' between organizational culture and market environment is important for short-term economic performance.

But:

(4) Tight fit can be undermined by a changing environment.
(5) In a competitive market, the way managers serve stockholder needs is to focus on customers and to support employees.

Organizations that do not focus on stockholders, customers, and employees tend to focus on 'Themselves'.

Source: Derived from J. Kotter and J. Heskett, *Corporate Culture and Performance* (New York: The Free Press, 1992).

WHAT IS ORGANIZATIONAL CULTURE?

Over the past thirty years enough has been written about the topic of organization culture to provide good guidance to the practising manager. The perspective adopted in this chapter is to assume that culture is something that all organizations have to a greater or lesser extent. It is a variable, and so it makes sense to find out whether different types or amounts of culture are related to other aspects of organizations. For example, Exhibit 6.1 indicates that organizations with a strong, balanced culture perform better in the marketplace than organizations with a weaker or unbalanced culture. Also, as outlined later in this chapter, different types of cultures can enhance or inhibit internal communication in an organization. These are the types of issues that management researchers and consultants consider.

A good working definition of organization culture is the following:

The system of shared values (what is important) and beliefs (how things work) that interact with a company's people, organizational structures, and control systems to produce behavioral norms (the way we do things around here).[4]

A somewhat more 'academic' definition is:

The pattern of basic assumptions which a group has invented, discovered or developed, in learning to cope with problems in its environment, which have worked well enough to be considered valid and therefore to be taught to new members as the correct way to perceive, think, and feel in relation to those problems.[5]

A number of aspects of these definitions are worth elaborating. First, cultures are developed by people (a group), and they are comprised of their beliefs, feelings, corporate values, and assumptions. These beliefs and values will vary, depending on the nature of the work group to which a person belongs, and the types of problems they face in the work environment. Broad national cultural factors and general workplace cultures will also affect an organization's culture. For example, in many countries workplace unions have a legitimacy in society and a major impact on what workers and governments perceive as acceptable conditions and pay rates for various types of work.

A second aspect of organizational culture is that it filters information coming into the organization. The positive result of this process is that the filtering removes extraneous information. The negative result is that it can also systematically remove important and relevant information. Companies with a more balanced culture, as described in Exhibit 6.1, may achieve a better balance between these two outcomes.

Harrison Trice and Janice Beyer suggest that what a culture 'does' in an organization is to help: manage shared uncertainties; create social order; promote continuity and learning; create collective identity and commitment; and encourage ethnocentrism.[6] These powerful effects are conveyed by the organization's symbols (e.g., a high-profile CEO, a well-recognized corporate logo), performers (e.g., in 1986 and 1987 scientists working for IBM won Nobel Prizes in physics and were featured in some of the company's corporate advertising), staff training (e.g., Citibank is known as the 'university bank'), language (e.g., internal jargon, and the corporate slogan used in advertising), narratives (stories and myths), and practices (rituals and taboos). Sometimes these conveyors of corporate culture can form a barrier for new entrants—even a new CEO. For example, when Lou Gerstner took over IBM he had to learn a new language: 'big iron'—mainframe computers; 'crisp up'—improve an overhead presentation; 'goat-roping'—a gathering of key players needed to resolve an issue; 'hypo'—a high-potential employee, usually destined for management; 'nonconcur'—to disagree; 'reswizzle'—to improve something.

One aspect of organizational culture stands as a warning. It is that because an organization's culture is conditioned more by its history than by its current state, the culture-bound actions of managers and employees may be more appropriate for the past than for the future.

It is important to be able to map the organization's culture and identify how it links to the formal policies discussed in Chapter 5. That is, to make 'the invisible web' (the subtitle of this chapter), visible. Figure 6.1 shows a

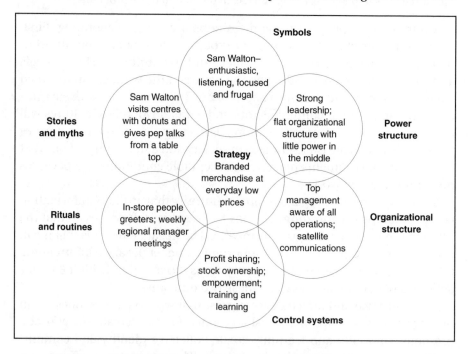

Figure 6.1. A culture web of Wal-Mart

Source: J. Davis and T. Devinney, *The Essence of Corporate Strategy* (Sydney: Allen & Unwin, 1997), 52.

stylized culture web for the Wal-Mart company (in 1993) which illustrates some of the key components and linkages (i.e., fit) of one of America's most admired companies.[7] These culture webs are a good way to communicate to both internal stakeholders (like new employees) and external stakeholders (like stock market analysts) the essence of a company's strategy and culture. Measuring organizational culture is an important first step in the process of evaluating the strengths and weaknesses of the culture and how it can be used to help develop a desired corporate image. For example, the Wal-Mart culture web shows a good fit between the anthropological nature of the organization's culture (symbols, stories and myths, rituals, and routines) and its structure (power structure, organizational structure, control systems). Note also that Sam Walton was important as a symbol, a leader, and an internal and external communicator.

Subcultures

The variety of factors that can affect an organization's culture means that within any medium to large organization, we should expect to find subcultures. For example, the head-office planning group's view of the organization is likely to differ from that of the workers on the production line. In the field of retail banking, the culture in the branches often differs from the culture in head office. One of the principal reasons for this is the lack of face-to-face dealings with customers by head office managers. Regional diversity can also encourage the formation of subcultures. For example, in the early years of the American Express Company, the company's Eastern (New York) and Western (Chicago) Departments had two very different subcultures. In the East, J. C. Fargo's autocratic leadership was followed to the letter, while in the West, the 'Chicago Rule' prevailed. It said: 'J. C. Fargo could be persuaded, and if he could not be persuaded, he could be deceived.'[8]

For an organization's subcultures to unite and drive its overall desired image and reputation, they must share a dominant core set of values. One way to achieve such integration is to use the vision statement and other forms of internal communication as vehicles to promote these core values. Another approach involves trying to align the organizational culture around a specific 'functional culture'. Two currently popular functional cultures focus on quality (via total quality management—TQM) and marketing (via customer service). For example, for a number of years the Ford Motor Co. used the slogan 'Quality is Job 1' in much of its advertising. SAS

(Scandinavian Airlines System) and other marketing-driven companies put customers at the top of the organization chart to signal their importance (and that of marketing) to employees.

When a core set of values is agreed to, the CEO and other senior managers need to monitor and manage the unique beliefs, feelings, and values that characterize the various subcultures. There can be some cultural diversity within an organization—but not too much, otherwise it becomes dysfunctional. Research has uncovered three types of 'pure' subculture that play different roles in shaping an organization's overall culture and thus its desired image.

The first case is where one subculture drives the overall culture of the company. For example, in the early days of the Apple computer company, the technical development people created a distinct subculture based on their unusual work habits and dress code. This subculture was often used as a way of demonstrating to visitors that Apple and its products were innovative—look at the people who created them! Another example is the R&D unit of the German car maker Mercedes-Benz. The values of engineering excellence and technological leadership, that this group hold, were reflected in the company's advertising for many years. The brand/corporate advertising slogan 'engineered like no other car' was thought to reflect this internal culture, and hopefully a desired customer benefit.

A subculture which drives the overall culture of the organization has been labelled an 'enhancing subculture'.[9] The problem with managing enhancing subcultures is to ensure that they do not come to completely dominate the way the organization views its competitive environment. If either Mercedes-Benz or Apple believe that their products are their key success factor, then they run the real risk of trying to fit their customers to their products (a product-oriented business philosophy), rather than being responsive to customer needs (a market-oriented business outlook). In fact, many business commentators accuse both these companies of focusing more on themselves than on their customers. (This is the problem identified in Exhibit 6.1.)

A second type of subculture is one that tries to have little or nothing in common with the overall organizational culture, or other subcultures. These groups create their own unique set of values that coexist, but do not compete with the organization's core values. An example of such a subculture is sometimes found in organizations that have their own internal legal department (e.g., in television stations and newspapers), or IT group. Here, the professional values or technical knowledge associated with the specialist activities of the group dominate its culture. The management task here is to assess whether or not such a coexisting subculture enhances or detracts from the functioning of other groups and the parent organization.

The third type of 'pure' subculture is one that is in conflict or incompatible with the dominant organizational culture. In the 1970s and early 1980s in Australia, many craft-based unions had a set of social values and assumptions about 'workers versus managers' which were directly opposed to the efficient and effective functioning of the organizations which employed their members. The result was very high levels of workplace disputation, and the use of government industrial tribunals to arbitrate these disputes. The extent of this workplace disruption ultimately led to Australia gaining an international image and reputation as a country with an uncooperative workforce.

Subcultures that diverge from the dominant culture can, in some cases, serve useful purposes for an organization. For example, in companies that do not have a culture of new product development, subcultures can create safe havens in which groups or task forces can create new products. They may also provide management with a breeding ground for the initiation of change. If a group is perceived by others in the organization as being more innovative, then management may be able to make use of the internal image of this group to start a new project or initiate change throughout the organization. My current employer, the Australian Graduate School of Management, has sometimes filled this role within its parent university. As a business school it was one of the first units of the university to introduce a scheme of performance-based salary supplementation. It was also an early adopter (in the Australian public university system) of the practice of charging student fees for an MBA degree. Both these initiatives were compatible with the image of a small innovative business school, but at the time of their introduction, they sat uncomfortably in a government-funded university system.

Culture strength

The research by John Kotter and James Heskett cited in Exhibit 6.1 makes the point that strong cultures are equally likely to be associated with either above- or below-average financial performance. The reason for this is that they may not fit the prevailing market conditions. This was one of the criticisms levelled at IBM in the 1990s for its poor financial performance. (Another criticism was that its product portfolio was too heavily reliant on mainframe computers.)

While the strength of organization culture is not, by itself, a good pre-dictor of superior financial performance, strong cultures do, however, seem to drive strong images and reputations. For example, in its formative years under Tom Watson, Sr. (and then Tom Watson Jr.), IBM developed a strong functional culture that revolved around its marketing, sales, and superior customer service. It became so feared and respected in the mar-ketplace that customers and competitors often referred to IBM using the nickname 'Big Blue' (blue being the corporate colour).

One company with a strong internal culture that drives a strong corpor-ate image and unrivalled respect in its market is the firm of management consultants McKinsey & Co.[10] Over the years they have built a special kind of firm through: their recruiting policies (often hiring people with MBAs from the world's leading business schools); the internal 'training' (sur-vivors feel as if they have gained a new degree—an McK); the McKinsey method of consulting (a cool, analytical approach to management that challenges assumptions and wishful thinking); the fostering of rigorous debate over the right answer without that debate resulting in personal criticism; and the Darwinian up or out policy of advancement. McKinsey builds its culture through these policies, and is known by its employees as 'a very kind place and a very cruel place'.

Many of McKinsey's key policies were developed by Marvin Bower, the legendary spiritual leader of the firm. As managing director from 1950 to 1967, this Harvard-trained lawyer brought the professional standards of a top-flight law firm to management consulting. One key principle is that the client comes first. Another is to be secretive and elitist by design. They call themselves 'The Firm'; they do 'engagements', not jobs; and The Firm is a 'practice', not a business. Their external reputation is so strong that CEOs who hire The Firm are seldom challenged by their boards or their rank and file employees.

In companies with strong cultures like McKinsey & Co. and IBM (in its early years), employees who elect to stay in the organization tend to be loyal and to enjoy their work. These organizations also tend to have a high level of consensus among employees about what basic assumptions and values guide them. For example, in IBM, nearly every senior executive in the early years came up the organizational ladder via the marketing route. In McKinsey, the hiring and training process preconditions The Firm's culture. While there may be various subcultures in these organizations, they are all subservient to a common set of core values. In a strong culture there is also likely to be a good fit between the organization's reward and control systems and acceptable behaviour.[11] The visitor to an organization with a strong culture can often see a certain 'style' of employee behaviour (e.g., the dark-suited, serious banker) or 'feel' the atmosphere of work (e.g., the currency trading room of a bank). In this way, strong cultures spill out of organizations to influence the images held of them by outsiders.

When aspects of the organization culture can be used to enhance the desired corporate image and reputation, then a communication strategy is necessary to get the message across to external stakeholders. For McKinsey & Co. this occurs primarily through their alumni (previous employees) and the 'old-boy' network. Often CEOs become a key part of this communication: Sam Walton's frugality signalling Wal-Mart's low-price strategy, Jack Welch's combative management style signalling GE's competitiveness, and Richard Branson's adventures signalling Virgin's challenging various well-established companies. More typically, publicity and corporate advertising are the primary vehicles used. For example, many companies have featured their employees in their ads to signal to them, and outsiders, how important and respected they are. Other companies feature customers in their product advertising to signal a customer focus. Another tactic is to have employees participate in (high-profile) community and environment-protection activities. Whatever the strategy, if part of the internal culture reflects values which are important to external stakeholders, then it can be used to help project a more desirable corporate image and reputation.

CHANGING ORGANIZATIONAL CULTURES

The definitions of organizational culture given earlier provide some insight into how to change and manage culture. For example, Kotter and Heskett divide organizational cultures into two sets of factors, which differ in their visibility and their resistance to change. At a deeper, less visible level are the values that are shared by people in a group. These tend to persist over time, even when there is some change in group membership. At a more visible level, culture represents the behaviour patterns, symbols, and style of the organization. These aspects tend to be easier to change than values about work. As we will see in Chapter 8, which deals with corporate identity symbols, some consultants think that changing the corporate logo will have a major positive impact on organizational culture, and corporate image. Only rarely will this occur.

A good way to illustrate the dynamic aspects of culture is to consider its role in a new, founder-dominated organization. Here, the main issue is how to form a number of individuals into a work-group, and to establish a growth path for the organization. The work-group, which is the organization at this particular time, needs to establish an identity, and to develop work procedures to accomplish its tasks. The emerging culture will act as a touchstone to test different perceptions of the goals of the organization, and how it should interact with its key stakeholders. Culture changes that occur during this early formative stage of development are concerned with clarifying the dominant beliefs and values of the group. These are typically strongly influenced by the personality of the founder, as shown by Sam Walton's prominence in the culture web in Figure 6.1.

As new organizations grow, an effective culture emerges. If it did not they would not survive. To change the culture of these organizations requires an appreciation of how the culture originally developed. This is especially important when some of the original members of the organization still hold positions of power and influence. The classic example of this situation occurs when the original founder of a company is about to abdicate his/her position, and the new management team (which may include one or more family members) charts a course to 'modernize' the company. There may be a feeling, at this crucial transition stage, that some major changes are necessary. The new team feels that the founders held too tightly to a set of values that were applicable to a past era. Culture change in this situation can be traumatic, and may result in the replacing of key people who want to hold on to the old culture.

In mature organizations that have a history spanning two or more generations of managers, the early history of the organization may provide only limited insight into the key factors which have shaped and which reinforce the existing culture. In these organizations research is necessary to describe culture strength, the existence of subcultures, the signalling devices used to communicate culture, and the degree of internal fit between strategy, structure, and culture. It is also necessary to assess the external fit between the demands of the organization's markets and the internal factors which shape its response to these markets. Culture change is typically extremely difficult for large, mature organizations and often requires a major external shock to stimulate action. A well-documented example of an organization which experienced such a shock, and which spent years trying to change its culture (and strategy and structure) to survive in a changing market, is the story of Lee Iacocca's reign at the Chrysler Corporation.[12]

Forces driving culture change

When Lee Iacocca took control of Chrysler in 1979 there was a huge gap between the way the US car market was evolving and the company's strategy for serving this market. (This was the era when small Japanese cars were making significant inroads into the market.) There was an equally big gap between Chrysler's flawed strategy and the organization's capability to implement it. In short, Chrysler was in deep trouble—it faced a crisis of survival. The pressure for change was enormous, and employees understood the consequences of failing to change. Iacocca's appointment as the new chief operating executive gave him the mandate to make vast changes in the Chrysler empire.

When thinking about how to change Chrysler's, or any organization's culture, a good metaphor is that of an iceberg. The part we can see above the waterline is only a small part of the total iceberg. Likewise with organization culture. Changing the bits that are easy to see such as rituals, vision statements, and corporate logos will have only limited effect on the overall culture. To significantly change an organization's culture often requires 'unfreezing' the total iceberg, and then refreezing it into a different shape. Now, whether the organization's culture is a strong or a weak force in determining its success, will determine whether you set out to unfreeze/ refreeze an iceberg (as in the case of the Chrysler Corporation) or an ice-block!

Consultants who help organizations to change their cultures often approach the problem using a simple model of change.[13] The first element to consider is whether or not there is significant pressure for change. This pressure may result from a crisis, such as the death of the founder, or an accident, like the grounding of the oil tanker *Exxon Valdez*. It may also emanate from an environmental threat such as the entry of a powerful competitor into the marketplace. IBM's entry into the personal computer market is a good example. When this occurred, all the PC suppliers realized that Big Blue's marketing muscle and its image of strong customer service would fundamentally change the nature of the PC market. When a significant threat occurs, both management and employees must agree that the consequences of failing to respond to the threat will cause serious problems for their organization and themselves. If they do not reach agreement on this, the organization is likely to defer change in the hope that things will return to normal.

When employees accept the need for change, a clear shared vision for the direction of change must be established. Top management play an important role in articulating this vision and demonstrating that they are fully committed to its implementation. The leadership role of the CEO is a critical success factor here because, unless employees understand the nature of the company's changed circumstances, management's new direction may appear illogical and/or unreasonable. Lee Iacocca at Chrysler, John Sculley at Apple, Jan Carlzon at SAS, Jack Welch at GE, and Lord King and Sir Colin Marshall of British Airways have all been credited with having a big impact on gaining commitment for their company's new direction, and for mobilizing the human resources necessary to implement such change. Chapter 11 reviews some of the different approaches these men used within their organizations.

The next factor that determines the potential effectiveness of change is whether the organization has the capability to change. These capabilities are of two types: people and business systems. Many people responsible for a particular job are ill equipped to change. Sometimes the problem can be rectified by training, while in other cases the information on which decisions are based is inadequate. Much change also falters because of the poor design of business systems. In the area of customer service this is a common problem. For example, many large retail banks have customer service systems that have been designed to facilitate the bank's individual account keeping requirements rather than to provide an integrated money management service to customers. The large scale of the investment in these systems makes it almost impossible for the banks to make a rapid response to changing customer needs, and/or to tailor their services to different segments of the market. In effect, the bank's systems and infrastructure constrain its capacity to make anything other than incremental change.

The final factor necessary to effect culture change is to ensure that change will be rewarded—in both the visible and invisible spectrums of the organization. Visible rewards need to be more than a series of public 'thank you' speeches and reports of progress from senior management. They need to be linked directly to the employee performance-appraisal system. Invisible rewards refer to the underlying feeling of successful change. How these factors combine to cement culture and organization change is well illustrated when employees are (first) given shares in their organization. Their performance and that of co-workers is reported daily on the stock exchange, and many people feel more direct ownership and rewards from their decisions and behaviour. When the employee stock-ownership scheme was implemented at United Airlines in 1994, positive effects on culture and performance were quickly evident.[14]

A crucial step in the change process is to get started. The actionable first steps should be simply stated and clearly demonstrated, and they should lead to some successful outcomes. In other words, it is necessary to get some early successes to signal and publicize the change process and outcomes. Then those people who have been instrumental in helping to achieve these successes should be publicly rewarded. Because people tend to do what is inspected, more than what is expected, compliance with the desired changes should be tied directly to the organization's reward system. The reward system—who gets rewarded and why—is an unequivocal statement of the organization's beliefs and values. It is a key to understanding and influencing the organization's culture and the images formed by employees.

Successful cultural change is a function of the four factors outlined in Figure 6.2. Each factor is necessary but not sufficient to change an organization's culture. The timeframe over which such cultural change is likely to occur is typically slower than anticipated by many managers. The main reasons for this are that it is often necessary to raise the 'cultural awareness' in an organization before embarking on a programme of change. Also, it takes time to get a widespread commitment that change is necessary, and to develop a clear, shared direction for change.

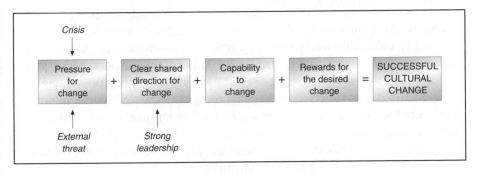

Figure 6.2. Forces driving organizational culture change

Cultural change can be of two types—evolutionary or revolutionary. Which type is necessary will depend on the degree of internal, and/or external misfit currently being experienced by the organization. Evolutionary change does not destroy the basic underlying beliefs and values of the culture—it merely modifies them. This type of cultural change typically leads to incremental changes in the organization's behaviour. Revolutionary cultural change, however, sets out to replace one system of beliefs and values with another system that, it is hoped, will be more appropriate for the organization's survival. It is usually accompanied by significant organizational restructuring, and changes of key personnel.

Many organizations forced to confront this type of situation will use an external consultant and a new CEO to facilitate the process. One ruthless 'fixer' during the 1980s and 1990s was widely known as Chainsaw Dunlap. (He was a specialist at downsizing and cost cutting.)

MEASURING ORGANIZATIONAL CULTURE

Much of the discussion in the two previous sections has assumed an ability to know, or to measure, an organization's culture. For example, it would be difficult to evaluate the success of a culture change programme if it was not possible to describe the old and the new culture. Also, it would be foolhardy to try to change various beliefs and values if you did not know how strongly and widely held they were. Measuring organizational culture transforms an 'invisible web' to a 'visible web'. When it becomes visible, it can be used to help monitor and shape employee behaviour, which in turn will have a big impact on the signals employees send to customers and other external stakeholders.

An outsider (e.g., a consultant, an investor, a potential employee) seeking to measure the culture of an organization is generally forced to rely on its visible indicators and identity symbols. A site visit may show a new building, quality furnishings, expensive cars in the carpark, open-plan offices, well-dressed people, et cetera. Also, the organization's advertising—the media in which it appears, its tone of voice, and its frequency—may provide clues about certain aspects of its culture. Other sources of cultural information are publicity, the annual report, and internal company newsletters. Information from such visible indicators is only partially representative of the true, underlying culture.

To measure the true culture you need to get inside the organization. Once inside, there are various ways to map the various subcultures. At one extreme is the type of research done by cultural anthropologists. They live in and become part of the organization for an extended period of time, studying the internal workings, decision-making processes, and rituals of the organization. Another version of this approach is the (investigative) journalist who writes a history of the organization.[15] Both approaches require a lengthy period of research and writing before the author produces his/her description of the organization's culture, based on his/her perceptions, as an 'expert witness'. Charles Handy's popular book, *The Gods of Management*,[16] describes four basic types of organizational cultures which he has gleaned from this type of research:

- *Zeus*, the patriarch of all the gods, represents the culture of charismatic leadership, where professionals are free to follow their instincts.
- *Apollo*, the god of rules and order, represents the culture of traditional bureaucracy and management control.
- *Athena*, the patroness of Odysseus, problem-solver of craftsmen and pioneering sea captains, represents the culture of project-based teamwork.
- *Dionysus*, the god of wine and song, represents the culture of individualism and independence.

There is a quicker route to culture mapping than the anthropological approach. It involves doing some type of survey among a representative sample of employees at all levels, and in all places of the organization. The three main survey techniques are: (a) in-depth personal interviews, (b) focus groups, and (c) self-completion questionnaires. In-depth personal interviews on a one-to-one basis can be time consuming, and if they are unstructured, the information they provide can be difficult to interpret. A focus group is composed of six to eight people plus a professional moderator to guide the discussion. The interaction among the individuals will usually stimulate thoughts and insight not easily obtained from individual interviews. Personal interviews and focus groups are valuable for building up an understanding of the way people think about the organization, and for discovering the language they use to describe their relationship with it.

A widely used method of data collection is to start by interviewing some of the longer-serving members of the organization and some people who have recently joined the organization. If possible, these people should be sought in various parts of the organization, and at various levels in the hierarchy. Stage two is to use the information gained from these interviews to select people to participate in two or three focus group sessions. (The number of focus groups is typically determined by the number of subcultures that seem to exist in the organization.) The information from the personal interviews and focus groups is then used to construct a questionnaire to be completed by a representative sample of employees. The individual and group interviews ensure that the questionnaire reflects the beliefs, values, language, and customs of the organization, that is, the elements in Figure 6.1.

The major alternatives to this in-house approach are to: (a) modify one of the various questionnaires available in the published academic literature,[17] or (b) employ a human resources consultant who specializes in measuring organizational culture. The use of this second approach can add an extra dimension to culture mapping, as these consultants can often compare the profile of the organization under consideration with those of other similar organizations.

The first time a culture survey is conducted it is difficult to predict how employees will react to the exercise. Hence, it is wise for organizations conducting such a survey to use the services of someone regarded by employees as independent, to send out the questionnaires, to carry out the data tabulation and statistical analysis, and to provide feedback of the results—quickly. Employees who fill in a questionnaire like feedback, fast enough so that they can remember what they have said—any longer than one month is too long.

When analysing data from a questionnaire, what is sought is a pattern of results. For example, is there a heavy emphasis on internal rituals and ceremonies but little emphasis on outwardly visible signals? What types of rituals and ceremonies do various parts of the organization use? Is fun at work something that only parts of the organization seem to indulge in? Do only some levels in the organizational hierarchy think that the reward system is fair and equitable? How do different parts of the organization regard customers? (For example, some bank employees label customers as 'credit risks'. The internal language used can sometimes give a good indication of the respect in which customers are held.) A good organization culture profile is one that has a balance among such factors, and that stresses those aspects that contribute to internal and external fit, and the desired corporate image and reputation.

CONCLUSIONS

Culture in large organizations is like national culture: it is reinforced and modified over many years. It is rooted in the countless details of organizational life—how rewards are administered, how plans are made, how conflict is resolved, how the CEO interacts with staff, et cetera. We have come to realize that significant strategic and structural change cannot take place unless it is supported by the organization's culture(s). Many organizations have also discovered that a key success factor in the management of their external images and reputations is the management of the internal culture. If the various subcultures can be organized around providing value to customers, employees, and stockholders, then this should facilitate good financial performance. Also, if they can be moulded into a force which projects a consistent set of signals to outside stakeholders, then there is potential to use the organization's culture as a powerful force to help shape its desired image. Body Shop has successfully achieved this. An organization with a healthy inside is one that is more likely to project a good image to outside stakeholders.

If you compete in an industry where product and service offerings are all fairly similar, then it is the company and its people that may be your best source of image advantage. Moulding a strong culture to add a personal or emotive attribute to your desired corporate image may be all that it takes to get ahead of a competitor. Recall the discussion of Southwest Airlines in Chapter 4, where this is what was achieved.

NOTES

1. For some of the historical background of the 'discovery' of organizational culture see J. Kotter and J. Heskett, *Corporate Culture and Performance* (New York: The Free Press, 1992).

2. The study was conducted by Universum International, a research company based in Sweden for the accounting firm Coopers & Lybrand. It was reported in P. Gollan, 'Careers Don't Always Come First', *Australian Financial Review* (5 Aug. 1997), 17.

3. K. Bates, S. Amundson, R. Schroeder, and W. Morris, 'The Crucial Interrelationship Between Manufacturing Strategy and Organizational Culture', *Management Science*, 41, 10 (1995), 1565–80.

4. B. Uttal, 'The Corporate Culture Vultures', *Fortune*, 17 (Oct. 1983), 66–72.

5. E. Schein, 'Coming to a New Awareness of Organizational Culture', *Sloan Management Review*, 25 (Winter 1984), 3–16. The interested reader could consult the following sources for more information on organization culture: A. Pettigrew, 'On Studying Organizational Cultures', *Administrative Science Quarterly*, 24, 4 (1979), 570–81; B. Arogyaswamy and C. Bayles, 'Organizational Culture: Internal and External Fits', *Journal of Management*, 13, 4 (1987), 647–59.

6. H. Trice and J. Beyer, *The Culture of Work Organizations* (Englewood Cliffs, NJ: Prentice Hall, 1993).

7. G. Johnson, 'Managing Strategic Change: Strategy, Culture and Action', *Long Range Planning*, 25, 1 (1992), 28–36.

8. P. Grossman, *American Express: the Unofficial History of the People Who Built the Great Financial Empire* (New York: Crown Publishers, 1987).

9. J. Martin and C. Siehl, 'Organizational Culture and Counterculture: An Uneasy Symbiosis', *Organizational Dynamics*, 12, 2 (1983), 52–64.

10. J. Byrne, 'The McKinsey Mystique', *Business Week* (20 Sept. 1993), 36–41; J. Huey, 'How McKinsey Does It', *Fortune* (1 Nov. 1993), 108–30.

11. J. Kerr and J. Slocum, 'Managing Corporate Culture Through Reward Systems', *Academy of Management Executive*, 1, 2 (1987), 99–107.

12. L. Iacocca with W. Novak, *Iacocca: an Autobiography* (Toronto: Bantam Books, 1984).

13. I was first introduced to this framework by Dr Norman Chorn of Gattorna Chorn Strategy Consultants, in Sydney, Australia.

14. S. Chandler, 'United We Own', *Business Week* (18 March 1996), 40–4.

15. A good example of a study of the inside workings of an organization—in this case an advertising agency—is A. Coombs, *AdLand* (Melborne: William Heinemann Australia, 1990).

16. C. Handy, *The Gods of Management* (Oxford: Oxford University Press, 1995).

17. See the sources listed in n. 5 above.

7

Corporate Communication: What to Say

Corporate advertising and sponsorship are often oversold as mechanisms for creating a better corporate image and reputation (as is corporate identity—discussed in the next chapter). Ralph Nader once made the comment: 'I don't care how many lobbyists [here read advertising] you have. If you're weak in the streets, you're weak.' Nader's advice reflects an age-old marketing 'law' that says that stakeholders, and especially customers, are more interested in what companies do for them than in what they say about themselves.

Advertising, sponsorships, and other forms of communication, such as direct mail, websites, identity symbols, publicity, and the sales-force are all important devices that organizations use to help project their desired image. Advertising is the best researched, and thus the best understood method of communication. Corporate advertising typically focuses on broad issues relating to the organization, while product advertising emphasizes one or more products. Corporate advertisements have traditionally been classified as image or issue ads, with each type broken down into the various categories shown in Table 7.1. The amount of advertising in each category varies by country. For example, Japanese companies seem to do more goodwill and corporate awareness advertising than US companies.[1]

Rather than focus on the company and try to answer the questions posed in Exhibit P.1, the McGraw-Hill advertisement, in the Preface to this book, many advertising agencies advise their clients to anchor all advertising to the company's best products or services. This strategy is designed to maximize the sales potential of the advertising and is adopted by most small-budget, and many big-budget advertisers. (For example, BMW often advertises its 7- and 5-series cars to sell them and its 3-series cars.) The task here is to make a connection between the product and the company that stands behind it. This is not always easy to do. For example, there has

Table 7.1. Types of corporate advertising

Type	Characteristics
Image advertisements	
A. *Goodwill*	Corporate philanthropy, cultural promotion, celebration/congratulation, corporate solutions to problems, public education/advisory.
B. *Charity*	Public or special interest group support.
C. *Financial*	Reporting financial results or new initiatives, stockholder fights, defence against takeover.
D. *Employee*	Recruitment, thanking employees for contributions.
E. *Awareness*	New Identity symbols, plant openings, innovations, social/civic activities, etc.
Issue	
F. *Position*	On social or business issues, ally recruitment.
G. *Counter*	Resolving a misunderstanding, counter editorial.

Source: D. McLeod and M. Kunita, 'A Comparative Analysis of the Use of Corporate Advertising in the United States and Japan', *International Journal of Advertising*, 13, 2 (1994), 137–52.

been an enormous amount of advertising and publicity for the wonder drug Viagra but do you know the name of the manufacturer?   (*Answer*: Pfizer.)

One company that has successfully blended its product and corporate advertising is Intel. In a trademark case in March 1991, Intel lost the right to prohibit other computer chip manufacturers using the numbers '386' (or 486 or 586—the intended product evolution) to designate its microprocessors. Over the next few months, the decision was taken to brand the company, as opposed to its products. The corporate brand was to be built on the twin attributes of safety and technology, and to inspire confidence that a PC with the latest Intel microprocessor was a safe choice. In late 1991 this concept was presented to consumers as the now-familiar 'Intel Inside' logo. To enlist support of original equipment manufacturers (OEMs) who were using Intel chips, they were offered a co-operative advertising deal whereby Intel would pay between 30 and 50 per cent of print advertising costs if the Intel Inside logo appeared in the manufacturer's ads and on the PC. In effect, Intel migrated its product advertising into a very successful corporate advertising campaign.[2]

A review of corporate advertising in the USA found that it has experienced a number of shifts of emphasis. In the 1970s the primary focus was on goodwill (e.g., public relations and public service). In the 1980s two themes were prominent, namely, hybrid ads which combined the promotion of products and services with general messages about the company, and advocacy and issue ads which promoted political, social, and economic ideas.[3] In the 1990s, many corporate ads were designed to keep customers and the public better informed of the customer-oriented nature of business activities. For example, 3M talked about its innovation process, Ford about its quality techniques, and Motorola about participatory management.

Estimates vary, but 'pure' corporate (image and issue) advertising seems to account for less than 3 per cent of US advertising expenditure. In dollar terms this is less than the amount spent by the USA's biggest advertiser, Procter & Gamble, which has an annual ad budget of $2.5 to $3.0 billion. Television and magazines are the two most preferred media with Internet websites growing in popularity. The giant companies AT&T, Chevron, General Electric, Du Pont, and Westinghouse have used corporate advertising for decades.

In the world of sponsorship, US companies spent an estimated $6.2 billion in 1998. Sports took 73 per cent of this money with the arts, festivals and fairs, and tours and attractions sharing the rest fairly equally.[4]

An issue which troubles many communication managers is what proportion of product, hybrid (i.e., product and/or sponsorship and/or corporate), and corporate communication will give an organization the most effectiveness per dollar spent. This is a question that often raises strong opinions within organizations and advertising agencies. However, there is no simple answer! Hence, what I will do in this chapter is to analyse the major components of corporate communication. Advertising is used to anchor the discussion for two reasons. First, all other forms of corporate communication to (external) stakeholders are really advertisements in disguise, and second, we know far more about how advertising works than about any other form of corporate communication.

The next section suggests five instances where corporate advertising plays an important role in the corporate image formation process. Following this discussion, the chapter sets out the factors that need to be taken into account in order to use advertising effectively. A look at sponsorships, philanthropy, cause-related marketing, and annual reports concludes the discussion. The chapter is followed by an extensive case study of the effectiveness of corporate advertising.

WHEN TO USE CORPORATE ADVERTISING

As to when companies should use corporate advertising, the five most important situations are:

(1) *When you need to put across a point of view or tell a story.* The different types of corporate advertising listed in Table 7.1 suggest that when a company wants to take a public stand on an issue, it should divorce this message from its product/service advertising. (During a product crisis this advice may not be applicable.) Also, when a company wants to talk to special non-customer groups such as a local community, politicians, and stockholders, corporate advertising is appropriate. Exhibit 7.1 provides an interesting example of the effectiveness of corporate advertising targeted at the financial community.

(2) *When the customer buys the company as well as the product.* Here, the reputation of the company becomes an important attribute in the consumer choice process. Product categories where customers have to trust that the company has designed the product correctly, or that it will still be in existence when needed, or that staff have been well trained or undertaken their duties properly, include: airlines, banking, construction, consulting services, insurance, pharmaceuticals, etc. In situations such as these, companies should tell their customers who stands behind the product. If customers do not really care who made the product they are using (e.g., a book publisher), then product-focused advertising is probably more effective.

(3) *When the length of the purchase cycle is long.* When customers make (very) infrequent purchases, as is the case for many types of consumer durable and industrial products, then a great deal of product advertising is wasted. Customers who are 'out of the market' tend to screen out most product advertising messages.[5] Corporate advertising can, however, be an effective vehicle whereby companies keep their names and desired image in the public domain. Currently, the big Dutch electronics company Philips is using corporate advertising to tell (potential) customers and the general public about its wide-ranging activities. Philips' print advertisements have a consistent style that acts as a memory trigger or a retrieval cue. This helps people identify these ads and others in the campaign as 'a Philips ad'. Good (corporate) advertising owns a style.

Exhibit 7.1. Advertising to investors: its effects on stock volume and price

Many research studies have suggested a relationship between corporate advertising and image—the more the better. However correlation does not mean causality. Two US researchers, George Bobinski and Gabriel Ramirez, conducted a study to determine if corporate advertising in the *Wall Street Journal*, which is targeted at the market makers, would have any effect on the company's trading volume and/or stock price.

Advertising theory says that it should—increasing awareness and a favourable message should generate a more favourable corporate image. Finance theory says that it should not affect stock prices because such ads would be unlikely to contain any new or relevant information that the market did not already have from a more reliable source. Stockmarket theory, however, would accommodate the hypothesis that a corporate ad might cause individual investors to alter their expectations about the stock, and because each may interpret it differently, the trading volume of the stock may rise.

The researchers collected 227 advertisements for listed companies during the period 1988–9, and using an event-study methodology (which assesses the prices and volumes before and after the appearance of the ad), they tested the effects of the ads on price and volume changes. They found no effect on stock price, but a significant positive effect on trading volume. This trading effect was bigger for smaller (less well capitalized) firms, and it only occurred the first time the ad appeared.

From a managerial perspective, the results indicate that if a firm is concerned about thin trading volume, or is planning to raise new equity in the capital markets, corporate advertising aimed at the financial community may be useful because it has the potential to increase trading volume.

Source: Derived from: G. Bobinski and G Ramirez, 'Advertising to Investors: The Effect of Financial-Relations Advertising on Stock Volume and Price', *Journal of Advertising*, 4 (Dec. 1994), 13–28.

(4) *When the company name and the brand name overlap.* There are two main instances where this occurs, namely, (a) when the company name is used in conjunction with a brand name—Nestlé and Nescafé instant coffee, or (b) when the company and product (brand) names are the same, such as the automotive divisions of BMW and Mercedes-Benz. In the latter case, corporate advertising directed to consumers is not necessary because the product advertising conveys both the brand and corporate images. Corporate advertising may be desirable, however, for communicating with other stakeholder groups. In the first case, where the corporate and brand names are used together, corporate advertising can be used

to create an umbrella image for the different brands. This is the strategy used by 3M. Its umbrella image is to position the company and its products as innovative. 3M signs off many of its product and corporate ads with the slogan 'innovation'.

(5) *When you want to thank your employees.* When employees deserve public recognition for their efforts some companies thank them in corporate advertisements. A common strategy is to highlight the contribution of employees to the company's success. After one such series of advertisements by United Technologies that ran in the *Wall Street Journal* and the local papers of the locations of the company's various businesses, the CEO Thomas Haas received letters of thanks from his employees saying that their family and friends now better understood their jobs, and why they had to travel so much to visit customers.

Many corporate campaigns featuring employees are linked to the company's product development process—as with many of the Philips ads mentioned earlier. The Saturn car company also features its employees and their jobs in many of its advertisements. While these ads thank current employees, they also target potential employees by projecting an image of an exciting and rewarding place to work. Given the importance of employees, and the buzz people get from seeing themselves or a co-worker in the press, it is surprising that we don't see more employee heroes and heroines.

The dark side of featuring employees in corporate advertising occurs when the motivation is to 'threaten' rather than thank them. In these ads, the employees are shown providing the excellent service levels that customers can expect when using the company. These ads put employees on public notice about what customers expect from them. They may be good for attracting customers, but can make it more difficult for front-line customer service people to respond when their support systems are inadequate.

In huge multinational companies, corporate advertising is a way of talking to a diverse group of employees about the corporate vision and mission. When it is impossible for the CEO to spread the corporate message in person, the question arises as to what is the next most effective channel of communication. Vision/mission statements, internal newsletters, email, and corporate advertising are all candidates. To the horror of many HR departments, sometimes corporate advertising in world-wide business magazines like *Review 200, Business Week, Forbes, Fortune,* and *The Economist* may be the most cost-effective medium. When companies state their strategy in this advertising (e.g., IBM and its 'e-business'), it talks equally to employees and customers.

PRODUCT *AND* CORPORATE ADVERTISING

The aim of corporate advertising is to project the desired image of the organization to create an overall feeling of familiarity, confidence, and trust. The job of product advertising is to focus on the functional, psychological, and economic benefits of the product/service. The exception to this 'rule' is when advertising products to very knowledgeable buyers. For these people, the message should concentrate on the (features of the) product because these buyers know all about its benefits. When product advertising is tied directly into corporate advertising, the aim is for the corporate image to support the product benefits. That, of course, is the theory. In practice, it is difficult, in many such advertisements, to find the link between attributes of the company and benefits of the product.

Many advertising agencies and managers, although not those who engage in it, regard corporate advertising as a waste of money. Such scepticism is healthy. One reason for this view is that much of this advertising is self-indulgent. Many of the ads are simply awful! They are long-winded and dull, or they are short and vague about what the company does. Look at the major business magazines like *Review 200*, *Business Week*, *The Economist*, *Forbes*, and *Fortune*. Many of their corporate ads are uninspiring. If they are lucky, they generate a 'Ho-Hum' reaction. If they are worse they are ignored. Worse still, and they generate a counter-arguing response such as 'Rubbish' or 'Says Who?'

A good example of a 'Ho-Hum' corporate campaign was the British oil company BP's 'For All Our Tomorrows' global ads. This campaign was designed to focus on three themes—environmental concern, community help, and research-based product development. The corporate ads showed BP conducting mineral exploration, shipping oil, building infrastructure, and providing solar energy systems to help developing countries. These advertising themes could however apply to any mining or oil company. There is nothing unique to BP about wanting to be a good corporate citizen—it should be a minimum requirement for a licence to do business. With such a broad set of claims, BP's advertising agency (Saatchi & Saatchi) had to be very creative to make the (TV) ads interesting enough to reward the viewer for their time and attention.[6]

Dick Wasserman, a noted US adman, says that many dull corporate ads go to air because corporate executives think that when they are spending a large amount of money, they should talk about something 'weighty'. Naturally, the tendency is to do this in a sombre tone. Unfortunately, this often leads to ads that sound like a corporate monologue and that are filled with abstract images or boring pictures of the company's activities. The closer the ads are to straightforward, literal speeches, or well-reasoned arguments, or declarations of solemn corporate credos, the less successful they are likely to be.[7] Wasserman says that since the reader or viewer of corporate advertising will not be rewarded with information about a tangible benefit, the reward for paying attention to the ad must be in the reading or viewing itself. Most successful corporate advertising must contain some sort of built-in tension producer, like an unusual twist or a surprise which makes the ad seem novel to the audience. It must also relate directly to what the company does.

Regardless of the type of corporate advertising used, the manager responsible for the ad campaign and the agency producing the ads must agree on a positioning for the company and a set of communication objectives. The next section outlines some positioning options available to companies. Attention then focuses on a communication planning frame-work. Together these two sections provide much of the information neces-sary to answer the question about what is the desirable balance between corporate and brand advertising for an organization.

POSITIONING: THE BATTLE TO BE IMPORTANT, DIFFERENT, AND RELEVANT

Positioning is arguably the single most important decision in designing a corporate (or brand) communication strategy. A positioning statement says what the company is, who it is for, and what benefits it offers. It does not spell out how to state the position. This is the function of the creative tactics from the ad agency. Advertising gurus John Rossiter and Larry Percy suggest a three-part positioning statement:[8]

(1) To (the target stakeholder audience).
(2) XYZ is the company (of this industry or to fulfil this need).
(3) That offers (these benefits).

A positioning statement containing these ingredients is the end result of the positioning decisions outlined in this section. Three linkages must be communicated for the company, namely, to which group of stakeholders, to what market (as defined relative to competitors or a customer need), and to a particular purchase or usage motivation (via its benefits). Some of these linkages may be implicit: for example, in a corporate recruiting video one does not need to spell out that potential employees are the target group.

In effect, positioning is all about the 'location' of the company in the stakeholder's mind. This location can be anchored to the market (viz., customer benefits or competitors) and a hero/heroine (viz., the company or stakeholder group). Figure 7.1 uses these anchors to derive some typical positioning themes.

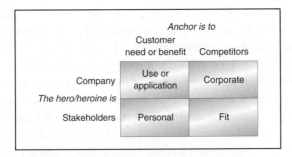

Figure 7.1. Corporate positioning themes

The four cells in Figure 7.1 reflect some of the common themes used in corporate positioning advertisements. For example, companies that adopt a 'use or application' theme establish the company as the vehicle to satisfy a broad stakeholder need. Often these ads have a 'try us' or 'we deliver' or 'this is our speciality' feel about them. In many cases this theme needs further support. A good example of such a positioning was Federal Express's slogan 'when it absolutely, positively has to be there overnight'.

When the stakeholder is the hero/heroine and the need or benefit is the anchor, the positioning theme is based on a personal, or 'what's in it for me' approach. The Michelin slogan of 'because so much is riding on your tires' reflects this theme.

When stakeholders are the focus and the company is compared (directly or implicitly) to a competitor(s), the theme is one of 'we can fulfil your requirements better than anyone else'. The famous Avis 'we're number two, we try harder' position is a clever example of how to support this theme. Their advertisements say that they are a car rental company, and the slogan gives the potential customer a logical reason to use them. (When Avis fell from its number two position, the advertising slogan was shortened to 'we try harder'.)

When the company is the hero and it is compared to competitors, these ads tend to have a very 'corporate' feel to them. Good examples are those (boring) advertisements of the financial statement type, found in business periodicals, and the 'tombstone' advertisements of investment banks which list the capital underwriting syndicate for the 'birth' of a new security.[9]

Figure 7.1 poses two implicit questions. First, how should the company be positioned with regard to the broad customer need it serves and its competitors? Second, when should the company rather than the stakeholder be the hero/heroine? Again, the Rossiter and Percy approach can be used to answer these questions.

A company can be positioned as the market leader, the industry standard, a successful pioneer, or a generic company serving a customer need. These are all examples of a central position within an industry. The market leader and/or industry standard and/or successful pioneer options (IBM in mainframe computers, Intel in microprocessors, McDonald's in fast food, and Xerox in photocopiers) define the major characteristics and performance levels in the industry. These companies can legitimately say that they are the best in their industry. This is a valuable position to reinforce and protect. A variation on this leadership theme is the 'club' position adopted by, for example: Fortune 500 companies, the Big Five accounting firms, the Top Twenty business schools, and the Big Three US car-makers.

Because this leadership position is so valuable, in terms of both customer consideration and management ego, there is always the temptation for the number two company in an industry to say that it is about to be, or wants to be number one. At the time of writing this chapter, Airbus is using the slogan 'setting the standards' on its corporate advertisements. Ask most people around the world who sets the standards in passenger aircraft design and manufacture, and more likely than not they will answer Boeing. Airbus needs a new position because even if its claim is correct, it is just not credible to most people.

The successful pioneer position is another powerful location in stakeholders' minds. It says: 'we created this industry or product category'. The critical issue here is that to credibly claim this position a company needs to be the *successful* pioneer—not necessarily the first company to enter the field. For example, which was the first company to make a personal computer? It was not Apple, but it tends to be remembered as *the* pioneer because it was the first successful manufacturer. Even in the late 1990s when the company was struggling in the marketplace, Apple could still claim this position.

The generic company option is really a 'me too' position. Me-too companies try to imitate the leaders and pioneers and they will only succeed if they can match the performance characteristics of these companies, but at a significantly lower price. Two old examples of successful me-too products (and companies) were the various brands of 'IBM clone' personal computers, and Pepsi in the Great Depression when it offered twice the amount of product for the same price as Coke. More recently, many store brands in supermarkets adopt this position.

Most companies cannot adopt a central position, and are forced to opt for a differentiation position. The crucial issue here is what the major differentiation options are. One alternative is to search for an attribute, or combination of attributes, that the leaders are not using. Low price is not an option here because it is generally the mainstay of the me-too companies. New attributes that are important to target customers and which competitors have not developed can be hard to find in mature markets. Harley-Davidson however, is a good success story. The company reflects the values of many of its customers in its bikes and clothing to differentiate itself from its Japanese competitors. The Japanese make technically better bikes, but Harley owns the position encapsulated in its motto— 'Live to ride, and ride to live'.

Another differentiation alternative is to locate the company in another industry—possibly even a new one that you create. Direct marketing companies did this when they split away from traditional advertising agencies. Management consultants created an industry when the big firms started to develop. McDonald's tries to do it every time it says it is a 'family restaurant'. As we saw in Chapter 5, Xerox tried to do this in the 1980s when it set out to become an 'information company' (Figure 5.3). My favourite discussion of positioning alternatives is by Al Ries and Jack Trout in their book, *Positioning: The Battle for Your Mind* (New York: McGraw-Hill, 1981, 1986). (These earlier editions are better than the latest book by Jack Trout with Steve Rivkin, *The New Positioning* (New York: McGraw-Hill, 1996).)

The second question implicit in Figure 7.1 is whether the company or the stakeholder should be the hero/heroine. This choice follows logically from the decision to adopt a central or differentiated position. Either of these positions can support a focus on the company or the stakeholder group. A stakeholder focus seems applicable when the company is a specialist that serves a tightly defined group. At one time SAS Airlines positioned itself as 'the business airline of Europe', and Caterpillar advertised '24 hour parts and service anywhere in the world'. Another situation in which the stakeholder can take centre stage is when the motivation to use the company is one of social approval. The world of management consulting provides an example of this with an interesting twist. Management consultants of the status of McKinsey & Co. are often chosen as much for their ability as for their social acceptability, namely, so that the CEO and the Board of Directors can feel comfortable among their peers concerning their choice of adviser.

In many situations companies are made the hero/heroine of the positioning. Their characteristics are the message. Companies can be described in terms of their vision (Chapter 4), formal policies (Chapter 5), culture (Chapter 6), products, range of activities, or size. A word of warning about positioning themes based on organizational characteristics is, however, in order. There are some which it is very difficult to make sound credible. One classic is the 'we have the best employees' position. If any company other than the market leader or the super specialist adopts this position, it invites counter-argument. (Many people believe that the best people really do work for the best companies.) Another dubious position is that of diversification. Positioning is all about focus, focus, and more focus. Strong corporate positions are not built on scattered foundations. Companies like General Electric, Philips, and Westinghouse, which are involved in many fields, have trouble standing for anything in stakeholders' minds. This is one reason why they use corporate advertising to try to establish *an* image.

Positioning options are only limited by a company's imagination and that of its advertising agency. Good options, however, pass the IDUS test. Is the position: *important* to stakeholders, *deliverable* by the company, *unique* to the company, and *sustainable* over time? The most difficult part of the test to pass is that of being unique (and/or authentic). Once positioning is agreed to, the task for the ad agency is to create an actual advertising campaign. The task for the company communication manager is to develop a communications plan.

PLANNING CORPORATE COMMUNICATION

Figure 7.2 outlines a generic communication planning framework.[10] Each step is briefly discussed below. In the real world of business, one seldom has the luxury of being able to plan in such an ideal way. Nevertheless, this is a useful way to think about the tasks involved in talking to external stakeholders. Communicating to employees is generally handled by the Human Relations Department and is mediated by the organization's various cultures (as discussed in Chapter 6). Here, the focus is on communicating with external audiences—with the reminder that employees will

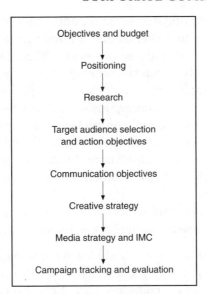

Figure 7.2. A communications planning framework
Note: IMC = integrated marketing communication.

critically evaluate these communications. Hence, it is important to make sure that they know about, and understand the reasons for any corporate communications to external stakeholders *before* they are used.

In planning a corporate campaign, managers need to ensure that it complements and, it is hoped, directly supports the company's other communications. A common criticism of corporate advertising comes from the sales-force and brand managers, who say that the sentiment of the advertising and the positioning of the company do nothing to enhance their marketing efforts. (In many cases this is an astute observation and it receives added credibility if it was the corporate affairs department that commissioned the advertising without input from the marketing people.) If they think that the money for the advertising in some way reduces the amount they would normally receive, then they can be quite vocal in their opposition to corporate, as opposed to straight product, advertising. Such internal criticism can quickly lower employee morale and devalue the positive effects that a good corporate campaign can have with employees.

Step two in Figure 7.2 is positioning, which was discussed in the previous section. Step three is research. This is discussed in Chapter 10. The aim of research is to discover what stakeholders currently think about the company so that these perceptions can be compared with the desired position.

Step four is target audience selection and action objectives. Figure 2.1 (in Chapter 2) classified stakeholders into four groups—normative (e.g., government), functional (e.g., employees), diffuse (e.g., the press), and customers. People within each customer group can be further divided into subgroups. For example, customers can be profiled as (a) potential new company users, (b) our-company loyals, (c) other-company loyals, (d) competitive, that is, customers who prefer us to any competitor, but for whom the difference is not great, (e) switchable, that is, customers who prefer a competitor to us, but for whom the difference is not great, and (f) multi-company loyals, that is, customers who use us and other companies to satisfy their needs.

Action objectives are statements of the type: 'What do we want people to do after they see the advertising?' Some typical action objectives are:

- potential new company users—to learn about the company using our information (rather than publicity, and/or word-of-mouth communication), and trial of the company's products or services;
- our-company loyals—increase use, and say favourable things about our company;
- other-company loyals—enquire/gather information about our company and its products or services, and consider using our company;
- competitives—develop a better image of, and a higher preference for our company;
- switchables—consider our company, and (re)try our company's products;
- multi-company loyals—maintain their image and patronage;
- key government employees—develop a favourable image of the company;
- financial analysts—ensure they give an accurate evaluation of the company's past performance and future prospects;
- journalists—ensure they give a fair reporting of events;
- employees—promote a more positive image and a greater feeling of attachment;
- investors—achieve a higher stock price, et cetera.

Each of these action objectives can then be linked to a communication objective.

Communication objectives ask the question: 'What factual or "image" (positioning) information should we communicate to achieve our action objective?' Advertising, direct marketing, sponsorships, public relations, promotion, and websites can help to achieve four communication effects:

(1) *Category need.* This occurs when the stakeholder (target audience member) seeks some type of benefit, or wants to solve a particular problem using the company or its products and services. Stimulating the category need is synonymous with stimulating primary demand. That is, it applies to all companies which offer these services. Apple Computer's long-used corporate advertising slogan 'The power to be your best' is a good example of advertising that applies to all PC manufacturers.

If the category need is not present, or it is weak, the company must 'sell' this basic need prior to selling the company. If the category need is latent, this need only has to be mentioned to remind the stakeholder of the previously established need. Companies selling infrequently purchased products, or new products for the first time (facsimile machines, mobile phones, MBA degrees, insurance, consulting services, etc.), will often need to sell the category *and* sell the brand.

(2) *Company awareness.* This occurs when a stakeholder recognizes or recalls that the company is involved in a certain industry, and/or sells certain products (brands). There has to be a link between the company and the industry or product category need. There is not much value in people knowing a company's name but knowing nothing about the company. The McGraw-Hill advertisement reproduced in Exhibit P.1, in the Preface to this book, is one of the best print ads to ever summarize awareness from a customer's (and many other stakeholders') point of view:

I don't know who you are.
I don't know your company.
I don't know your company's product.
I don't know what your company stands for.
I don't know your company's customers.
I don't know your company's record.
I don't know your company's reputation.

Now—what was it you wanted to sell me?

As a stakeholder gets answers to the questions posed in the McGraw-Hill ad, he or she will progress up the pyramid in Figure 7.3, and is likely to form a better corporate image and reputation.

(3) *Corporate image.* This refers to the stakeholder's overall evaluation of the qualities associated with the company, and the emotional reaction those qualities produce. This evaluation, like awareness, must be linked to the company's perceived ability to meet the stakeholder's current need. The link between image and need is via one of seven primary usage motivations. Four of these have a negative origin (problem removal, problem avoidance, incomplete satisfaction, normal depletion), and three a

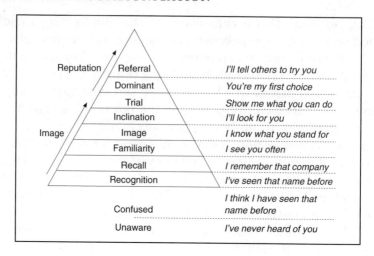

Figure 7.3. The image–reputation pyramid

positive origin (sensory gratification, intellectual stimulation or mastery, social approval). These motivations stimulate the stakeholder's relationship with the company and have an impact on the effectiveness of creative tactics used to spell out its desired image.

Depending on what research indicates, management may need to: (a) create a favourable image (for people previously unaware of the company), (b) enhance a weak favourable image, (c) maintain or reinforce an established very favourable image, (d) change an unfavourable image by correcting faulty beliefs about the company, (e) update people's images when they lag behind the company's activities, or (f) differentiate the company when competitors are seen to be very similar. (The example used to illustrate how to measure corporate images in Chapter 10 provides an example of an attempt to enhance the images of a company held by stakeholders.)

(4) *Delayed (soft sell) company consideration and support.* These occur when the corporate advertising can help to raise the levels of confidence and trust that internal and external stakeholders have in the company. As we will see in Chapter 10, this in turn leads to stakeholders supporting corporate activities, and under appropriate circumstances, being prepared to say positive things about it.

The first three communication effects are always communication objectives, while the fourth will occur as a natural outcome of good corporate (and product) advertising. The fundamental issue facing management is to develop a co-ordinated approach to corporate and product advertising, so that there is a positive carryover from each type of advertising to the other. When the company equals the brand, as is the case with BMW, Coca-Cola, IBM, Levi's, McDonald's, Sony, and so on, this carryover effect is automatic. Also, for many professional service providers (ad agencies, consultants, law firms, market research firms, etc.) corporate advertising is really brand advertising. Government agencies like health services, police services, and schools also fall into this category, that is, all their communications promote the body corporate.

Companies that have multiple brands or strategic business units often use corporate advertising as an umbrella. This can be effective, if it is embedded in an integrated marketing communications (IMC) programme. Such a programme recognizes that even though corporate communications are targeted at different stakeholders, the purpose should be to keep the same overall positioning of the company across all types of communications. When a company uses different advertising agencies for its divisions and/or for its brand advertising, it is difficult for it to project a consistent positioning.

Creative strategy

The next step is the creative strategy, when it is the turn of the ad agency to find a way to communicate the corporate position effectively. Generally, the most effective way of doing this is by developing a powerful creative idea. These ideas are generally very simple and attention getting, and have a direct relevance to the corporate image/position. The creative idea + message content + executional tactics = an advertisement. The ad agency is responsible for the creative idea and its execution, that is, the emotion and drama of the ad. The company is responsible for the overall message content, that is, the desired image/position.

The preceding description sets out what a rational approach to management says should happen. What often happens, however, is that the positioning statement developed by the company is weaker (i.e., vaguer) than the ad agency's creative idea. The agency then captures the whole process and the creative tactics redefine the company's desired position. If this results in a change for the better, then it should be adopted.

A creative idea and its message are only prescriptions for an advertisement. These have to be executed—that is, designed as an ad and put on paper or video. In most cases, this needs to be done so that the ad is amenable to multiple executions to produce a campaign. The manager's problem is to evaluate the rough advertising executions before large amounts of money are committed to production and media placement.

Extensive advertising research for products and services has revealed that the executional tactics should vary depending on whether the target audience member has a positive or negative motivation for purchase and whether the use is low or high involvement (i.e., whether the person perceives a low or high level of risk). For corporate image advertising, this research suggests that executional tactics should vary depending on the type of stakeholder group and the motivation for paying attention to the corporate advertising. Recall that in Chapter 2 stakeholders were divided into those whose primary interest was supervising or reporting on the company (normative and diffuse groups) and those whose primary interest was buying the company's products and services (customers) and working with or for it (functional groups).

In effect, normative and diffuse groups are somewhat less involved with a company than customer and functional groups. Also, the primary motivation of normative and diffuse groups is more informational, and that of customers and functional groups is more relationship oriented. Using the executional tactics that have proven effective for consumer brands, Figure 7.4 provides some suggestions for managers faced with the task of evaluating rough corporate ads from their agency.

	Informational ads	Relationship ads
Normative and diffuse groups	Claims about the company should be explicit A problem-solution format may be appropriate Don't overclaim or underclaim Consider the use of an expert presenter Consider a refutational approach The audience doesn't have to like the ad—but should believe it	
Customers and functional groups		Benefit claims should focus on the stakeholder Long copy is OK if it is well presented Tend towards overclaiming Repetition serves to build learning and image Audience must identify personally with company Audience should like the ad Lifestyle and emotions must be authentic

Figure 7.4. Guidelines for evaluating rough corporate image ads

SPONSORSHIPS: ADOPTED BY FIRMS BUT FORGOTTEN BY THEORY

The special report on sponsorship published by The Economist Intelligence Unit (1980) defined sponsorship as: 'the payment in cash or kind to an activity which does not form part of the main commercial function of the sponsoring body, in return for some publicity'. It is an advertising-like communication activity.

As noted earlier in this chapter, more money is spent on sponsorships than on corporate image advertising, especially when the hidden costs (entertainment, travel, and corporate overhead) are added to the direct sponsorship payment.[11] One reason for this is that sponsorship (especially sport) is more fun for employees than advertising. Notwithstanding this motivation, we know far less about how or if sponsorships work, and how to evaluate them, than we know about corporate advertising.

Because the goals of sponsorships and are advertising are similar, the corporate image advertising framework outlined in Figure 7.4 is as useful as any other for evaluating sponsorships—both the motivation for being involved and the evaluation of effectiveness.[12]

Various surveys have identified the types of events that companies sponsor most frequently:[13]

(a) sport (events, teams, individuals, leagues);
(b) the arts (visual, performing);
(c) community (projects, events, national days, state fairs); and
(d) trade shows.

These surveys reveal a wide range of motivations for sponsorships. For example:

(a) to help the sport, arts, community, etc.;
(b) to enhance community relations;
(c) to enhance the corporate image;
(d) to 'rent' some attributes of the item being sponsored that may be beneficial in marketing the company and/or its products (e.g., sponsoring sport and art allows the company to link with the highest aspirations of society);
(e) to provide corporate hospitality, namely, getting company personnel and client executives into events and meetings with the stars;
(f) to raise employee morale and inspire salespeople;
(g) as an advertising substitute—for products which have restricted

advertising opportunities (e.g., alcohol, tobacco), or where there is so much competitor advertising that any more would be ineffective (e.g., the very successful sponsorship of English test cricket by the Cornhill Insurance company[14]; and

(h) because the company cannot say no to a good cause or an influential executive.

These surveys also reveal that the effectiveness of many sponsorships are not formally evaluated. There are three main reasons for this:

(1) It is claimed to be too difficult to de-couple the effects of the sponsorship from the other marketing activities such as advertising and merchandising which often accompany a sponsorship.
(2) It is too costly, given the amount of money involved.
(3) It is not relevant because the sponsorship fulfils the personal objectives of the manager who champions the cause.

When sponsorships have been evaluated, the results are very often not encouraging. Rossiter and Percy suggest that sponsorships have a failure rate of approximately 50 per cent. For example, a national survey of Australians found that 97 per cent thought that sponsorship was a good idea, but nearly two-thirds were unlikely to notice corporate event sponsorships, less than a third were inclined to buy a sponsor's product, and 60 per cent believed sponsors act in their own self-interest.[15] Sponsorship of the arts rated no better, with just 21 per cent of people being able to name *any* arts sponsor.

When companies decide to sponsor a major sports event such as the World Cup soccer or the Olympic Games, the organizing committees tend to allow only one airline, bank, computer company, credit card, official time-keeper, et cetera as official sponsors. At the 1996 Atlanta games and prior to the 2000 Sydney Olympics some companies that competed with the official sponsors reaped many of the benefits of official sponsorship without paying the levy to the organizers. They did this by using Olympic athletes in their advertising. Surveys showed that a significant percentage of people thought that these companies were Olympic sponsors.[16]

A second problem with sponsoring major events occurs when (parts of) the organization of the event falls into disrepute. The way tickets were sold for the World Cup soccer matches in France and the Sydney Olympic Games tarnished the image of both events and thus devalued the official sponsorships.

A third problem with sponsoring major events occurs as a result of media clutter. The simple fact is that the more sponsors there are, the more difficult it becomes for each individual sponsor to stand out from the crowd of other sponsors. The paradox here is that the more successful the marketing of sponsorships for an event becomes, the less effective each individual sponsorship is likely to be for the sponsoring organization!

The publication of broad-based surveys about the lack of effectiveness of sponsorships is often accompanied by commentary from public relations and sponsorship agencies to the effect that sponsors need to be more innovative. There may be some justification to this criticism. Casual observation, however, often reveals a more deep-seated problem with many sponsorships, namely, that they have no obvious relationship (or 'fit') to the sponsoring company, to its desired corporate image or its brand images. With no logical link between the company and the sponsorship, it is harder for people to remember who (if anybody) sponsors what.

An example of a good 'fit' between sponsorship and corporate activities is the Ford motor company's participation in motor racing. (My argument here is that participation in motor sport is as much a form of sponsorship as it is a laboratory for product development.) It is easy for car buyers to see why any major car maker should participate in car racing—especially when the company uses the advertising slogan (as Ford does): 'We race. You win'. Some other Ford sponsorships have, however, been of questionable value (e.g., the multi-year sponsorship of English and European soccer at the end of which only 1 per cent of the public could link the Ford name with soccer).[17]

A critical factor that influences the effectiveness of a sponsorship is the marketing programme that supports it. Typically this consists of advertising, retail promotions, prizes, publicity, and the inevitable baseball hats and cheap ball-point pens. Marketers will argue that the level of marketing support should be at least equal to the cost of the sponsorship.

If these two factors are combined, they suggest that sponsorships will be most effective when there is a good 'fit' between the company (its products/services) and the sponsorship, and when the company's expenditure on marketing support is large. The further a company departs from these two conditions, the more innovative, and/or long term the sponsorship will need to be in order to provide a return on the expenditure equivalent to, say, corporate advertising.

CORPORATE PHILANTHROPY: ECONOMIC RATIONALISM VERSUS CHARITY

Pure philanthropy is based on charity and altruism, and will go largely unnoticed. (Did you know that Exxon is one of the world's biggest corporate donors?)[18] Companies with such philanthropic views give to charities and good causes or establish foundations simply because they believe in them. The tradition of corporate giving is far better established in some countries (e.g., the USA) than others (e.g., Australia). One reason for differences between countries is the tax deductibility of the corporate philanthropic donations.

Governments argue that corporate philanthropy is all about forging a social coalition between government, business, the environment, and welfare. It is hard to argue against such a general proposition—unless one is a strident financial economist.

The alternative perspective is that the role of business is to make profits, pay taxes, not damage the environment, and obey all the laws of the land. Such a role fits with a company's statutory and fiduciary duties to shareholders. The major social contributions of business, apart from paying taxes to government, are the creation of jobs and the provision of products and services to enhance people's lives. If shareholders want to give away their own dividends that's fine—but it is not the role of company managers to give other people's money to their own favourite causes.

During the 1990s a middle ground began to emerge between the 'give generously and give often' philanthropists and the 'give nothing' rational economists. In part it was a response to opinion polls that reported that many people believed that a primary role of business was to help build a better society.[19] The middle ground is one of synergy.

Companies around the world seem more willing to give—with no strings attached, if there is some link (visible to external stakeholders) between the company and the cause. The existence of such a link avoids the problem of philanthropic donations having no effect on corporate image or reputation (because so few people know about the donations). The most recent variation of this trend is discussed next.

CAUSE-RELATED MARKETING

As I write this chapter, there are a number of consultants advising managers that the way to the hearts, minds, and loyalty of employees and customers is by instituting a programme of cause-related marketing (CRM). CRM differs from philanthropy by explicitly building a public relationship with a cause for mutual benefit. The motivation for this image-building tactic is the belief that while many people no longer trust institutions and are cynical about their marketing practices, aligning the company to a worthy cause will reverse this attitude.[20]

Advocates of CRM believe that if companies and brands are aligned with causes people feel strongly about, it will be possible for social capital to be created and a strong relationship will be built between companies and customers. You will recall from earlier discussions in this book that this is one of the platforms that has made companies like Body Shop such a success. Another internationally successful CRM programme is McDonald's Roland McDonald House for terminally ill children. Exxon adopted this approach in an attempt to recover from the oil pollution of Prince William Sound in Alaska in 1989.

A word of caution is appropriate here. While CRM consultants are extolling the virtues of linking companies to good causes, it is unrealistic to expect that this (alone) will cause customers to change their well-established patterns of purchase behaviour. For example, if you do not like opera, then you are not going to start going to the opera just because they support the Multiple Sclerosis Society. Also, if a person is a cynic about how companies do their marketing it is highly likely that such a person will evaluate these programmes cynically.

One of the ways in which CRM programmes can have a significant impact is when employees become involved. Active participation makes the employees feel as though they are making a contribution, and it provides visible evidence that the company is donating one of its most valuable resources to a project, namely, employee time. Many companies now encourage and support their employees in community and cause-related activities.

ANNUAL REPORTS AND OTHER OCCASIONAL ACTIVITIES TO MANAGE THE STOCK PRICE

A key concern of the senior executives of listed companies is to ensure that the traded stock of the firm is not undervalued. To this end, most big listed companies use three forms of spin doctoring (or, more formally, corporate communication)—the annual report, investor relations teams, and public relations. In some exceptional circumstances, a fourth strategy may be undertaken—voluntarily disclosing more information than is required by accounting standards and SEC regulations, and occasionally changing accounting procedures. Healy and Palepu describe how a change to accounting policies resulted in a correction to the stock price.[21]

Creating annual reports is a time-consuming and expensive process for most companies. It can cost as much as $25 each to create and mail printed versions. Electronic versions are located in some corporate websites. Some of these offer SEC filings and contain more information than the printed versions. For example, 3Com allows some financial tables to be downloaded as Excel spreadsheets for customized analysis.

Regardless of the production format, annual reports nearly always result in executive emotional stress. This becomes apparent when every director suddenly becomes an expert on grammar, writing style, the real meaning of words, and photographic layout. When directors start having this type of input, annual reports can range from the bland to the eccentric (e.g., the Campbell Soup Company's 1995 report).

Investor surveys repeatedly indicate that most annual reports are of doubtful value to all but the uninformed investor. Investors and their advocates (such as shareholder associations) say that more detailed information about company performance and investment value should replace the gloss and beautifully styled photographs found in many reports.[22]

Gone are the days, it seems, when the dominance and personality of the chief executive is enough to hold sway with brokers, the financial press, and institutional investors. Organized investor relations programmes and more general public relations (PR) activities are now touted as essential to get a company's message across to the financial community. Investor relations activities include activities such as calming anxious investors who do not understand how tax changes will affect their investment, explaining the long-term strategy of the company to the market, and cultivating an investor base which has the expertise to evaluate the company and its industry (thus reducing the chance of misunderstandings).

In 1994, 56 per cent of Fortune 500 companies had an investor relations department. A study by Hayagreeva Rao of Emory University suggested that companies which established these departments had: (a) a greater variability in financial performance, (b) a greater number of anti-management resolutions from stockholders, (c) a greater number of analysts following the company, and (d) more direct ties through board members to other companies which had such a department and/or more competitors which had an investor relations department. Interestingly, companies in which a high percentage of shares were owned by institutional investors were no more likely than other companies to create an investor relations department.[23]

Investor and PR activities have the same aims as a good brand man-ager—two-way communication with customers, and the management of the expectations of the key (opinion-leader) investors (customers). And like a brand manager, they must balance the functional (strategic, com-pany, and financial information) with the psychological (the spirit of the CEO and the culture of the company). In communications with investors in different cultures, the emphasis on these two aspects might have to dif-fer (e.g., more emphasis on numerical information in the USA than, say, in Asia and the UK). PR and investor relations staff used to sit outside the board of directors meetings waiting for a statement to be distributed to the press. Nowadays, they tend to be at the boardroom table, involved in much decision making.

CONCLUSIONS

While corporate images and reputations are driven mostly by the need to offer good value to stakeholders (employment, products, and services, etc.), corporate communication has a vital role to play in image formation. First, it can publicize an organization's strengths and successes. Second, it is the primary vehicle for positioning the ideal image of the organization. Finally, it may be the only way to signal to stakeholders that what the organization is doing supports one of their free-standing values. Recall that it is the linkage of the corporate image to these values that helps cre-ate good reputations—and thus corporate super-brands.

For some companies in the risk management business corporate com-munications are doubly important. These companies sell products and services which many people think are risky to make or to use, e.g., airlines, chemicals, nuclear power, pharmaceuticals, and so on. Hence, they rely on public trust in order to carry out their basic operations. To a lesser extent, banks, carmakers, insurance firms, public transport operators, and schools also rely heavily on trust. One trap that these companies fall into is to try to advertise (shout) that they are trustworthy. This strategy only works if the company already has a good reputation and the advertising reminds people of this fact. A more subtle, and I think equally ineffective, approach adopted by some companies trying to gain trust, is to use a heri-tage theme in their advertising. The implicit idea is that 'because we have been around for a long time, we are trustworthy'.

New companies have to *prove* that they are trustworthy. So do companies with a poor track record. When Richard W. Sears started the mail-order business of Sears Roebuck he understood a basic principle of trust, namely, he had to trust the customer before he could ask for trust in return. Sears told their customers to 'Send No Money'. Business boomed.[24] Many modern-day companies would do well to be less suspicious of their customers.

One means through which the major companies in an industry can build awareness, familiarity, and respect for industry participants is corporate advertising. It requires long-term investment, and can also be undertaken by an industry association on behalf of all its members. Accountants, advertisers, bankers, container manufacturers, farmers, foresters, lawyers, miners, and other industry groups often use advertising and PR activities to help educate various stakeholder groups about their contribution to society and their stewardship activities. Sometimes these associations even take a leaf out of the packaged goods marketers' handbook, and create a brand name for their members. For example, the letters CPA, which stand for Certified Practising Accountant (in Australia), and Certified Public Accountant (in the USA), effectively signal a certain minimum standard in these accounting professions.

With all forms of corporate communication, managers and their advertising agencies need to avoid vague and meaningless messages about the company. Stakeholders tune into only one radio station in the world of advertising and corporate communications: Radio Station WII-FM, or 'What's In It For Me!'

NOTES

1. D. McLeod and M. Kunita, 'A Comparative Analysis of the Use of Corporate Advertising in the United States and Japan', *International Journal of Advertising*, 13, 2 (1994), 137–52.
2. K. Keller, *Strategic Brand Management* (Upper Saddle River, NJ: Prentice Hall, 1998), B-1 to B-23.
3. D. Schumann, J. Hathcote, and S. West, 'Corporate Advertising in America: A Review of Published Studies on Use, Measurement, and Effectiveness', *Journal of Advertising*, 20 (Sept. 1991), 35–56; P. Alvarez, 'Overall Media Buying Stagnates but Targeted TV Booms', *Public Relations Journal*, 49 (Aug. 1993), 14–17. For some good examples of corporate campaigns see J. Gregory with J. Wiechmann, *Marketing Corporate Image* (Chicago: NTC Business Books, 1991).
4. M. Hiestand, 'Marketing Research: Trying to Measure Exposure, Its Value', *USA Today* (18 Nov. 1998), 38.
5. Try this 'test' on yourself. Think back to the last business magazine or newspaper that you read, and see how many ads you can recall. For most of the man-

agers in my executive programmes, the answer is zero. A few managers will recall one—often because they are in the market for that type of product. The other main reason that ads are noticed is that it is the manager's company that is advertising. The lesson of this test is that it is managers like the readers of this book who authorize the ads in these magazines—and hardly anybody notices them!

6. Another problem with these ads was that they replaced some very successful parochial campaigns in different countries. G. R. Dowling, 'BP Catches the Global Brand Fad', *Australian Institute of Management Magazine* (Feb. 1991, NSW edn.), 7–8.

7. D. Wasserman, *That's Our New Campaign* (Lexington, VA: Lexington Books, 1988).

8. J. Rossiter and L. Percy, *Advertising Communications & Promotion Management* (New York: McGraw-Hill, 1997), ch. 6.

9. There is much hidden reputation meaning in these tombstone advertisements. For example, the level at which firms are bracketed in the ad (from top to bottom), and the order in which names appear, both signal to competitors and clients the status of the firms.

10. This section is based on Rossiter and Percy, *Advertising Communications* (n. 8 above).

11. A rough 'rule of thumb' is to double the direct cost of the sponsorship to cover advertising, merchandising, and the 'hidden' costs.

12. This comment is made with the understanding that the measurement of the effectiveness of sponsorships should be undertaken from a broad perspective against a set of clear objectives. It should *not* be done merely in terms of media equivalences, that is, tallying up the free coverage a sponsorship has generated, then determining how much it would have cost to purchase an equivalent amount of ad space. See also Rossiter and Percy, *Advertising Communications* (n. 8 above), ch. 11, Appendix 11D.

13. See, for example, D. Marshall and G. Cook, 'The Corporate (Sports) Sponsor', *International Journal of Advertising*, 11, 4 (1992), 307–24; R. Javalgi, M. Traylor, A. Gross, and E. Lampman, 'Awareness of Sponsorship and Corporate Image: An Empirical Investigation', *Journal of Advertising*, 23, 4 (1994), 47–58; and Hiestand, 'Marketing Research' (n. 4 above).

14. T. Meenaghan, 'The Role of Sponsorship in the Marketing Communications Mix', *International Journal of Advertising*, 10, 1 (1990), 35–47; C. Culligan and A. Harvey, 'The Links Between Objectives and Function in Organizational Sponsorship', *International Journal of Advertising*, 10, 1 (1990), 13–33.

15. C. Snow, 'Setbacks and Some Scoring Chances for Sports Sponsors', *Australian Financial Review* (5 March 1996), 35.

16. 'Qantas & NAB Deny "Hijack" Charge', *Marketing* (Sept. 1997), 9.

17. 'Sponsorship Fails at Ford', *Marketing* (Australia), (March 1994), 9.

18. In America there is a strong tradition that corporate philanthropy is expected of major companies. The tradition is not as developed in other nations. Some

of America's biggest corporate philanthropists are: Exxon, General Motors, Wal-Mart, AT&T, Johnson & Johnson, Ford Motor Corp., Citicorp, J. C. Penney, Chevron, Boeing, State Farm, Levi's, and Sara Lee.

19. B. Hale, 'Do Good, or Else, the Public Warns', *Business Review Weekly* (5 Nov. 1999), 94–5.
20. R. Burbury, 'The "Third Wave" of Branding', *Australian Financial Review* (15 March 1999), 15–16.
21. P. Healy and K. Palepu, 'The Challenges of Investor Communication: The Case of CUC International Inc.', *Journal of Financial Economics*, 38 (1995), 111–40.
22. A.-M. Moodie, 'Taking the Gloss off Annual Reports', *Australian Financial Review* (15 May 1998), 55.
23. H. Rao, 'The Rise of Investor Relations Departments in the Fortune 500 Industrials', *Corporate Reputation Review*, 1, 2 (1997), 172–7.
24. R. Tedlow, *New and Improved: The Story of Mass Marketing in America* (Boston: Harvard Business School Press, 1996), ch. 5.

7.1

Chevron: Corporate Image Advertising and Research

INTRODUCTION

This case history describes how Chevron, an integrated petroleum company, designed and implemented a successful corporate image advertising campaign. The campaign started in 1985 and continues to run.

Why this case study? First, Lewis Winters, Manager, Strategy & Opinion Research at Chevron, has made public the information described below.[1] A more important reason, however, is that Chevron is a company in an industry with a poor image and reputation. Hence, if it is possible for Chevron to enhance its corporate image in such a hostile environment, then it should be possible for many other organizations to make substantial improvements.

Some key issues are highlighted in this case. The first is the relationship between a person's values and their corporate images and reputations. As suggested in Chapter 1, we would expect that people with different values will have different views of the reputations of a particular company. The following research illustrates this phenomenon. A second is the length of time it takes to see some tangible results. Another is the use of consumer research to measure corporate images and monitor the effectiveness of corporate advertising. Research helps to suggest changes and to justify the advertising investment. A fourth is the relationship between the industry image and that of a particular company: they are correlated. A fifth is the theme used in corporate advertising: the more specific the better.

INDUSTRY AND COMPANY BACKGROUND

The 1970s were not a good period for US and European oil companies. The OPEC cartel had formed and was restricting supply and raising prices in world markets. In the USA prices rose tenfold and there were supply shortages at the pump in 1974 and 1979. By the early 1980s there was public distrust of the oil industry: its approval rating nationwide was less than 50 per cent. Figure 7.5 chronicles Americans' opinions of their oil industry from 1974 to 1992. It shows that each major crisis had a significant negative impact on the industry image.

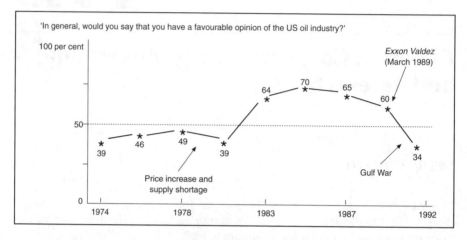

Figure 7.5. Favourable opinions of the US oil industry

Chevron's public opinion research showed that the company's overall image was consistently better than that of the industry. However, the Chevron image rose and fell with the industry image. Chevron's research also revealed that the image of the worst oil company was more strongly correlated with the industry image than the image of the best company. Bad companies, it seems have a bigger impact than good ones.

In early 1982, Chevron's Public Affairs Department began a systematic research programme under the direction of Lewis Winters to understand the factors that shape the image of the oil industry and the various oil companies. The broad aim was to see if it was possible to improve people's images of Chevron. This research also provided a better understanding of the relationship between Chevron's prod-uct/retail marketing efforts and the overall Chevron image.

In 1984 Chevron acquired the Gulf oil company in what was, at that time, the biggest merger in US history. This merger presented Chevron with a huge chal-lenge—how to integrate the brand personalities of two corporate giants? Chevron was widely known in the South-East and Pacific regions while Gulf was the major brand in the South-West region, especially the state of Texas. Chevron's manage-ment decided that the company would market a single brand of petrol throughout the country. This decision meant converting approximately 3,000 Gulf stations to the Chevron name in Texas, Louisiana, Arkansas, and New Mexico.

Management looked on this challenge as an opportunity. Rather than merely change the identity symbols of the petrol stations, there was an opportunity to introduce the company to its new customers and create a personality for the Chevron company and brand. The company committed $50 million to this task.

OPINION RESEARCH AT CHEVRON

In 1974 Lewis Winters started a survey entitled 'Public Opinion Monitor'. This survey gathered data on Americans' overall attitudes to Chevron, its competitors, and the oil industry. Figure 7.5 is derived from this research. The survey also measured how people rated Chevron on a number of corporate image attributes. For example, the 1981–2 annual survey had people rate Chevron on the following sixteen attributes. Do you agree or disagree that Chevron:

- contributes money to meet the health, education, and social welfare needs of the community;
- shows concern for the public interest;
- pays its fair share of taxes;
- contributes money to cultural, music, or arts organizations;
- sponsors radio and television programmes on the Public Broadcasting System (PBS);
- provides good service at its stations;
- would be a good company to work for;
- is a good stock investment;
- charges fair prices for its products;
- makes too much profit;
- makes high-quality products;
- is seriously concerned with protecting the environment;
- cares about how people feel about them;
- makes public statements that are truthful;
- is making efforts to develop alternative forms of energy;
- is making efforts to find new sources of oil and gas, including drilling offshore?

Using a statistical technique called factor analysis, Winters and his research team discovered that these sixteen attributes combined to form three broad corporate image factors:[2]

(1) marketing and business conduct;
(2) environmental/business conduct;
(3) corporate contributions.

Winters' training as a psychologist led him to speculate that the relative importance of these three factors (and their underlying attributes) would be driven by a person's values. On a visit to Stanford University he became aware of a research

programme called 'VALS' (Values and Lifestyles) which provided a systematic clas-
sification of American adults into nine value and lifestyle typologies. In 1983 the
lifestyle types were (ranked from worst to best): survivors (4 per cent), sustainers (7
per cent), belongers (35 per cent), emulators (9 per cent), achievers (22 per cent), I-
am-me's (5 per cent), experientials (7 per cent), societally conscious (9 per cent),
and integrated (2 per cent).[3] Figure 7.6 illustrates how these segments of the population are further classified according to Maslow's hierarchy of needs and the concept of social character.

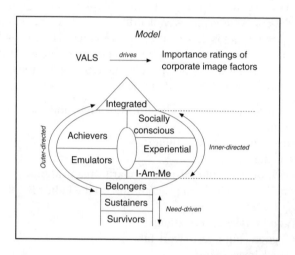

Figure 7.6. VALS: the values and lifestyle programme

In order to test his speculation, Winters commissioned a study to examine
whether the inner-directed groups had a different image of Chevron from that
held by the outer-directed groups. The results showed that they did, especially in
Chevron's home state of California. California also had a higher proportion of
inner-directed than the USA as a whole (28 per cent versus 21 per cent). Another
interesting finding was that the rank order of importance of the three corporate
image factors differed across the two groups. Table 7.2 shows that the inner-
directed group rated the environment as the most important contributor to
Chevron's corporate image, followed by marketing and business conduct, and
lastly corporate contributions. The outer-directed group rated marketing and
business conduct as the most important factor, then the environment, and lastly
corporate contributions. For both groups the corporate contributions factor
ranked a distant third.

On the basis of these research findings, Chevron decided to develop a corporate
advertising campaign targeted primarily to the inner-directed group in California.
The international ad agency J. Walter Thompson was briefed for the assignment.

Table 7.2. Values drive corporate image

Corporate image factor	Group[a]			
	Inner-directed		Outer-directed	
	Rating[b]	Importance[c]	Rating	Importance
Marketing and business conduct	4.0	2	4.1	1
Environmental and Social	3.2	1	3.6	2
Corporate contributions	3.6	3	3.8	3
Average favourability[d]	5.0		5.3	

Note: a = all respondents; b = average value on a 5-point (dis)agree scale; c = importance rank; d = average value on a 7-point scale.

THE CORPORATE CAMPAIGN

J. Walter Thompson, San Francisco, organized six independent creative teams to develop a range of creative executions around a broad environmental theme. In 1970, Chevron had used a similar theme in some corporate advertisements. From the variety of ideas generated by the creative teams, six were converted into rough television commercials for testing. The ads were called:

(a) *Go softly and gently* (upon the land with what you build and what you plan).
(b) *Kids* (are asked why we need clean air).
(c) *Water* (recycled water from a Chevron oil refinery is shown with fish swimming in it).
(d) *Friends* (children talking about what makes a good neighbour and friend).
(e) *Rabbit* (a farmer ploughing a field comes to a nest of rabbits and ploughs around it).
(f) *Colour it* (child draws a landscape picture to show the world he wants to live in).

Each of these rough ads cost between $5,000 and $10,000 to produce as against a cost of approximately $200,000 for a finished commercial.

Chevron had a policy of pre-testing both its product and corporate advertisements using the method developed by the McCollum-Spielman Worldwide research firm. While all such pre-testing approaches have their shortcomings, Lewis Winters adopted the philosophy of using a well-recognized method and sticking with it. This enabled Chevron's ads to be compared with the McCollum-Spielman effectiveness norms as well as previous Chevron pre-test scores.

The McCollum-Spielman advertising pre-test methodology involved inviting 100 people to a small theatre to view pilot television programs. Like all TV programmes, these would be interspersed with a number of different ads. Before viewing the programmes, each person filled in a questionnaire that gathered data about their attitudes towards the companies and their purchase behaviour in relation to products for which test ads would be shown that evening. When this information was gathered, the respondents did not know that they would be viewing ads for these products and/or companies. For the Chevron pre-test, the respondents also completed a short set of questions which enabled the researchers to classify them as either inner-directeds or outer-directeds.

The McCollum-Spielman pre-test method set out to measure three outcomes of the advertisement:

(1) *Cut-through awareness*: the respondent should be able to recall an advertisement thirty minutes after seeing it and know what product or company sponsored the advertisement.

(2) *Main idea*: the respondent should understand the intended message of the advertisement and be capable of 'playing back' the main idea.

(3) *Attitude change*: the advertisement should have a positive impact on the respondent's overall attitude, or in this case the respondent's image of Chevron.

Table 7.3 summarizes the results of the pre-tests.

Table 7.3. McCollum-Spielman pre-test results

| | Advertising Effects | | | | | |
| | *Awareness*[a] | | *Main idea*[b] | | *Image change*[c] | |
Ad name	*Total*	*Inner-Ds*	*Total*	*Inner-Ds*	*Total*	*Inner-Ds*
Go softly	46%	45%	39%	46%	+18%	+16%
Kids	42	36	35	35	+14	+11
Water	37	44	29	45	+32	+36
Friends	34	47	24	38	+5	−9
Colour it	39	32	20	15	+12	+1
Rabbit	47	45	35	35	+3	+1
Norm (range)	11–87		7–75		−4 +33	

Note: a = unaided awareness 30 min. after seeing the ad; b = recall the main idea of the ad; c = before/after exposure image change.

The pattern of results in Table 7.3 shows that the six test commercials were about average in terms of the McCollum-Spielman norms. They also scored well against the earlier Chevron corporate ads. The Water ad, however, had a significantly better result for the inner-directed group, especially the societally conscious sub-segment. This ad used an emotional soft tone and illustrated something specific that Chevron was doing to protect the environment. This creative approach was adopted to develop a corporate campaign named '*People Do*'. Each subsequent Chevron corporate TV ad was 'signed off' using the voice-over—'Do people care about the environment? People Do'.

The *People Do* campaign was launched in California in 1985 with an annual budget of $5 million. In order to determine if the campaign was effective, Chevron conducted tracking research. A sample of the target audience was surveyed before the campaign was screened on television to establish a benchmark, and then reinterviewed usually a year later to gauge changes in the level of awareness, sponsor identification, favourability of attitudes towards Chevron, and petrol purchase.

During 1985–6 Chevron management was thinking about how to convert their Gulf service stations to the Chevron brand. It was decided that the *People Do* ads could be used as a pre-conversion advertising campaign before the names on the Gulf service stations were changed. This was going to be one of Chevron's toughest tests because research had shown that Gulf customers had a different VALS profile to the typical Chevron (California) customer, namely, a higher concentration of belongers (part of the outer-directed group) who valued security, conformity, tradition, and major established brands.

Research conducted in early 1987 showed that some Gulf customers had strongly favourable images of the Gulf brand and that Gulf had become part of Texas history. Thus, the marketing problems associated with converting the brand went beyond customers' utilitarian issues of good service, convenient location, and low prices to include emotional ones like pride in Texas. In fact, one survey showed that 54 per cent of Gulf customers would consider defecting if Gulf petrol stations became Chevron stations. Since the four states (Texas, Louisiana, Arkansas, New Mexico) represented 25 per cent of Chevron's total US volume, there would be a significant negative economic impact if vast numbers of Gulf customers deserted these petrol stations.

With this knowledge, Chevron's main goal was to use corporate advertising to introduce Chevron to customers in order to retain them when the gas stations were rebadged. Because the psychographic profiles of the California and Texas markets were different, J. Walter Thompson was asked to produce two new ads that might be suitable for the Texas market. McCollum-Spielman benchmark tested these two ads against one of the *People Do* commercials that was running in California. The tests were undertaken in three cities: New Orleans, Dallas, and Houston.

The *People Do* ad tested was called *Eagle*, and a print version is reproduced in Exhibit 7.2. In terms of potential awareness, *Eagle* scored slightly above average. On correct message communication it also scored slightly above average. It was given above-average scores on descriptors such as 'imaginative', 'believable', and 'interesting'. Most importantly, the commercial received very high persuasion scores, namely, a positive attitude shift of 34 per cent. Also, three out of four pretest respondents said that they would be more likely to buy Chevron petrol after seeing the ad.

The *People Do* corporate campaign began running in each conversion market approximately three months before any physical changes to service stations were

Exhibit 7.2. Chevron's Eagle advertisement

made. It was supported by product advertising created by the ad agency Young & Rubicam. For example, a print ad that ran in Houston with the headline—'I heard Gulf stations are changing to Chevron. What's that mean to Houston?'—provided information about the conversion.

DOES THE *PEOPLE DO* CAMPAIGN WORK?

In California during the period 1985 to 1993, the *People Do* campaign registered a steady rise in awareness from 36 per cent to 71 per cent. Between 1986 and 1987, the campaign achieved a 10 per cent increase in the inner-directeds' favourable images toward Chevron and a 22 per cent increase in sales as measured by 'the brand last bought'. Further details are shown in Table 7.4.

Table 7.4. 1986–7 Results (per cent)

	Image change towards Chevron: California inner-directeds		
Attitude change	Unaware of Chevron ads	Aware of Chevron ads	Overall ad effect
Favourable	+7	+15	+8
Unfavourable	−3	−5	+2
Net	+10	+20	+10

	Purchase impact on California inner-directeds					
Chevron last brand bought	Unaware		Aware		Overall ad effectiveness	
	Total	Inner-Ds	Total	Inner-Ds	Total	Inner-Ds
Jan. 1986	24	26	9	10		
Jan. 1987	26	21	19	27		
Net	+2	−5	+10	+17	+8	+22

In mid-1989 a second study was conducted in the Houston, Dallas, and New Orleans markets for comparison with the 1987 study. Although it was not possible to attribute specific improvements to either the product or corporate advertisements, the overall research results were favourable. The comprehensive communications campaign had improved awareness of the Chevron-Gulf merger by 17 per cent. Also, the number of customers who said that they would defect from the new Chevron stations fell from 54 per cent to 4 per cent by 1989. Two other indices of the effectiveness of the two campaigns are that by the early 1990s Chevron had the near top market share in Houston, and it was rated as the oil company that could be most trusted to handle an environmentally sensitive project in a responsible manner.[4]

Chevron continued to conduct an annual review of the effectiveness of its corporate and product advertising. While it is almost impossible to de-couple the effects of the corporate campaign from those of the product advertisements, senior managers were convinced that both types of advertising made a positive contribution to Chevron's corporate image and its sales at the pump.

UPDATE

In 2000, the *People Do* campaign continues to run in California, Texas, Louisiana, and other US locations—see www.chevron.com/environment/peopledo. Over this time there have been more than twenty different creative executions to keep the campaign fresh. Periodically the creative team gets tired of the theme and wants to change it. Management has so far resisted their requests because the research results suggest that neither consumers nor employees are tired of the campaign.

A side-effect of the corporate campaign not anticipated in 1985 was that employee pride in the company and its stand on environmental protection has increased. In 1989 this corporate-environment ethic was incorporated into a comprehensive document known as *Policy 530*, which was formally adopted by the Board of Directors in 1992.

NOTES

1. This case is based on the following sources: Lewis C. Winters, 'Does It Pay to Advertise To Hostile Audiences With Corporate Advertising?' *Journal of Advertising Research*, 28, 3 (1988); Lewis C. Winters, 'The Role of Corporate Advertising In Building a Brand—Chevron's Pre-Conversion Campaign in Texas', paper presented to The Tenth Annual Advertising and Consumer Psychology Conference (16–17 May 1991, San Francisco); John A. Quelch, 'Chevron Corporation', Harvard Business School, Case 9-591-005 (June 1993); Lewis Winters, personal presentation to MBA students at the Australian Graduate School of Management (Oct. 1994).
2. Factor (or principal components) analysis is a statistical procedure that is frequently used to analyse people's ratings of a large number of attributes which describe a brand or a company. Because many of the attribute ratings are correlated with each other, it is possible to reduce the set of attributes to a smaller set of underlying factors.
3. Arnold Mitchell, *The Nine American Lifestyles: Who We Are and Where We're Going* (New York: MacMillan, 1983).
4. This research also indicated that the biggest group of respondents did not trust any US oil company to handle an environmentally sensitive project responsibly. Lewis Winters says that the Chevron board is fully aware that Chevron is 'second to none' in this survey.

8

Corporate Identity: What You See Is Often Less Than What You Get

This year, with the help of corporate identity consultants, hundreds of organizations will change one or more of their identity symbols. For a big company these changes are expensive. For example, it has been estimated that it cost International Harvester between $13 and $16 million to change its name to Navistar (consultant expenses, signage, stationery, etc.); the change from Burroughs and Sperry to Unisys about $15 million; UAL Inc. to Allegis a bit more than $7 million, and AT&T's spin-off Lucent Technologies $50 million.[1] These dollar costs exclude the management time taken to effect the changes, and the emotional costs of the people involved with the change. Arguably, many such corporate identity changes will not achieve a positive return on the fully costed investment. Because organizations invest so much time, money, and emotion in their corporate identity symbols, there is a need to demystify the ability of these symbols to have a positive impact on the performance and corporate image of an organization.

In 1987 and 1989 two research studies suggested that a corporate name change could have a significant impact on the stockmarket valuation of a company.[2] 'Great news', I hear you say—especially if you are a CFO or a corporate identity consultant. However, both studies found that the effect only accrued to a certain type of company, namely, those which had just completed, or were demonstrably in the process of some type of major change—such as a change in management, a new product offering, or a corporate restructuring. Also, the effect on stock prices was only modest and transitory. In fact, what these studies found was that a corporate name change was a good way of *signalling* to investors (probably only the smaller, less informed ones) that there had been some significant changes *inside* the company.

There is other evidence to suggest that much of the investment many companies put into the promotion of their corporate identity symbols has only a limited pay-off. For example, a study of the effect of a change of name for 140 US colleges and universities found no significant effect on enrolments.[3] Also, surveys often find that even the identity symbols of many nationally advertised companies are poorly recognized.[4] Recall that the discussion of sponsorships in Chapter 7 comes to a similar conclusion—put corporate names and logos on sportspeople's clothing and all over sporting venues and hardly anyone remembers.

The counterpoint to this evidence comes in the form of some spectacularly successful corporate (and/or brand) identities. Four of the best-known of these belong to Coca-Cola, McDonald's, Harley-Davidson, and Nike.[5] For example, the Harley-Davidson name and logo is thought to be the most popular tattoo in the United States.[6] And the Nike swoosh is so well known that Nike can use it in its advertising without the company name. The crucial question for managers is: 'How likely is it that we, or our identity consultant, can come up with such a stand-out identity?'

To answer this question requires that we unpack the idea of corporate identities. The first part of this process started in Chapter 1, where the case was put that corporate image and corporate reputation are not the same as corporate identity—they are much more. The subtitle of this chapter suggests how I will extend this argument. It is meant to be mildly provocative, especially to those corporate identity consultants who believe that the change of a company's visual presentation—its identity—will significantly change the image people hold of it, and then, it is hoped, people's reputation of the company.

While the argument is easily advanced that an identity change by itself is insufficient to have much effect on the images that people hold of most companies, over the years, many CEOs and their senior management teams have been seduced by consultants into believing otherwise. The seduction works so often because when an organization tries to change its image, it can change either its advertising, identity symbols, product/service quality, and/or its behaviour. What is the easier to change? What is quick to change? What can easily be seen to have been changed? Without doubt, a clean, simple solution is to employ an ad agency or a design consultant to help change the advertising and/or identity; and to be seen to have made an explicit attempt to improve the company's desired image.

This chapter has four aims. First, to draw attention—yet again—to the fact that corporate identity is only a signpost for corporate image. It may be a visible element of an organization's communication with its stakeholders, but it is only a minor part of the overall corporate image formation process. The second, and most important aim is to outline if and when identity symbols are likely to influence the desired image of an organization. The third aim is to suggest how a company and its consultants can search for a powerful set of identity symbols. Finally I identify some common corporate identity traps which can catch an unwary manager. These post the following warning: 'What you see is often less than what you get'. We first examine a common management dilemma.

THE MANAGER'S DILEMMA: IT'S TIME FOR A CHANGE

While nobody is complaining about them, most corporate identity symbols are part of the corporate landscape. Occasionally, however, something triggers the suggestion that 'it's time for a change'. The most common triggers are:

(a) a new CEO or Director of Corporate Affairs who decides to signal his or her arrival with a corporate identity overhaul;
(b) a design consultant, public relations firm, or ad agency which sells the idea to the Corporate Affairs Department;
(c) a customer survey that indicates that few people can recall the corporate identity;
(d) the top management team may decide that a change is required to reflect a change of operations or a merger.

When change is initiated, it usually follows that a firm of design consultants is engaged to create the new look. Some of the big consultants are: Anspach Grossman Enterprise (www.enterprisegrp.com); Landor Associates (www.landor.com); Lippincott & Margulies (www.lippincott-margulies.com); and Wolff Olins/Hall (www.wolff-olins.com). The Design Management Institute publishes its own journal that contains many case studies (see www.dmi.org).

While the approach of each consultant differs, the usual *modus operandi* is to start by reviewing how the current identity symbols are used. Often the opinions of customers and other stakeholders are also sought. From this base, and discussions with senior management, the consultants then create a number of designs to reflect the desired qualities of the company, reduce these to a shortlist, and then present them for discussion, possible further development, and final selection. To select the final design and ensure that senior managers support the new identity symbols, a common approach is to form a steering committee of executive managers and the lead consultant. At first glance, this seems to be a good approach to gain access to the skills of professional designers and the commitment and enthusiasm of internal and external stakeholders. In some crucial respects however, the way that this process unfolds is flawed! See Exhibit 8.1: Developing a new corporate identity.

The change of corporate logo for Australia's biggest retail bank is a good example of the issues involved in many corporate identity redesigns.[7] In 1991 the Commonwealth Bank of Australia launched its new corporate logo—an obscure geometric representation of the Southern Cross star constellation (which appears on the Australian flag). The old corporate colours were retained. The thirty-year-old previous logo was a map of Australia surrounded by three concentric circles. To redesign the logo and change all the signage, stationery, staff uniforms, and advertising cost the bank millions of dollars and took over two years to complete. Staff were informed of the change three weeks prior to launch.

The bank stated three main reasons for developing a new identity. First, it was a very different bank to the one that existed when the previous identity was designed. Second, the old logo and identity symbols were used inconsistently. Third, the bank wanted to project itself as modern and dynamic and the old logo was perceived as old-fashioned. The new corporate image was to support the bank changing from government ownership to a public company.

Journalists who commented on what was at the time Australia's biggest corporate identity change exposed three common corporate identity mistakes. First, most people did not understand the meaning designed into the new corporate logo. The effect was customer confusion and public ridicule. Second, the change in the bank's identity symbols was not accompanied by any appreciable improvement in its products, pricing, or standard of service to customers. The effect was a feeling among many customers that the bank was wasting their money on cosmetic changes. Also, the changes occurred when economic conditions were depressed, and in an overall atmosphere of antagonism to the four major Australian retail banks. The bank's third mistake was to replace its very memorable advertising campaign with one that was easily forgettable. A few years, and a couple of ad campaigns later, they quietly reintroduced the old corporate slogan.

This case illustrates the dilemma faced by many organizations which embark on a change to their corporate identities. The change has strategic merit, but it fails to convince external stakeholders, and in many cases company employees, that it has been well thought through. The case also alludes to a major theme of this chapter, namely, that there is often as

Exhibit 8.1.   Developing a new corporate identity

Developing new corporate identity symbols is similar to developing a new advertising campaign. Over the past twenty years the high failure rate of new ad campaigns has stimulated research on how to improve development procedures. What this research has discovered is that there are three critical facets to developing successful advertising (for which, read corporate identity) using an outsourcing arrangement.

The first is that generally too few creative ideas (or identity elements) are generated *and* tested before one is selected for use. The theory of 'random creativity', as it has been called, suggests that between five and 94 creative ideas (or sets of identity symbols) should be tested, depending on how confident the manager or the design consultant needs to be in coming up with a 'real winner'.[a] (Whether a small or large number is required also depends on (a) how accurate the testing procedure is—the higher the accuracy, the more ideas should be tested, (b) the average hit rate of the agency—this is inversely proportional to the average creativity of the source, and (c) the variability around that track record—greater variability requires more ideas to be tested.)

The second facet is that managers (and consultants) should *not* try to select the 'real winner' identity. The reason for this is that when judging creative advertising ideas, managers are just as likely to pick a loser as a winner.[b] Why should their intuition be any better when selecting identity symbols? (Consultants typically use their judgement to come up with a shortlist to be evaluated by management. There may be some formal testing of the shortlisted ideas with stakeholders, but senior management will reject any designs they do not like.)

The third facet relates to how one writes an incentive contract with an outsourced supplier (an ad agency or a corporate identity consultant) to maximize the chance that a 'real winner' identity is developed. Contracting theory suggests that a fee for service arrangement will not be as effective as some form of incentive contract based on the effectiveness of the advertising (or corporate identity).[c] (Few, if any, contracts with designers contain an incentive component.)

Sources:
[a] J. Rossiter and L. Percy, *Advertising Communications & Promotion Management* (New York: McGraw-Hill, 1997), ch. 7.
[b] See L. Bogart, B. Tolly, and F. Orenstein, 'What One Little Ad Can Do', *Journal of Advertising Research*, 10, 4 (1970), 3–13; and G. McCorkell, *Advertising That Pulls Response* (Maidenhead, UK: McGraw-Hill, 1990), 10–13.
[c] T. Devinney and G. Dowling, 'Getting the Piper to Play a Better Tune: Understanding and Resolving Advertiser–Agency Conflicts', *Journal of Business-to-Business Marketing*, 6, 1 (1999), 19–58.

much potential for an identity change to cause a negative reaction among key stakeholder groups, as there is for it to have a major positive effect. The Allegis case in Exhibit 8.2 provides another example of such problems. The first step in helping to avoid the problems associated with changing corporate identities is to be clear about the nature and the role of corporate identity symbols.

Exhibit 8.2. The Allegis débâcle

Many commentators, and even Clive Chajet, CEO of Lippincott & Margulies, the firm responsible for the name change, consider it a débâcle. In short, Dick Ferris, CEO of UAL Inc., the holding company of United Airlines, Hertz, Western, and Hilton Hotels, wanted a new name for the holding company in order to better communicate its diversified nature to financial analysts. He subsequently decided to use the new Allegis name as a marketing tool for the integrated travel services of the group. This is when the trouble started, because people thought that the airline was being rebadged—with a name that sounded like a new disease (a Donald Trump observation). Both the board of directors and outside commentators began to question Ferris's judgement about why UAL needed a new name. They and the financial community then began to question his judgement about the worth of creating an integrated travel conglomerate. Ferris was soon forced to resign, the Allegis name was scrapped, and the conglomerate disbanded.

How did the new name cause people to change their image of the company? First, it created increased awareness and interest. Then it got outsiders (market analysts, commentators, and corporate raiders) thinking about the viability of Ferris's new strategy. This in turn stimulated insiders (the board of directors and employees) to reconsider their support for the CEO and his strategy. In effect, the new name acted as a catalyst to accelerate events happening both inside the company (union discontent), and outside the company (the financial restructuring of many companies in the late 1980s). What really destroyed the UAL/Allegis group was not its new identity, but the manifestation of some strong forces both inside and outside the organization.

Source: Derived from: Clive Chajet and Tom Shachtman, *Image by Design* (Reading, MA: Addison-Wesley, 1991), 104–9.

THE ROLE OF VISUAL IDENTITY

There are four basic components of an organization's identity: its name, logo/symbol, typeface, and colour scheme. In addition to these, the company's buildings, office decor, signage, stationery, uniforms, cars and trucks, and so on can all play a part in helping stakeholders and other people to identify the organization. All these elements are visual.[8] Companies often combine them to create a visual style which can help to make a statement to people about what the company hopes to stand for. For example, many professional service firms design the office decor, staff dress, letterhead, and so on to project an image of high quality. The Transamerica financial services company uses a picture of the famous San Francisco landmark as its logo with the slogan, 'The people in the pyramid are working for you'.

Hence, a second aspect of the definition of corporate identity stated in Chapter 1 is that the organization's various identity symbols try to represent 'the visual manifestation of the organization's desired image'. Just how difficult this is to do is illustrated in Exhibit 8.3.

The primary roles of corporate identity symbols are to: (a) create awareness, (b) trigger recognition of the organization, and (c) activate an already stored image of the organization in people's minds. In this way, identity is more tactical than strategic. Whether the organization's tactics (the way it co-ordinates its identity symbols) support its strategy (its desired image and reputation) is a question best answered by research. As an aside to Exhibit 8.3, it may be of interest that the consultants who designed both the Lucent Technologies and Imation names had to complete their tasks in a very short time period (three and eight months respectively). They did not have the luxury of being able to test whether the names really did evoke (support) any of the twenty listed corporate traits (desired image).

Figure 8.1 offers a useful framework for identifying the potential failure points which stop a company's identity symbols 'working'. The first potential failure point is that the identity is not noticed. Attention is a simple binary (yes/no) gateway. Two factors enhance the attention-getting potential of corporate identity symbols, namely, salience, and vividness. Salience occurs when a person's attention is directed to one part of their environment rather than to other parts. It can be achieved by making the corporate identity novel, extreme, colourful, or large, or by incorporating it in a distinctive context. Salience is, however, becoming more difficult to achieve in an increasingly more cluttered visual environment. Also, many corporate identities lose much of their salience when reproduced as black on white (e.g., in newspaper advertisements).

Vividness is the ability to attract and hold a person's attention and to excite the imagination. Information will be vivid to the extent that it is (a) emotionally interesting, (b) concrete and imagery provoking, and (c) proximate in a sensory, temporal, or spatial way.[9] A good example of a

Exhibit 8.3. Leaving home and creating a new identity

1996 saw two of the biggest 'start-up' companies in US corporate history—the $20 billion Lucent Technologies and the $2 billion Imation. Two of the world's leading corporate identity firms helped the managers of these start-ups choose their new names and identity symbols. The goal of both companies was to build on the previous parent company strengths, leave behind perceived weaknesses, and introduce new traits that would define the new company's personality and positioning.

How well do you think that the two names signal these goals? Listed below are twenty traits that could be associated with each corporate name. Which, if any, of these are evoked by each name? (You can choose as many or as few as you like for each company. Also, the same trait can apply to both companies.)

1.	Aggressive	11.	Innovative
2.	Agile	12.	Reliable
3.	Creative	13.	Stature
4.	Visionary	14.	Speedy
5.	Results driven	15.	Energetic
6.	Decisive	16.	Flexible
7.	Global	17.	Customer focused
8.	Leaders	18.	Confident
9.	High-tech	19.	Imitative
10.	Focused	20.	Establishment

Lucent Technologies was spun off from AT&T and Imation from 3M. Traits 1–11 were desired by Imation, 9 by both companies, and 12–17 by Lucent Technologies. Traits 18–20 were desired by neither company. How many did you correctly evoke?

If, like me and most of the executives to whom I have presented this task, you did not do particularly well, it indicates that the corporate advertising of both companies has a big job to do.

Sources: Derived from: P. Kavanaugh, 'Creating the Identity for a $20 Billion Start-up', *Design Management Journal*, 8, 1 (1997), 20–5; A Schechter, 'Building a Global Brand', *Design Management Journal*, 8, 1 (1997), 40–4.

company which has a salient and vivid corporate (and brand) logo is the Arnott's Biscuits Company in Australia. (Its majority shareholder is the Campbell Soup Company.) It paints its delivery vehicles red (the corporate colour) with a large, very colourful picture of a Rosella parrot eating a cracker biscuit. The vehicles are *always* immaculately presented and act as a moving advertisement for the company and its products.

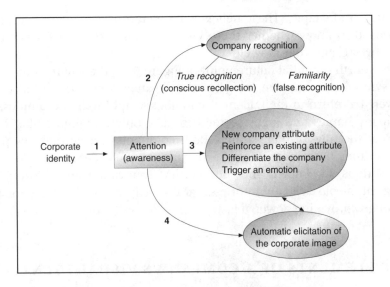

Figure 8.1. Failure points for corporate identity

The second potential failure point involves recognition. Is it true recognition based on a conscious recollection (from past exposure), or an illusion of recognition based on the similar corporate identity of another organization? From a strategic standpoint, true recognition is valuable to a company. When the company falsely recognized has a good image, false recognition can also be valuable. Recognition, either true or false, can improve evaluation and stimulate positive emotions.

The third failure point involves the ability of the corporate identity to influence a person's beliefs and/or feelings about the company. Exhibit 8.3 was an illustration of this. For most people, neither name automatically generates a clear set of meanings. Also, the corporate logos of these two companies have to be explained to people before they understand their relationship to the corporate name, and the company. For example, the Lucent Technologies logo is a hand-drawn circle rendered with a single brush stroke. Both name and logo are meant to convey the themes of creativity and light (a metaphor for visionary thinking), and system and connection (to reflect the nature of the industry). Given that a ten-minute corporate video was used to explain these meanings to employees, what chance did other stakeholders have of understanding this built-in meaning?

Corporate identity designers need to know what associated beliefs and feelings different stakeholders automatically attribute to names, colours, pictures, and shapes. These beliefs will be culture dependent. Designers also need to know whether these beliefs are important to stakeholders, and how strongly they are held.

The fourth potential failure point in Figure 8.1 is the ability of the identity symbols to evoke an image of the organization in the mind of the viewer. To return to the Lucent Technologies and Imation examples, the company names and logos seemed to have only a limited ability to do this—at the time of their launch. Both companies recognized this problem, so they both incorporated a slogan into their identities—'Bell Labs Innovations' for Lucent and 'Born of 3M Innovation' for Imation. The image of the old Bell Laboratories or 3M is retrieved and linked to the new company, providing power at last!

THE ELEMENTS OF A COMPANY'S VISUAL IDENTITY

Of the various parts of an organization's visual identity, by far the most important of these devices is the corporate name. There are two reasons for this. First, names tend to describe organizations—what they do, what they stand for, their aspirations, and so on. Second, a name is generally the first meaningful point of contact with an organization. And, for some reason, people seem to assign greater importance to information they receive first.[10]

Company names

In the early days of commercial enterprise, many companies were named after their founders, as a way of assuring customers and investors that a (noteworthy) person stood behind the company. This naming practice is still common among professional service firms, where the names of the founders often crowd the firm's letterhead. Another early practice was to name a company after its generic product, examples being, Campbell *Soup* Company, Chase Manhattan *Bank*, US *Steel*, and China *Light & Power*. In each case, the name communicated the company's core products or services, and probably helped to sell the product category as well as the company. For example, if you are an early entrant into the cash register market, then you may as well be known as the 'National Cash Register' company.

Advertising gurus Al Ries and Jack Trout revived interest in names.[11] They argued that a company's name is usually the first point of contact for a stakeholder. Because names denote and connote meaning, then a good name can enhance communication with people. In their terminology, the name helps to position the company in a person's mind. To illustrate, consider how the following names tell customers about the product's core benefit:

- Compaq personal computers;
- Weight Watchers, Lean Cuisine, and Healthy Choice (frozen) foods;
- Head & Shoulders shampoo;
- Intensive Care skin lotion;
- Close-Up toothpaste;
- DieHard batteries;
- U-haul trailers.

Ries and Trout argue that many special interest groups recognize the power of a good name, for example, British Design Council, Right to Life, Freedom from Hunger, Greenpeace. Sometimes governments also effectively position their legislative endeavours: fair trade laws, consumer protection, child safety campaigns, and so on. During the Pierre Trudeau administration in Canada, a two-word naming system was adopted for identifying government departments—the Canadian Ministry of Air Transport became Air Canada; the Ministry of Health & Human Services became Health Canada; the Taxation Ministry became Revenue Canada, etc.[12]

Many companies struggle to derive the full value from their name. Sometimes this is the result of industry convention, but often it results from failing to appreciate the marketing power of a good name. For example, most accounting, engineering, management consulting, and law firms are named after the founding partners. One problem with founder names is that they signal who are, and who are not, the most important people in the firm. When the founders are still with the firm, clients not served by one of these owners may think that the service has been second-class. Alternatively, when the founders are no longer with the firm, it is debatable what value the original names contribute. A second problem is that unless the founder names are associated with an already established image and/or reputation, they do nothing to help new clients choose a firm that may offer the type of service they require. In the world of professional communicators, namely, advertising and public relations, this tradition lives on. I suppose that one should never underestimate the feeling of seeing one's own name in print (or in neon lights).

One way to calibrate the communication value of an organization's name is to compare it with the names of competitors. This can be done formally using various consumer research techniques, or it can be done by comparing it with the various alternative types of company names in common use. Table 8.1 lists ten commonly used types of company names, and examples of each. Scanning this list usually raises two questions.

(1) What is an appropriate type of name for our company?
(2) Should we change our company name?

Table 8.1. Types of company names

Type	Examples
1. Founder names	Ford, Philips, Rolls-Royce, Hewlett-Packard, Nestlé
2. Location	Lloyd's of London, Saks-Fifth Avenue, Zurich Insurance
3. Animal, etc.	Caterpillar, Shell, Apple, Jaguar, Cobra Golf
4. Descriptive	Abbey Healthcare, Boston Beer Company, Holiday Inn
5. Abbreviated	Pan Am, Nabisco (The National Biscuit Co), PetsMart
6. Initials	ABC, BP, IBM, NEC, Qantas (Queensland and Northern Territory Air Service)
7. Abstract	Exxon, Kodak, Navistar, Unisys, Xerox
8. Analogy	Burger King, Cadillac (Canadian Chief), Nike (Greek goddess of victory)
9. Dynamic	Whirlpool, Travelers Insurance, Surf, Dive & Ski, Four Seasons, Speedo
10. Coined	Coca-Cola (from the coca leaf and the cola nut), Allegis (from 'allegiance' to signal loyalty and 'aegis' to signal protection)

Wally Olins, one of the most prominent corporate identity consultants, says that the naming process usually 'works' when the company is committed to it, and fails when it is not.[13] I think this is good advice. However, we have learnt that poor names often require brute-force commitment (often in the form of a large advertising budget) to be successful. This can be expensive if the name breaks some of the 'rules' discovered by advertisers and communication researchers. Here are some of these rules (or traps to avoid) which seem to make sense:

(1) Names (and advertising copy) often communicate better in print if they are designed for radio first. That is, if the name sounds good to the ear then it is likely to communicate well in any medium. Mostly, however, names are created in the reverse order!

(2) Only when a company pioneers a new product or service that customers really want is it safe to use a mean-nothing name like Kodak, Coca-Cola, Xerox, and so on. When the new product is good, customers are willing to learn that Xerox means photocopiers, Coke means cola, and Kodak means film.

(3) Avoid 'alphabet soup' names like ABC, CBS, CNN, CNBC, ESPN, NBC, and so on. (Which one is the news specialist?) Only when a company dominates a category (hence most customers know who it is anyway) is it safe to use the company's initials. Until research shows that customers and other stakeholders are starting to abbreviate the company name, it is best to use the words. For example, many people were using the names IBM and FedEx before International Business Machines and Federal Express officially changed their names.

One reason that many companies shorten their name is because the letters of the name are used in normal conversation among managers and on documents inside the organization. For example, in the business school where I work—the Australian Graduate School of Management—we call ourselves the AGSM. What typically happens is that when employees become comfortable using the shortened name, it soon appears on corporate signage. However, just because the shortened name is used 'inside the tent' does not mean that outsiders are using it.

(4) Have a name that is easy to pronounce, spell, and remember in the countries in which it is used. In Australia and the United States the German pharmaceutical company Hoechst has found that customers could not pronounce its name. They periodically run television advertising to demonstrate the correct pronunciation, and to help customers recognize the name! The German company Siemens has also found that people outside Germany often have trouble spelling its name. There is only negative equity in a meaningless name. Bayerische Motorenwerke solved this problem by calling themselves BMW—so occasionally letter names 'work' (when backed by a good product and extensive advertising).

(5) Try to avoid new names beginning with the country name, or the words 'Continental', 'General', 'Global', 'International', 'National', and so on. These words are now overused, and mostly they reflect the company's aspirations rather than commercial reality. Also, if a company has one of these 'big-sounding' names, then people will expect it to act 'big' (and tough, and impersonal, etc.).

(6) Do not play semantic, or other games with the company name. A good name is the first phase of seduction, but it should not be a mystery. For example, a small Australian design consultancy calls itself the Leda Consulting Group. Most people might expect that Mr or Ms Leda was the

founder. Not so—the first page of their corporate brochure links the origins of the *Leda* name to the father of the gods, Zeus. Interesting to some people—but do potential clients really care? Also, if people do not ask the company for a brochure they do not get the message!

(7) Be careful when considering a name change. Many long-established names have built up customer equity. While they may no longer accurately reflect what the company does, they may stand for a set of corporate values (like trust, reliability, quality, service) that are important to customers. Sometimes these names need to be repositioned, rather than changed. A good example is American Express. This company stopped doing what its name suggested in 1918 (when it lost its US express delivery business). Its travellers cheque business, and then its credit cards, have created such strong equity for the corporate name that it would be unfortunate if the company stopped using the name American Express. Also, some of the big Japanese conglomerates have built up such strong equity in the name that it can appear on a wide variety of products and services, an example being Mitsubishi, used for automobiles, a bank, electrical products, heavy industry, etc. A brand/company name can be extended considerably.[14]

(8) A frequent reason for company name changes is to reflect a merger or acquisition. In the field of professional business services (accounting, advertising, law, management consulting, and so on) this type of activity produces some of the worst corporate names. For example, in 1970 Charles and Maurice Saatchi founded the UK advertising agency Saatchi & Saatchi. In 1975 they merged with the Garland-Compton agency to become Saatchi & Saatchi Garland-Compton. The agency later became Saatchi & Saatchi Compton Worldwide. Throughout this period however, it was generally known as just Saatchi & Saatchi. The name of the international accounting firm KPMG Peat Marwick LLP is a good example of how difficult it is to reflect the heritage of various mergers in a name that is short enough to fit on a business card.

The merger of two companies does not have to result in a double-barrelled name. For example, when the computer companies Burroughs and Sperry merged they became Unisys, with the slogan 'the power of 2'. Better still is the name adopted after the merger of BOAC and BEA—British Airways.

(9) One of the risks of using any short name is that people who dislike the organization for some reason will use the letters in the name to make fun of the company. For example, this occurred when sports car drivers in the United Kingdom started to say that the name Lotus stood for 'Lots Of Trouble, Usually Serious'. Also, many flyers on Belgium's national airline

Sabena often refer to it as 'Such A Bad Experience, Never Again'. In the USA, Ford has been renamed 'Fix Or Repair Daily'.

Logos and symbols

What flags are to countries, and heraldic shields and banners are to families, logos are to the founders of companies. They are a badge of identification and membership. They also signal consistency of product and service. For example, the giant US food company RJR Nabisco's logo is based on a medieval Italian printer's symbol. It is a cross with two bars on top of an oval (which contains the word Nabisco). Originally the symbol represented the triumph of the moral and spiritual over the evil and the material.[15] (The irony of this is that the RJR part of the company is the R J Reynolds Tobacco Company.) The giant Swiss food company Nestlé also has a name and logo with symbolic meaning. Nestlé means 'little nest' in the Swiss German dialect, and the logo depicts a bird feeding its young in a nest (which seems very appropriate for a food company). To a suggestion that the Nestlé nest logo be replaced by the cross which appears on the Swiss flag, Henri Nestlé is reported to have replied: 'The nest is not merely my trademark, it is also my coat of arms'.[16]

A good logo can be a distinctive point of eye contact. Most logos, however, are remarkable for their anonymity. Wally Olins suggests that one reason for this is that at least boring, anonymous logos are 'safe'.[17] They are unlikely to upset too many people inside the organization.

A few logos have gained widespread recognition. Internationally, the most recognized logos are the Christian cross, the Olympic rings, the Red Cross, the Star of David, and the swastika. In Australia, the Qantas logo of a flying white kangaroo set in a scarlet triangle is probably the most recognizable corporate logo. In the USA the Nike swoosh and McDonald's golden arches are probably best known. The Apple computer company's rainbow-coloured apple with the bite missing from it is claimed (by Apple) to be one of the world's best known corporate/brand logos. Another well-known logo is the Shell petroleum company's shell. Shell's trade mark is registered in more than 170 countries, and over the years it has been changed without customers being conscious of the change. The guidelines for managing this logo and the other elements of Shell's visual identity are recorded in a manual several inches thick.

Unlike the Apple and Shell logos, many, if not most, corporate logos can be accused of having intrinsic meaning only to their designers. They seem to be chosen because they look like a corporate logo rather than for their ability automatically to enhance the company's internal or external communication. To help overcome this problem, the Marketing Science Institute has supported research to identify the characteristics of recognizable logos.[18] If a company is going to spend a lot of money promoting its logo and thus wants people to be able to identify it quickly and accurately, then the logo should emphasize a simple natural design (i.e., something real or identifiable). Alternatively, a company with a smaller budget may prefer to develop an immediate sense of familiarity (i.e., false recognition). In this case, it should choose a less natural, more symmetric, elaborate (more complex) design. Further guidelines are noted in Exhibit 8.4.

Exhibit 8.4. Getting noticed and remembered

Semiotic and psycholinguistic research can be used to help understand how the symbols and words in corporate identities are interpreted to have social relevance and meaning. Research consistently shows that pictures are better attention-getters, and are more easily remembered and recognized than words. Also, concrete words are better than abstract words. Occasionally, a familiar sound can be used (e.g., the toll of a bell) or a very distinctive sound such as the rumble of a Harley-Davidson motorbike.

As indicated in the body of the chapter, designs for creating immediate familiarity (false recognition) differ from those for achieving true recognition. Also, certain colours have cultural significance—what is good in the West, however, may not be so good in the East.

Some suggestions to facilitate recognition and recall are:

(1) Weave the company name and logo together (Apple's rainbow-coloured apple).
(2) Choose a logo that evokes the company name (Chevron, Jaguar, Shell).
(3) Provide people with a slogan for the logo (and/or company name) so that they learn the desired association (3M—innovation).
(4) Use a symmetric pattern in preference to an asymmetric one (the Nike swoosh versus Imation's hand waving a wand out of which come colourful dots and crosses).
(5) Link the identity to the advertising (the bell in Taco Bell, a 'look for the Bell' theme in advertisements, and the sound of a bell).
(6) Display your identity as often as possible on product and corporate artifacts.

Sources: Derived from: G. Dowling, 'Corporate Identity Traps', Working Paper 96-002, Australian Graduate School of Management (Feb. 1996); P. Henderson and J. Cote, 'Designing Recognizable Logos', Working Paper 96-124, *Marketing Science Institute* (Dec. 1996).

Colour

Colour is often the final decorative element of a corporate identity. Left to the designer's or corporate management's whim, a potentially important part of an organization's visual identity can be chosen without regard to the psychology of the effects of colour on people's emotions. People are thought to notice colour more readily than form or shape, and it is thought to hold their attention longer. The red and white of Coca-Cola, the blue of Ford, the yellow arches of McDonald's, and the yellow of Kodak are now important parts of the corporate landscape. Most company colour schemes, however, do not elicit strong recall from stakeholders. Some companies will even use different colours to sign their name. For example, I wrote my first book on an IBM personal computer where the IBM letters were printed in silver on the computer, brown on the keyboard, white on the monitor, and black on the printer. (And to think that IBM was once known as 'Big Blue'!)

Research has shown that certain colours can cause predictable emotional and physiological effects. We also learn to respond to them in certain ways: for example, in all the world's traffic signals, red means stop and danger, while green means go. The cultural context within which a colour is used, however, can be an important factor to consider. For example, white often signals purity and cleanliness, but in some cultures it is the colour of mourning. Red is a lucky colour in many Asian cultures. Colour researchers have documented many generalizations regarding the effects of colour on people.[19] For example, in Western cultures:

- red is often perceived as more energetic, passionate, and extroverted;
- blue implies authority, responsibility, and calmness;
- brown is an earthy, no-nonsense colour;
- green is cool, refreshing, and tranquil;
- grey creates a mood of dignity and safety;
- yellow is friendly and cheerful, it is the happiest of colours;
- darker colours are 'stronger';
- black and white and gold and silver are the prestige colours.

In short, many colours are liked or disliked intuitively, as clothing manufacturers see (to their cost) each fashion season.

Typeface

A look through any business magazine shows the variety of typefaces used by organizations to present their names. In fact, there are hundreds of different faces from which a typographer can choose. In addition to selecting a face, the typographer needs to select the size of type, and the form (upper and/or lower case, light, bold, italic, etc.) in which it will appear. With so many possible variations, one would expect that no two companies would use similar typefaces. Not so. Advertisers have found that relatively few are suitable for easy communication and recognition. For example, even though UPPER CASE is more difficult to read, this is a favourite option for many single-word corporate names.

Apart from the distinctive way that Coca-Cola writes its name, I struggle to recall the typefaces used by ten of the world's most recognized companies: Coca-Cola, Sony, Mercedes-Benz, Kodak, Disney, Nestlé, Toyota, McDonald's, IBM, and Pepsi.[20] How many typefaces can you recall? (Sony, Toyota, IBM, and Pepsi all commonly write their names in upper case.) Better still, how many of your own company's customers would know how your organization writes its name?

A question often asked is, who cares how our company writes its name (or what corporate colors we use) as long as it stands out from the crowd, is clear and legible, and easy to reproduce? The answer is that some typefaces may transfer subtle meanings about a company. For example, it has been suggested that tall, narrow letters with serifs (those small cross lines at the top and bottom of letters) seem elegant; rounded, full letters without serifs seem friendly; a typeface that seems almost handwritten will convey a people orientation; upper case letters convey authority.[21] If people really do make these inferences, I suppose that it is best to find out prior to deciding on a particular typeface.

There is one time when it *is* very important to understand all the inferences that people make from the way a name is written. It is when a company takes its name into a different culture—especially Asia. For example, keeping a Western corporate name and spelling is likely to be more successful in Japan than in China because Japanese are more familiar with the Roman alphabet. If a Western name is translated into Chinese characters, then different writing systems and styles can impact on people's perceptions of the company. This occurs because the visual characteristics of a name are important to native speakers of Chinese. In short, the cultural and linguistic aspects of corporate identity in the East are different from those in the West.[22]

A fascinating way to test your company's typeface is to write it in several different styles, some of which are used by your competitors. Ask (different sets of) customers to rate each typeface on the attributes which you hope they will use to describe your company's or brand's desired image (e.g., product quality, customer service, etc.) The results might surprise you. For example, a study of audiotape buyers showed that most customers preferred the Memorex name written in the typeface used by Maxell, a key competitor.[23]

Corporate slogans

Many corporate identities contain a slogan as one of their integral parts. These are used for a variety of purposes. For example, the Mitsubishi car division's slogan asks the customer for some action—'please consider', while the Lexus slogan makes a customer promise, and reminds employees about the car's desired quality—'without compromise', and BMW's provides a reason to buy—'the ultimate driving machine'. Some slogans, however, are forced to explain who the company is (e.g., ANA—'All Nippon Airways') or what it does (e.g., Allson—hotels and resorts). These last two expose the weakness of the corporate name.

The main criticism of corporate slogans is that many are meaningless to outsiders, and often to employees. Others are platitudes or self-congratulatory statements that invite a cynical response from both insiders and outsiders. A study of corporate slogans found that approximately 50 per cent of them were caught by this trap.[24] While they may have some meaning to the wordsmith who wrote the slogan and the senior managers who signed off on it, many corporate slogans are mystifying to people.

In Chapter 4 I recommended that one way to help 'sell' a company's vision to both insiders and outsiders is to translate it into a corporate slogan. If customers 'buy' the company as well as its products and services, then a corporate slogan that says something meaningful about the company or its products to customers is a useful device. For example, the old Leo Burnett advertising agency once used the slogan: 'If you reach for the stars, you will never come up with a handful of dirt'. The die is now cast to create great advertising.

THE LACK OF CONSISTENCY TRAP?

In many organizations it is easy to find examples of the inconsistent presentation of corporate identity symbols. Many identity consultants argue that anything less than a perfectly consistent presentation of these symbols will harm the corporate image. (Given the discussion of Figure 8.1 earlier, this seems an unlikely outcome.) The problem with direct comparisons of identity symbols used on communication materials aimed at different target audiences is that trivial differences often look more significant than they really are. The reason is that most people will not notice a small difference, especially when they see the identity symbols on different occasions. Hence, a small variation in the presentation of corporate identity is more untidy than potentially disastrous.

There is, however, one case where perfect consistency makes sense. This is when a person simultaneously sees multiple uses of the same company's identity. The example I noted earlier about one of my IBM personal computers is a case in point. If different versions of corporate identity are seen together, then they can look untidy and possibly confusing. For example, when I noticed the differences I then looked to see where each component was manufactured. To my surprise, each came from a different country.

IS THERE ANY MEANING IN THE MESSAGE?

All organizations have a visual identity even though they may never have employed a design consultant to integrate the various elements into a coherent whole. The difference between the visual identity of McDonald's and most other companies is that of consistency and uniformity of presentation. McDonald's family restaurants (or fast food outlets, depending on your image) have a similar 'look' all over the world. This makes them easy to recognize for people of all ages, and it reminds travellers to expect similar fare as at their local McDonald's. Few other multi-outlet organizations (with the notable exception of some petrol service stations) manage their visual identities so well.

The minimum any organization should seek to achieve is to co-ordinate all aspects of its advertising and visual identity. This will help it present a consistent style to its internal and external stakeholders. What will have even more impact, however, is if the organization can fuse its values, strategy, and organizational culture with its visual style. The aim here is to create a single value proposition that includes the company name and logo, and to communicate this to every stakeholder. A corporate slogan is one way to 'force' this integration.

There is a note of what I think is healthy scepticism in the discussion in this chapter about the ability of an organization's identity elements automatically to elicit strong meanings in the minds of stakeholders. My position, and possibly yours if you failed the test in Exhibit 8.3, is that such powerful identities are the exception rather than the rule in Corporate America, Corporate Asia, and Corporate Europe. It is extremely difficult to design an identity that breaks through the clutter and evokes corporate traits that are immediately valued by many stakeholders. I also believe that some of the identity changes that are often commissioned are a blatant waste of money. Such a classic is illustrated in Exhibit 8.5.

Exhibit 8.5. Digital Equipment Corporation changes its logo

In 1993, seven months after Robert Palmer became CEO of digital to redirect the company, it launched an updated corporate logo. Peter Phillips, director of corporate identity and design, said that the logo was updated rather than radically altered to maintain a sense of the thirty-five-year tradition in the old logo. The update was achieved by making three changes: (1) the letters 'd', 'g', and 'a' in the name 'digital' were made more proportional to the boxes on which they are written, (2) the 'i's' were topped with dots instead of squares, and (3) the colour of the corporate logo was standardized to burgundy. The rationale by Sampson Tyrrell, the London-based design house responsible for the changes, was that the first two modifications would make the name 'digital' read more fluidly. The problem was that the journalist who wrote the article on which this case is based, could not pick the difference in the proportional spacing.[a] (With the old and new logos next to each other, nor could I.) The crucial question is whether such a subliminal change is likely to be effective.

The reason for standardizing the colour from blue for stationery, black or white for literature, and grey for products to all burgundy was that the use of different colours damaged the company's image. It seems that digital did some research which suggested that some customers were confused by the different colours. Their research, however, uncovered a bigger source of confusion. Some people referred to the company as DEC—a name it used in its mainframe days, while others knew the company as digital. People who knew the company as DEC thought it was an old, stale, hardware company. People who knew the company as digital had more favourable perceptions.

cont.

Exhibit 8.5. *cont.*

It is not uncommon for a company to be remembered by its old name. A classic case is the Datsun becomes Nissan story in the USA.[b] In the USA and many other countries, Nissan sold its cars under the Datsun name. In Japan the company and its cars were known as Nissan. In pursuit of a global strategy, the decision was made to change to the Nissan name. At least this was the public story. Industry observers speculated that the most important motivation was to make Nissan as big a name as Honda and Toyota had become. This would help the company market its stocks and bonds in the USA, and enhance the status of its executives in Japan.

The change was implemented in the years 1982–4 and supported by about $240 million of advertising and $30 million of dealership sign changes. A national survey in 1988 found that the recognition and esteem of the Datsun name was essentially the same as of the Nissan name. Well into the 1990s, many people still remembered the Datsun name.

Back to the digital case. What we have here are three forces acting together to drive a corporate logo change. A new CEO wants to signal the new direction of his company to employees, customers, and industry analysts. Research suggests that some people confuse DEC with Digital. Third, the company has a thirty-five-year-old logo. Add to this a company director charged with the responsibility for corporate identity, and it is not surprising that digital changed its logo.

What is questionable, however, is whether the company spent its money in the most cost-effective manner. Digital's biggest problem was that some people held an out-dated image of the company. Was the best way to overcome this problem a subliminal change to the corporate logo, or would some other marketing initiative have been more effective? It is easy to argue that (corporate) advertising to the group with the out-of-date image would have been more effective.

Sources:
[a] Y. A. Venable, 'New Logo Preserves Brand Equity', *Business Marketing* (Aug. 1993), 18.
[b] D. Aaker, *Managing Brand Equity* (New York: The Free Press, 1991), 56–8.

Corporate identity seems to 'work' when it is 'sold' well to both internal and external stakeholders. This takes time and often a great deal of money. One of my favourite examples of this use of visual identity is the way that the British Royal Family have mastered the art of creating images of splendour and tradition with a range of ceremonies and identity symbols. This skill, however, has not been sufficient to compensate for the damage to the reputation of the House of Windsor that the poor behaviour of some of its members has caused.

CONCLUSIONS—THE CONTRIBUTION OF CORPORATE IDENTITY

This chapter suggests that sometimes there are literal meanings and inferential beliefs which automatically attach to, or which can be engineered into, corporate identity symbols. If these exist, and they are favourable to the *raison d'être* of the company, then they can help promote the company to its internal and external stakeholders. This Language School of corporate identity advocates searching for the power of corporate identity in semiotics (the social meaning of signs and symbols), psycholinguistics (the meaning of words and their imagery), and phonetics (the science of speech sounds).

The opposing school of thought can be illustrated by that famous quotation from Shakespeare's *Romeo and Juliet*—'that which we call a rose, by any other name would smell as sweet'. Here, the basic driver of a successful corporate identity is marketing muscle. That is, with sufficient and effective promotion any corporate identity symbols can be made to work. For example, over time people have become accustomed to names (and sometimes the logos) of companies like BMW, Exxon, Harley-Davidson, Marriott, Philips, Shell, and Toyota, and they associate them with the products and services these companies offer.

The central argument of this chapter is that the main reason why companies waste money when changing their identity symbols is that they do not fully appreciate the difference between the Language and the Romeo and Juliet schools of corporate identity. Here, I suggest that most consultants belong to the Language School of corporate identity, but most stakeholders act as though they belong to the Romeo and Juliet School. For external stakeholders, corporate identity is used mainly as a signpost—to help recognize an organization and recall their image of it. Internal stakeholders use identity mainly as a badge—to signal their association and commitment to an organization.

The visual symbols an organization uses to identify itself are no substitute for the corporate image (beliefs and feelings) that people have of the organization. With this distinction in mind, it is hard for an organization to be convinced by an external consultant that a cosmetic change to the corporate name, typeface, logo, or colours will have a significant impact on how stakeholders evaluate that organization. The time to change your corporate identity is *after* there have been significant changes in the company's operations or market offerings, that is, after changing the factors that drive corporate image. Then there is a good chance that both stakeholders and the stockmarket will enhance their images and valuation of the company. A company that changes its identity symbols at the same time that it says that it is trying to change its behaviour is often evaluated scornfully.

NOTES

1. These estimates were reported in: *Wall Street Journal* (17 Nov. 1986), 33; *USA Today* (4 May 1987), 5B; *Business Week* (2 March 1987), 54; D. Barbuza, 'Now That It Is a Separate Company, Lucent Is Spending $50 million to Create an Image', *New York Times* (3 June 1996), D9.

2. J.-C. Bosch and M. Hirschey, 'The Valuation Effects of Corporate Name Changes', *Financial Management* (Winter 1989), 64–73; D. Horsky and P. Swyngedouw, 'Does It Pay to Change Your Company's Name? A Stock Market Perspective', *Marketing Science*, 6, 4 (1987), 320–35.

3. P. S. Koku, 'What is in a Name? The Impact of Strategic Name Change on Student Enrollment in Colleges and Universities', *Journal of Marketing for Higher Education*, 8, 2 (1997), 53–69.

4. L. Bird, 'Eye-Catching Logos All Too Often Leave Fuzzy Images in Minds of Consumers', *Wall Street Journal* (5 Dec. 1992), B-1.

5. Nike is an interesting, and some would say a virtual company. It has relatively few employees. About the only functions that it does perform are designing its product range, organizing production and distribution, and counting its profits. Its other major functions—advertising, distribution, and manufacturing—are outsourced. It is one of the few companies whose brand-mark is truly valuable in its own right.

6. D. Aaker, *Building Strong Brands* (New York: The Free Press, 1996), 138–41.

7. This information is sourced from various newspaper and magazine articles and discussions with some of the bank's personnel.

8. Some auditory identity elements are: the tolling of church bells, the firing of the noon-day gun in Hong Kong, the rumble of a Harley-Davidson motorbike. Music in corporate advertising such as United Airlines' use of Gershwin's *Rhapsody in Blue* can also help identify a company.

9. R. Hoverstad, 'Vividness as a Means of Attracting Attention: A Revised Concept of Vividness', in R. Belk, G. Zaitman, R. Bagozzi, D. Brinberg, R. Deshpende, A. Firat, M. Holbrook, J. Olson, J. Sherry, and B. Weitz (eds.), *AMA Winter Educators Conference* (Chicago: American Marketing Association, 1987), 245–8.

10. S. Asche, 'Forming Impressions of Personality', *Journal of Abnormal and Social Psychology*, 41 (1946), 258–90.

11. A. Ries and J. Trout, *Positioning: The Battle for Your Mind* (New York: McGraw-Hill, 1981).

12. E. Selame and J. Selame, *The Company Image* (New York: John Wiley & Sons, 1988).

13. W. Olins, *Corporate Identity* (Harvard: Harvard Business School Press, 1989).

14. See D. Aaker, *Managing Brand Equity* (New York: The Free Press, 1991), ch. 9; D. Aaker, *Building Strong Brands* (New York: The Free Press, 1996); K. Keller, *Strategic Brand Management* (Upper Saddle River, NJ: Prentice Hall, 1998).

15. B. Burrough and J. Helyar, *Barbarians at the Gate* (London: Arrow Books, 1990).

16. D. Heer, *Nestlé 125 Years 1866–1991* (Vevey: Nestlé, 1991).

17. Olins, *Corporate Identity* (see n. 13 above).

18. P. W. Henderson and J. A. Cote, 'Guidelines for Selecting or Modifying Logos', *Journal of Marketing*, 62, 2 (1998), 14–30.

19. J. E. Miner, 'The Colour of Money', *Marketing* (Dec. 1991–Jan. 1992), 8–10; B. Schmitt and A. Simonson, *Marketing Aesthetics* (New York: The Free Press, 1997), 92–7.

20. Landor Associates top ten most recognized companies (1990), company press release, San Francisco.

21. Schmitt and Simonson, *Marketing Aesthetics* (see n. 19 above), 97–8.

22. B. Schmitt and Y. Pan, 'Managing Corporate and Brand Identities in the Asia-Pacific Region', *California Management Review*, 36, 4 (1994), 32–48.

23. D. L. Masten, 'Logo's Power Depends on How Well It Communicates with Target Market', *Marketing News* (5 Dec. 1988), 20.

24. G. R. Dowling and B. Kabanoff, 'Computer-Aided Content Analysis: What Do 240 Advertising Slogans Have in Common?', *Marketing Letters*, 7, 1 (1996), 63–75.

9

Country, Industry, Partner, and Brand Images: Leveraging Secondary Associations to Enhance a Corporate Image

People often associate certain types of products with a particular country. For example, to many people Italian leather goods, French wine, Chinese food, Swiss watches, Japanese cameras, and US films are all special. Within these product categories brands like Gucci have helped enhance the image of other Italian leather manufacturers, and famous French champagne brands like Moët & Chandon have helped to promote the French wineries. This chapter focuses on the relationship between country, industry, company, and brand images. To illustrate the importance of understanding these relationships for an organization consider how two UK companies enhanced their corporate/brand images by linking them to their US parent company.

In the early 1980s, General Motors was manufacturing and selling cars and trucks in the UK and Europe under the names Vauxhall and Bedford. The Vauxhall and Bedford companies, like others in the GM family (e.g., AC Spark Plug, Delco Products), operated largely independently of each other. They did, however, co-operate through a group known as the Public Affairs Council (PAC). The PAC decided to investigate the potential for linking together companies like Vauxhall and Bedford by identifying them and their products with General Motors.[1]

It was not clear that such a clear identification with the giant US parent company would be beneficial to the various operating companies. Most people in the UK saw GM's various companies as solidly British. Would identifying these companies as part of the General Motors USA family damage this parochial relationship? In effect, the PAC needed answers to the following questions:

- Would linking the companies to General Motors USA provide a greater sense of identity, cohesion, and purpose for the UK operations?
- Would there be any adverse effects of this strategy on customer preferences and loyalty?
- What were the relative strengths of the GM corporate image which could support such a communication strategy? What weaknesses needed to be avoided?
- What would be the overall effect of the strategy on the corporate standing of both GM and its individual operating companies?

A major research project was undertaken in the UK. It showed that there were considerable benefits to be gained from being known as a GM company. The PAC then used advertising, promotion, branding, and other communication strategies to build the GM association, and capitalize on this positive linkage. In effect, Vauxhall and Bedford were able to 'rent', or to use more formal terminology, to 'gain marketing leverage' from the General Motors name.

How times have changed for GM. When they set out to build a car called Saturn, their research showed that linking the car (and separate division) to the GM name resulted in lower perceptions of quality and credibility by (potential) customers. Hence, the car is called a Saturn—not a General Motors Saturn. Toyota also found that its corporate image was a liability when it developed the Lexus. For most consumers Toyota could not credibly make a premium-priced luxury car. Hence, Lexus was launched as a stand-alone brand through a separate dealer network.

The aim of this chapter is to explore some ways to rent the positive associations of other images. In particular, how can an organization get leverage from its high-profile brands (or vice versa)? Should it emphasize its links with a particular industry; should it promote the fact that some product ingredients are made by other manufacturers; or should it try to position itself using a nationalistic theme to share the parochial values of its stakeholders? While we see many examples of companies that use each of these strategies, there are few guidelines to help managers answer the questions posed above.

A NETWORK OF IMAGES

Figure 3.4 (Chapter 3) shows that external stakeholders' images of an organization can be affected by country, industry, and brand images. That is, when most people think about an organization, they do so within a relevant context. This context may be the industry in which the company operates or the brands it sells. For example, depending on what people know about American Express they may think of it as a type of financial institution, or as a company involved in travel services. (When it originally started out in 1850 it did exactly what its name says—it was an express company which transported small parcels and cash throughout the east coast of the USA.) Hence, American Express belongs to an industry. Because some industries have more favourable images than others, a company like American Express could choose to associate itself with financial services and/or travel services.

The word *American* in the name American Express also automatically associates the company with the USA for most people. In this case, the image of America can be a positive or a negative attribute, depending on what people think of America, and the American finance and travel industries. If these linkages in people's minds generate positive associations, they represent an important source of leverage for a company's image—for companies such as American Express, American Airlines, American Home Products, and the American Marketing Association. If these linkages are negative, then the organization can try to distance itself from its country of origin.

On the eve of the 1992 Barcelona summer Olympic Games, Spain launched one of the costliest public relations campaigns in history. This was aimed at changing the European stereotype of Hispanics as lazy, uneducated, corrupt, and cruel. This stereotype has its roots in the Black Legend, which was formed during the sixteenth century by the enemies of Spain. They could not defeat the Spanish armed forces, so they attacked Spain with words. The English, Dutch, Germans, Italians, French, and later the Americans accused Spain of atrocities during their conquest of the Americas, and in the conduct of the Inquisition. These charges were embellished and repeated so often over the next four centuries that many Spaniards even believed them. To help repair Spain's global image, the country hosted a number of public relations events, such as the Barcelona Olympics and Expo '92 in Seville. It also became a full member of the European Community, embarked on a nation-wide programme to restore its museums and monuments, and started to actively promote Hispanic culture to the world. It will take some time before we can tell whether these actions will change what is written in the history books and what people think about the country and its people.

What we know is that the image of countries like America, Britain, France, Hong Kong, Italy, Japan, and Spain can enhance or detract from the images people hold of their companies, industries, and brands. Also, research in psychology indicates that what people have learnt about companies, industries, and brands may be used to make inferences about other companies to which these are linked. These different types of images exist in a network as shown in Figure 9.1. Each arrow represents a source of potential corporate image leverage.

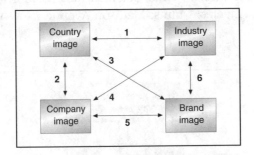

Figure 9.1. A network of images: six potential sources for leverage

The strength of the six arrows in Figure 9.1 will be determined by three factors:

(1) Whether people are aware of and knowledgeable about the linkage. For example, the old Bell Laboratories (now Lucent Technologies) was a part of AT&T, which was the biggest American telecommunications supplier.
(2) The relevance of the entity's associations for the stakeholder. For example, does it matter to a person buying Pert hair shampoo that Procter & Gamble is an American company?
(3) The degree of fit of a positively valued characteristic of one entity with the desired image of the other entity. For example, is it appropriate to link British-style tradition and fair play to the practice of law?

The stronger an arrow, the more opportunity there is explicitly to enhance the desired image of an organization by linking the two entities.

Arrow No. 1 in Figure 9.1 indicates that certain countries are known for their excellence in certain industries, namely, Australian wool, French perfume and wine, Irish (Waterford) crystal, Italian sports cars, Japanese consumer electronics, Saudi oil, Scotch whisky, Swiss (discrete) banking, US military weapons systems, and so on. Sometimes countries are also known for their expertise regarding a particular industrial process, for example, Finnish and Swedish design, French and Italian fashion, German engineering, Japanese production systems, and US advertising and finance. (See Figure 9.2 for how the image of German engineering is used to position some of the world's finest cars.) Often cities or areas may become associated with particular industrial activities. For example, Wall Street (New York)—finance; Harley Street (London)—medical specialists; Detroit (USA)—cars; Akron (USA)—tyres; Silicon Valley (California)—computers; Hollywood (Los Angeles)—films; Madison Avenue (New York)—advertising; and so on.

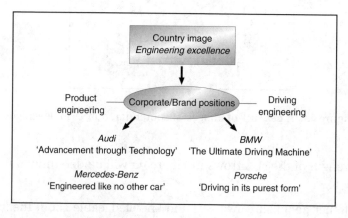

Figure 9.2. German engineering: carmakers dancing on the head of a pin

Arrow No. 2 in Figure 9.1 links country and company images. Many companies like to associate themselves implicitly or explicitly with their country of origin. One example is Nestlé. The company has a policy of maintaining a majority of its share capital in the hands of Swiss citizens.[2] This is important to employees and the Swiss government. A better example of renting the Swiss country image is the Zurich Insurance Company. In Switzerland and around the world, this company has outgrown its original name. It is now a major financial services company with a range of products that create wealth (e.g., funds management) and protect wealth (viz., insurance). In the mid-1990s it traded under the names of

Zurich (Australia), (USA), and so on, and used the corporate slogan 'Global strength. Local knowledge'. Its corporate advertising emphasized the financial astuteness and conservativeness of the Swiss. This was a good fit with the expressed needs of its target customers and the 'financial philosophy' of its managers.

This company–country association is most often signalled through the choice of the company name, as we saw with American Express and Zurich Insurance. It can also be communicated with the corporate slogan, for example, Qantas—'The Spirit of Australia', Lufthansa—'German Airlines', ANA—'Japan's Best to the World'. The perceived value of being associated with one's country often seems more important to senior managers (and employees) than to customers. For example, one of Australia's major domestic airlines started out being called Trans Australia Airlines. It then shortened its name to TAA, and later changed it to Australian Airlines. As luck would have it, Australian Airlines and Qantas were merged and now fly under the Qantas name. (They were both government owned.)

In the 1980s, TAA was known as the government airline (with government procedures and attitudes), and its only domestic competitor Ansett (named after its founder Reg Ansett) was known as the private sector airline—with all the positive associations of private enterprise. Perceptions of government can be an important asset or liability for host-country companies, as Exhibit 9.1 outlines.

A look in any phonebook will illustrate that many companies believe that incorporating the name of their country, region, or city in their corporate name has image and/or marketing value. The interesting question to ponder when adopting such a naming strategy, however, is whether there is an order-of-entry limitation to using such a strategy. That is, does only the first company to use the country/region/city name in an industry gain the advantage? For example, once Australian Airlines had adopted its new name, was it too late for Ansett to gain any leverage from any Australian connection? (Its full name is Ansett Australia even though most people refer to the airline simply as Ansett.) While there is no specific research on this topic in the public domain, it seems reasonable to believe that if customers already associate one company with a country/region/city, then the value for the later users of this naming convention will be diminished.

Like the first two arrows in Figure 9.1, arrow No. 3 is double headed. The double-headed arrows are used to indicate that either entity can rent the image of the other entity with which it is paired. In the case of the connection between country image and brand image (arrow No. 3) this two-way influence is a common occurrence. For example, on a grand scale, brand

Exhibit 9.1. The government's image

A 1997 World Bank report made the point that an effective government is essential for a prosperous economy. In many countries, governments still own businesses, run banks, build protectionist barriers, manipulate foreign exchange, and create webs of regulation and red tape—often with disastrous results. Economists now argue that effective institutions matter as much as sensible policies. To many businesspeople, this sounds like a BGO (a blinding glimpse of the obvious).

Businesspeople, however, always seem to complain about governments. But it is striking how much their perceptions of the credibility of government seem to matter. In a survey of 3,600 entrepreneurs in sixty-nine countries, the World Bank asked respondents about how well they thought such basic government functions as securing property rights and creating a reliable judiciary were fulfilled. It then aggregated the responses into an overall index of government credibility.

The results were disconcerting for many governments. Countries with higher credibility rankings enjoy higher investment and faster economic growth. In fact, just two factors, per-capita income and government credibility, explained about 70 per cent of the difference in investment rates from one country to another.

Because perceptions are most people's reality, it seems that many governments have a big corporate image problem. Also, the old saying of 'I'm from the government, I'm here to help you', is not a positive selling point to many entrepreneurs.

Source: Based on 'It's the government, stupid', *The Economist* (28 June 1997), 83–4.

names such as Apple, Boeing, Coca-Cola, Disney, Ford, IBM, Kodak, Levi's, McDonald's, and Xerox have helped shape the image of America. Also America's image as a fast-moving business and consumer society helps these brands to be successful outside the USA. Similarly, brands such as Canon, Fuji, Honda, Mitsubishi, Nikon, Panasonic, Seiko, Sony, Suntory, Toshiba, Toyota, and Yamaha help define the image of Japan, and are supported by Japan's image for quality products. On a smaller scale, the advertising for KLM, the Royal Dutch Airline, has helped shape the image of Amsterdam and the Netherlands. Likewise, the use of Paul Hogan (alias Crocodile Dundee) in advertisements for the Australian Tourist Commission in the USA, and for Foster's beer in the United Kingdom, has helped to shape the image of Australia.

An interesting use of the country-of-origin associations of a brand has been to help develop many global brands. Traditional approaches to global branding emphasize selling more or less the same product, in the same way, in different countries. The assumption is that standardization allows economies of scale and scope to be achieved, and lower prices for consumers.[3] The giant British advertising agency Saatchi & Saatchi has been a strong advocate of this strategy. While there has been considerable argument about the pros and cons of global branding, one way in which it has worked successfully is when a brand has a strong country heritage which consumers in other countries value. For example, one of the attributes of Coca-Cola, Harley-Davidson, Levi's, and McDonald's is that they are American brands, and represent aspects of the lifestyle which appeal to people in other countries. In a similar way, Gucci fashion and Chanel perfume have become global brands outside their country of origin, in part because they are associated with the elegance and *savoir-vivre* of the Italians and French.

While there has been little research on relationship No. 4 in Figure 9.1, it seems that the key anchor point in this relationship is the industry image. Many industries have inherently more favourable images (health care, entertainment, education, the arts) than others (gambling, weapons manufacturing, nuclear power, tobacco). If you are in a 'good' industry, any implicit or explicit associations will help. If you are in a 'bad' industry, then the typical strategy is to hide the association. (For example, how many weapons manufacturers can you name?) If you cannot hide because you need to advertise to attract customers, then change your industry name to something more socially respectable (e.g., gambling to gaming) and link it with an industry with a better image (e.g., gaming and entertainment). If you can also locate in an area which your non-customers (with their unfavourable images) can easily avoid (e.g., Las Vegas) all the better. Another corporate hiding strategy is to brand your products without reference to the company name (e.g., Marlboro cigarettes).

Many big diversified companies like the Japanese *zaibatsu* (Mitsui and Mitsubishi) and their US and European counterparts (General Electric, Westinghouse, Du Pont, Philips) have the opportunity to use corporate advertising to inform (business) people about the range of industries in which they participate. The implicit assumption here is that there is value in explicitly promoting these associations—especially if these industries are driven by a core set of value-enhancing activities like electronics, production expertise, research and development, and so on. One of the failings of the older Philips corporate advertisements referred to in Chapter 7 is that they do not link the various products and divisions of the company together. The later ads try to do this through an emphasis on showing the people behind the products.

Another way in which diversified companies can get marketing leverage for their products is to rent the image of making products in one industry to promote a product in a different industry. For example, the Swedish car company Saab considers itself an aviation-fuelled car maker. The 1997 launch of its flagship model, the 9-5, in Sweden, was 100 metres away from where it built its first aircraft. The theme of this launch (and referred to in some of its advertisements)was the company's origins as an aircraft manufacturer.

As noted elsewhere in this book, companies which have a diversified portfolio of operations, all of which carry the parent company name, more likely than not present an unfocused image to stakeholders and the general public. In the game of image management, many commentators argue that it is better to be focused than unfocused.[4] In other words, it is better to be known for something specific than for being a part of everything. (Many major political parties might also reflect on this advice.)

Relationship No. 5 in Figure 9.1 reflects the common marketing strategy often referred to as 'umbrella' or 'family' branding. Some companies practise it, some studiously avoid it, and some cannot make up their minds and use a hybrid naming system. For example, at the time of writing BMW identify their cars as a BMW: 316, 318, 323, 328, M3, Z3, 523, 528, 535, 540, 735, 740, 750, 840. For years each BMW was positioned as 'The Ultimate Driving Machine'.[5] (An 840 is just a bit more ultimate than a 316!) Procter & Gamble, on the other hand, do not associate their brands with the company. For example, P&G make more than 350 brands, including Pert, Pantene, Pro-V, Head & Shoulders, Oil of Ulan, Crest, Pampers, Tide, Cheer, Bold, Pringles, and Folgers. There is no common selling proposition among the various brands either within or across product categories. The marketing strategy is to target them to different segments of the market which value different attributes, and thus gain more market coverage.

In any single market it is common to find competitors using different corporate and brand-name strategies. Each has its advantages and disadvantages, which any good marketing text will elaborate.[6] The point here is that a company can give marketing leverage to its brands by linking them to the corporate name. This is especially relevant when customers perceive risk when buying products and services. In this case, knowing the company that stands behind the product can help reduce this risk.

In the more general context, the issue that managers must grapple with is what type of branding hierarchy allows them to capture the potential leverage between the company and its product/service brands. In industrial or business-to-business markets one often sees a pairing between company brand and division brand, for example:

- Thermo Electron (parent company);
- Thermo Instrument;
- Thermo Process;
- Thermo Power;
- Thermo Cardiosystems;
- Thermo Voltek;
- Thermo Trex;
- Thermo Fibertek;
- Thermo Remediation;
- Thermo Lase;
- Thermo Ecotek;
- Thermo Spectra and, you guessed it, one last name to ruin a perfect example:
- Thermedics.

When the company makes products for consumer markets, various combinations of corporate brands, family brands, individual brands, and models can be used. For example, my current personal computer is a digital (corporate brand), Venturis (individual brand), FX-2 (model), while my current car is a Ford (corporate), Taurus (family), Ghia (model). There are no 'rules' to guide the combination of brands to use apart from the fairly obvious advice of attempting to harness the positive associations and mitigate against any negative associations—depending on the context.

Exhibit 9.2 provides an example of how attributes of the corporate image can affect consumer evaluations of new brands. In an interesting reversal of this strategy the Australian company Amatil rented the world's best-known brand name to give more leverage to the company name—it changed its name to Coca-Cola Amatil. Another Australian company, Elders IXL, changed its name to Foster's Brewing Group to gain the benefits associated with this well-known brand of beer. In the USA, Consolidated Foods Corporation renamed itself Sara Lee Corp after one of its better-known brands.

The last relationship in Figure 9.1 (arrow No. 6) reflects the influence that high profile brand names can have on the image of an industry. The images of Coke and Pepsi almost define the image of the soft-drink industry. Similarly, the images of McDonald's and Pizza Hut help many people form their image of the fast food industry. In effect, these are 'market-driving' brands. They influence the expectations of many people about how all the brands in the industry will perform. When the Taiwanese computer manufacturers wanted to enter the personal computer market they used the well-established image of IBM Personal Computers to help them

Exhibit 9.2. Stretching the corporate name over new brands

A question that has occupied the minds of many marketing managers is whether any of the attributes of their company would support the introduction of a new product. Kevin Keller and David Aaker designed an experiment to see if a company that was perceived as innovative, or concerned with the environment, or involved with the community, would have greater corporate credibility when introducing new products under the corporate name. Corporate credibility was measured in terms of the company's perceived expertise, trustworthiness, and likeability. Their hypothesis, which is compatible with the overall thrust of this book, is that being known for product innovation would have the strongest influence. Because the other two corporate characteristics are only tangentially related to the company's products, they would be less effective.

Keller and Aaker asked 256 students to evaluate some new products in four product categories (over-the-counter drugs, baked goods, personal care products, and dairy products). All products were sold by a company with a name chosen to be neutral and to convey no specific product information. Also, each new product (or corporate brand extension, to use the technically correct term), was one that was a moderate 'fit' with the company's existing products. For example, Medallion, the baked-goods company, was introducing rice.

The researchers found that being innovative provided the most valuable enhancements to the new corporate brand extension. Specifically, it led to the most favourable perceptions of corporate expertise, and it provided a substantial increase to both perceived product quality and the likelihood of purchase. Concern with the environment provided enhanced perceptions of corporate trustworthiness and likeability, but it had no impact on the attributes of the new product. Involvement with the community was the least effective corporate characteristic. It had a weak effect on trustworthiness and likeability.

If we extend these findings, it seems that a new product carrying the company name should be positioned to fit an attribute of the company that customers think is important to them. This will provide the best chance that the corporate image will support the new product.

Some companies refuse to recognize how corporate image can affect a new product introduction. For example, it is ironic, given the GM example discussed at the start of this chapter, that Ford Australia decided to manufacture a small sports car (the Capri) for sale in Australia and export to the USA. Australians do not generally regard US carmakers as having special expertise in the design of small sports cars, nor would Americans typically associate Australia with such cars. Hence, a small sports car from Ford Australia starts its life with a negative image. (Ford now concedes that the car was a failure in both the US and Australian markets.) Had Ford designed and built a four-wheel drive recreational vehicle in Australia, there would have been ample opportunity to use the image of the rugged Australian outback to add credibility to the brand image.

Sources: Derived from: K. Keller and D. Aaker, 'Managing the Corporate Brand: The Effects of Corporate Marketing Activity on Consumer Evaluations of Brand Extensions', *Marketing Science Institute*, Working Paper Report No. 97-106 (May 1997); B. Tuckey, 'Spring-Clean Gives Ford the Edge', *Business Review Weekly* (15 Jan. 1993), 26–7.

legitimize their products. They called their new, cheaper personal computers 'IBM clones'.

Which of the relationships discussed here will be more useful as a potential source of leverage for your organization's image is best determined by research. This is because the value of a country, industry, or brand image depends solely on how it is perceived by the particular stakeholder. Also, as Figure 9.1 indicates, two or more of these images may combine to affect your organization's overall image.

COUNTRY IMAGES

Research has shown that when consumers are not familiar with a country's products, then the image of the country may serve as the critical frame of reference for consumer evaluations of the product.[8] For example, if the product comes from France, it must be fashionable; if it is built in Germany, then it is probably well engineered; if it is Japanese, it will be reliable; if the consultant is American, he or she will be good; if the businessman is Chinese and is a resident of Hong Kong, he will be entrepreneurial; and so on. These stereotypes often frame an organization's images. Hence, it is worth briefly reviewing some of the major factors that may help shape the image of a country for a person who has not been there. (The images held by visitors and residents will tend to be shaped more by their personal experiences.) Figure 9.3 illustrates twelve such factors.

Few people have visited Iraq or Kuwait. The Gulf War in 1991, however, suddenly focused attention on both countries. CNN's television pictures from this conflict probably did more to shape the image of these countries than any other single event in their history. The news coverage also introduced many people to some of the cultural and religious aspects of life in

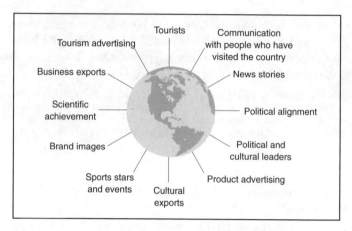

Figure 9.3. Factors that shape a country's images

this region of the world. In short, during a crisis, the power of the news media in shaping the images of countries can be significant, and often distorting. The mass media also put their own 'spin' on information about a country's business, culture, politics, and scientific and sporting achievements.

The old 'East versus West' political alignments helped to typecast many countries. They also offered an opportunity for countries such as Switzerland to adopt a non-aligned position, which its banking and ethical products industries have used to their advantage. To continue this theme, the space race between the USA and the USSR, and other such mega-programmes, helped to build a broad frame of reference within which people evaluated the potential for both countries to achieve their goals. The USA's achievements in space send a strong signal to the world that its companies can produce leading-edge technology and systems. In contrast, the way the USSR organized and publicized its space programme provided fewer spin-offs for its commercial enterprises.

A country's business leaders, multinational companies, global brands, sporting events, and promotions in a foreign country are other important sources of information which people use for forming their image of a country. For example, many Americans, Europeans, and Japanese have an image of Australia as friendly, fun loving, different, a bit mysterious, and a good place to visit.[9] It is also often referred to as 'the land of the long weekend'. Its cultural exports (TV soap operas, dramas, and films), international sports stars, cultural icons (kangaroos and koalas), tourist advertising, and direct consumer advertising (especially for beer and wine) reinforce this (outdated) image. Some of its high-profile business leaders, like the 1980s beer baron Alan Bond who won the America's Cup yacht race and the media mogul Rupert Murdoch, do little to dispel this image. How the country presents the 2000 Olympic Games will further (re)shape the image of Australia.

Different image problems face Finland, Taiwan, and Great Britain (or do they now prefer to be called the United Kingdom?). Outside Europe, Finland's next-door neighbour, Sweden, has a more established image as a country skilled in business. Companies such as Saab, Ikea, and Volvo have helped put Sweden on the (business) map. Finland, it seems, has both an awareness and an image problem. First, many (business)people know little about Finland or its major companies. Little knowledge, in turn, generally leads to a weak image. In the case of Great Britain, certain people want to reposition the country. The prime minister elected in 1997, Tony Blair, wants to help. Taiwan produces 20 per cent of the world's IT products, but the country does not really sit at the same table as the USA and Japan. Exhibit 9.3 describes how these two countries are tackling their problems.

Exhibit 9.3. Two countries with image problems

A new brand for Britain

Having redefined what it means to be left-wing, Tony Blair now wants to rebrand Great Britain. He wants to update the image of Great Britain as backward-looking and aloof, with its icons of Buckingham Palace, beefeaters, and the English bulldog. The aim is to reflect what Great Britain has become, and what it might be in the new millennium. In the process he would like to drop Lady Thatcher's concept of Britishness, with its imperialist overtones.

One of Blair's first steps was to get a debate started about what attributes the new Great Britain should project, for example, as a bridge between Europe and America; as a 'creative island'; as a nation of 'fair play'. One suggestion from this debate for how to rebrand Great Britain came from Wolff Olins, Britain's most famous corporate identity consultant. His advice was to drop the word Great. This, it is hoped, will aid recall of the country and reduce associations with the country's colonial past. Blair has also made some cosmetic changes in the government such as creating a new mission statement for the Foreign Office, and renaming the Department of National Heritage the Department of Culture, Media and Sport.

The real question, however, is: 'Can the government, or any government, help a country project a new, more desirable image?' The next example says yes, but only with the help of others.

cont.

Exhibit 9.3. *cont.*

Sources: Derived from: 'A New Brand for Britain', *The Economist* (23 Aug. 1997), 45–6;
M. Leonard, *Britain: Renewing Our Identity* (London: Demos, 1997).

Made in Taiwan

In the world of information technology, Taiwan is sometimes referred to as
'Silicon Island'. It produces about a quarter of the world's personal computers and many other high-technology information products. Yet for all this, the
USA and Japan are the world's most prestigious IT countries. The label 'made
in Taiwan' still carries the stigma of imitation and cheap. Part of the reason
for this relates to the days when Taiwan produced the 'IBM clone' personal
computers, and the fact that many of Taiwan's products carry another country's brand name.

Under the direction of Taiwan's Ministry of Economic Affairs, a strategy
was developed to update the image of Taiwanese high-technology products,
and thus the country itself. Two key aspects of this programme were to
improve: (a) the quality of Taiwanese products, and (b) product designs.
Improving both of these would add demonstrable value to products and
directly enhance the images of the companies (and Taiwan) that produced
them. The third part of the programme was to promote these changes
through an assortment of events, programmes to motivate industry to keep
improving its products, and a corporate identity campaign.

Taiwan's strategy is a long-term one, and it is based on good foundations—
offering better customer value. If Great Britain is to be rebranded it will also
need the co-operation of its industries and business leaders.

Source: Derived from: R. Blaich and J. Blaich, 'Made in Taiwan: Designing a New
Image', *Design Management Journal* (Summer 1993), 36–40.

For a company interested in renting the image of its host country, it is
important to understand the strength of the image of their country, the
attributes on which it is based, and whether any of these attributes help
people form favourable evaluations of the company or its products. These
attributes are the key to building associations in people's minds. They also
suggest which industries may benefit from a country association. For
example, if a target audience thinks that Australia is a 'lifestyle' country,
then there is potentially more marketing leverage to be gained by industries (and companies) which are associated with this image (such as
swimwear, sporting goods, skin cancer research, and tourism), than, say,
the elaborately transformed manufacturing industries. The only reliable
way to uncover which attributes define a country's images is to use

research. The research techniques outlined in Chapter 10 can also be used to profile country images. When you know what people think about your country, then it is relatively easy to decide whether or not to build an explicit country–industry–company linkage.

RENTING THE IMAGE OF A BUSINESS PARTNER

In the era of strategic partnerships, it is instructive to think about how partners rent each other's corporate images. For example, in the cosmetics industry, many manufacturers want to sell their expensive brands only through the more up-market retailers. The assumption is that the expensive (high-quality) brands 'fit' with the image of up-market retailers. In fact, a casual look at retailers suggests that most adopt one of four positions in the market: specialist retailing often in out-of-the-way locations; convenience retailing based on advantageous locations; hard discounting underpinned by 'every day low prices'; or large-scale value-quality retailing.[10] Each projects a different core image to customers which the manufacturer rents to a greater or lesser degree.

The quality of a wide range of products is not readily observable until they are used. Given that many consumers are willing to pay a higher price for a better-quality product, but it costs less to make low-quality products, a moral hazard problem arises. The manufacturer has an incentive to produce low-quality products and pass them off as high quality. Under such circumstances, a manufacturer producing high quality needs a way to signal such quality and thus be able to capture a higher price (and repeat purchases).

The common tools for signalling high quality are high price, extensive advertising, a long warranty, and an established brand name. However, if the manufacturer is a small start-up, or it is exporting to a new country, these tools may not be available. For example, who would believe a lifetime warranty from a new, unknown manufacturer? Under these circumstances, the manufacturer will often try to signal quality by selling through a reputable retailer. Research has shown that when the perceptions of store names are favourable, the buyers' perceptions of product quality are higher.[11]

One of the strategies of Asian firms entering the American market has been to produce their products to be sold under the name of a respected retailer such as Sears or J. C. Penney. Here, the retailer is posting its corporate reputation as a 'bond' and is signalling the quality of the product for the manufacturer. When respected retailers sell unknown brands they are posting a similar bond. In this case, however, they are allowing the unknown brand to rent part of the their reputation.

In business-to-business markets it is distributors which often play a key role in capturing and retaining customers. Take the case of Caterpillar, which make construction and mining equipment. Donald Fites, the chairman and CEO of Caterpillar, says that their single biggest marketplace advantage over competitors such as Komatsu, Hitachi, and Kobelco is their distribution system and product support.[12] The backbone of that system is their 186 independent dealers around the world. Most dealers are long-established members of their local communities, thereby holding positions that allow them to get closer to customers than a global company could on its own. In effect, Caterpillar 'thinks global but acts local'. It depends heavily on the good image and reputation of each of its dealers for much of its success. In return, the dealers rely on Caterpillar's image for product quality and back-up technical support for much of their success.

Another opportunity to rent a partner's image is when a manufacturer includes parts from other suppliers in its products. In the case of Nike, they choose not to publicize who makes their shoes. (Next time you are in a store, have a look at their shoes, and other well-known brands, to see where they are made. It might surprise you to note that the products of one of America's most prominent brands are not made in America.) In the case of many PC manufacturers exactly the opposite occurs. Most of the major brands of PC are happy to include the 'intel inside' logo on the advertising. In fact, the 'intel inside' advertising campaign is a classic example of creating what marketers call a 'branded ingredient'. The interesting thing about the Intel case is that it has been too successful from the point of view of many manufacturers. See Exhibit 9.4 for the inside story—the pun is intended.

Research indicates that an averaging process occurs when the images of two companies are mixed in a person's mind. The company with the better corporate image loses some of its gloss and the other company gains a little. Research has yet to calibrate how much is gained and lost, but the effect is there. As noted earlier, newly established business consultants understand this effect. Early on, they try to work for some well-respected organizations so that they can tell prospective clients the calibre of customers they have. The better the client list, the better the consultant's image.

Exhibit 9.4. 'intel inside'

In 1991, as part of the launch of its 486 chip, Intel made a co-operative advertising offer to any personal computer manufacturer that was using its microprocessors that few could refuse. Intel would pay up to half the cost of the advertising if the manufacturer would include the 'intel inside' logo in the ads. What a great deal! Few manufacturers, however, could foresee the consequences of telling customers that it was the Intel chip that was the heart of their PC.

Over the years Intel has run thousands of ads convincing less knowledgeable buyers that its chip is the heart of the modern PC. Its 'intel inside' logo has also appeared on thousands of PC manufacturers' advertisements. The more successful the company's advertising, product development, and market penetration became, the more customers changed the way that they ordered a new PC. In the days when the IBM PC dominated the market, most customers ordered a PC by selecting a manufacturer brand as one of the first and most important choice criteria. If you were risk averse, you ordered IBM. (Nobody ever got fired for buying IBM.) If you knew something about PCs and were price conscious you probably ordered a Taiwanese-made 'IBM clone'. Others ordered a recognized brand name machine. In short, the image of the manufacturer was an important choice attribute.

Compare this to the way many people chose a PC in the 1990s. Their first choice criterion was the type of Intel chip. 'I want a [386, 486, Pentium] machine.' Then they considered the manufacturer—its options, price, design, etc. Intel was now more important than Acer, Compaq, digital, Dell, Toshiba, and so on. And Intel machines were certainly more popular than Apple.

In effect, as the corporate image of Intel strengthened, the corporate image of the PC manufacturers weakened. During this time Intel went from a standing start to a top ten corporate reputation company in the Fortune 500 ranking (see Table I.1 in the Introduction). Other ingredient brands, like Dolby, Gor-tex, Lycra, NutraSweet, and Stainmaster have been successful, but their image rental value is not nearly as great as that of Intel.

COMMUNICATION STRATEGIES

The previous discussion indicates the role of brand, country, industry, and partner images as potential sources of leverage for a company's desired image. For leverage to occur, the stakeholder group must first be aware of the linkage between the company and the country, industry, partner, or brand, and they must hold a (potentially) favourable image of the other entity. (Favourable in this case means that one or more attributes of the other image will help people to form a favourable evaluation of the company or its products.) Lack of awareness is a relatively simple problem to overcome. As we will see below, advertising agencies can use a number of different communication strategies to build a linkage between two images. Often, the problem is to position, say, a country in people's minds so that it can be used to springboard the image of the country's industries, companies, and brands.

That founding father of modern advertising, David Ogilvy, and two famous, modern-day advertising consultants, Al Ries and Jack Trout, suggest that our mind sees many cities, countries, and industries as 'mental picture postcards'.[13] (Big countries may have more postcards than smaller countries.) Research can unlock the attributes that define these mental picture postcards.

To illustrate this idea, let us assume that research shows that most people know little about Finland, other than that it is next door (or close) to Sweden. Let us also assume that the images they hold of Sweden are favourable. How could advertising be used to (quickly) establish that Finland is a country worth visiting (for tourists), or doing business with. To borrow one of Ries and Trout's ideas, we might consider using the mental picture postcard of Sweden as the anchor for developing an image of Finland. The slogan 'Finland—the country next door to Sweden' might begin the process of building an image. Alternatively, we link Finland to its other well-known neighbour, Russia: 'Finland—the gateway to St. Petersburg'. (Ries and Trout once suggested positioning Jamaica as the Hawaii of the Caribbean. Everybody knew about Hawaii, but few knew anything distinctive about Jamaica.) Now, it is unlikely that the people of Finland would be too enthusiastic about either such positioning (they are very wary of the Russians and they do not like being compared to the Swedes), but the moral of the story here is to start with what your target audience will give you, namely, being a neighbour. It seems to be more cost effective to build on existing knowledge than to try to create a desired image from scratch.

In the rest of this section, let us assume that the images people hold of the country you are thinking of using have some positive attributes which your company can rent. The problem is: how do you signal an association between these attributes and your company? There are a number of possibilities, the most obvious one being advertising.

One approach is explicitly to tell people in the target audience about the association. For example, an advertisement for Audi cars started with the headline: 'Australia's Best German Luxury Car Value'. Another ad in the same newspaper had the headline: 'Sydney's Saab dealers offer Europe's best at prices to embarrass the Japanese'. A more subtle approach was used in a television ad for a brand of jeans. It showed two people arguing about the jeans in French. Not a word of English was spoken. The ad implicitly rented the fashion image of France. The oil company BP used a corporate advertising campaign called 'Britain at its Best' for a number of years. Many people had forgotten that BP stood for British Petroleum.

Corporate names are another important signalling device. It is not difficult to tell the country of origin of the following organizations: American Airlines, Boston Consulting Group, British Airways, London Business School, London Fog Clothing Co., Singapore Airlines, Texas Instruments, and USAir. It is a little harder to tell where these brands originate, although many people can make a good guess: Benetton, Fuji, Heineken, Lowenbrau, Mercedes-Benz, Perrier, Pierre Cardin, and Volkswagen. Sometimes when a company wants to signal its country of origin but its name cannot do the job, a tag-line or slogan may be used with the name. Two examples of this strategy have been referred to earlier: Lufthansa—'German Airlines', and Qantas—'The Spirit of Australia'. (Qantas also uses a picture of a flying kangaroo as its logo.)

A third type of signalling device is visual symbols. A variety of such symbols can be used to establish country-of-origin linkages. For example, a country's flag in an advertisement, or the major elements of the flag, can be an effective signalling device. Many people know the 'Stars and Stripes' of the USA, and the red maple leaf of Canada. An interesting twist to using a flag as a signal of a country occurred when Australia won the America's Cup yachting trophy. During this 'campaign', waged specifically against the New York Yacht Club, Alan Bond and his team unfurled their new flag. It was designed to serve the same purpose as the familiar pirate flag—the skull and crossbones. This one, however, was the 'Boxing Kangaroo'—a gold kangaroo standing on his hind legs, with red boxing gloves on his front legs, set on a green background. (Green and gold are the traditional Australian national sporting colours.) For a number of years after this sporting event, the boxing kangaroo flag came to symbolize Australian sporting achievement for nationals and many overseas people.

Each country typically has a number of cultural symbols. The Eiffel Tower of Paris, the Statue of Liberty of New York, the Golden Gate Bridge of San Francisco, the wooden clogs, tulips, and canals of the Netherlands, the Sydney Opera House, and Big Ben, and the Tower of London are all well-known cultural symbols. These pictures can be worth a thousand words as signals of country and cultural linkages.

A final way to advertise a country connection is to use the words 'made in . . .'. Research by David Head, of the University of Bath in the UK, indicates that 'made in' advertising slogans tend to fall into one of three categories.[14] The first category involves a direct appeal to the national pride of the target audience. As an example of this strategy he cites the German bank BfG, which used the slogan '100 Years of Made in Germany'. In Europe, the Dutch company Philips uses its advertising subtly to position itself as 'the European alternative [to the Japanese]'. Head's second strategy for using the 'made in' (country) connection represents the antidote to patriotism. It is characterized by drawing the attention of a foreign audience to positive, and usually stereotyped attributes of a country. The idea is to imbue the product or service originating from that country with these image-enhancing qualities. For example, Swissair printed this slogan over a full-page photograph of the workings of a (Swiss) pocket watch: 'Only the sum total of all the details shows how smoothly a Swiss airport operates'. The last strategy for this type of advertising derives from the allusion to a particular expertise that is associated with a foreign country. For example, outside Germany, German engineering is strongly associated with notions of workmanship, technology, and inventiveness. The electrical giant AEG used the following slogan in a British ad: 'AEG—ADVANCED ENGINEERING FROM GERMANY'.

If a country has a weak or neutral image, then the task is to sharpen the country image. As noted in Exhibit 9.3, one or two attributes are chosen that will support home company export drives. These attempts typically take a long time to bear fruit. There is however, one strategy that is fast-track, and very costly (in terms of dollars and the risk of public failure), and this strategy is one that governments fight for the right to use. It is called the Olympic Games. The argument is that if a country can put itself on the world stage for a two-week period, its athletes, government, business community, and organizers have the chance to demonstrate excellence, high performance, world-class quality and competitiveness. These are a good set of foundations from which to start to (re)position a country.

CONCLUSIONS

This chapter outlines some of the principal avenues open for renting the image of other entities to enhance the desired image of a company and its brands. While most of the discussion has focused on the images people hold of a company's country of origin, managers must remember that these images are often only useful for particular industries. Research is the key to finding out which attributes of a country's image are linked to a particular industry, and which may be used to provide image leverage.

Nationalism and patriotism are powerful forces in many cultures. They are not however, omnipotent in most advanced consumer markets. Yet this has not deterred some political and business leaders in countries like Australia, Britain, and the USA from trying to use a 'made in . . .' advertising campaign to stimulate demand for domestically produced products. A good example of how such a campaign can be less successful than expected is in the US automotive industry. In the 1980s, many US brands of car were advertised using a primary or secondary theme of 'buy American'. Sales of Japanese cars were hardly affected. A large segment of American buyers were buying Japanese cars because they perceived them to be of superior quality. Had the CEOs of the US carmakers understood this, more effort would have been directed to improving quality (what the buyer wanted), rather than reminding people of their patriotism (and trying to make them feel guilty). Advertising can help, but it has to be based on a thorough prior image investigation and a believable image proposition.

The guiding theme of this chapter is—do research to find out how your organization's stakeholders link their country, industry, company, and brand images. Opportunities exist to communicate linkages between two or more of these images to enhance the value of your corporate image. The search is for positive attributes in a country, industry, partner, or brand image that can be used to differentiate your organization favourably in stakeholders' minds. Consider how successfully the USA has exported its culture around the world through its sporting events, films, and brands, and how this has provided many opportunities for its businesspeople and companies to follow.

NOTES

1. E. Fountain, I. Parker, and J. Samules, 'The Contribution of Research to General Motors' Corporate Communications Strategy in the UK', *Journal of the Market Research Society*, 28, 1 (Jan. 1986), 25–42.
2. J. Heer, *Nestlé 125 Years 1866–1991* (Vevey: Nestlé, 1991).
3. T. Levitt, 'The Globalization of Markets', *Harvard Business Review* (May/June 1983), 92–102.
4. A. Ries, *Focus* (London: HarperCollins Business, 1996).
5. They now use the slogan 'Sheer Driving Pleasure'.

6. P. Kotler, *Marketing Management* (Englewood Cliffs, NJ: Prentice Hall, 1991); K. Keller, *Strategic Brand Management* (Upper Saddle River, NJ: Prentice Hall, 1998).

7. Keller, *Strategic Brand Management* (see n. 6 above), ch. 7.

8. C. Min Han, 'Country Image: Halo or Summary Construct?', *Journal of Marketing Research*, 26 (May 1989), 222–9; D. Maheswaran, 'Country of Origin as a Stereotype: Effects of Consumer Expertise and Attribute Strength on Product Evaluations', *Journal of Consumer Research*, 21, 2 (1994), 354–65.

9. 'Olympics 2000: Realizing Economic and Political Opportunities', *Committee for Economic Development of Australia* (Feb. 1995).

10. J. Corstjens and M. Corstjens, *Store Wars: The Battle for Mindspace and Shelfspace* (Chichester, UK: John Wiley, 1995).

11. For a discussion of these issues and references to other studies in this area, see: W. Chu and W. Chu, 'Signaling Quality by Selling through a Reputable Retailer: An Example of Renting the Reputation of Another Agent', *Marketing Science*, 13, 2 (1994), 177–89.

12. D. Fites, 'Make Your Dealers Your Partners', *Harvard Business Review* (March–April 1996), 84–95.

13. D. Ogilvy, *Ogilvy on Advertising* (London: Pan Books, 1983), ch. 10. A. Ries and J. Trout, *Positioning: the Battle for Your Mind* (New York: McGraw-Hill, 1981), ch. 15.

14. D. Head, 'Advertising Slogans and the "Made-in" Concept', *International Journal of Advertising*, 7 (1988), 237–52.

MANAGING CORPORATE IMAGES AND REPUTATIONS

10

Measuring Images and Reputations: What Do Stakeholders Actually Think?

One thing that we have learnt from the discipline of marketing is that *the most dangerous place to look at stakeholders is from behind a desk*. The simple truth of the matter is that the only way accurately to gauge what people think of an organization is to ask them. This is easy to say, but often difficult to do, because it takes (valuable) time; it costs money that has no direct contribution to generating bottom-line profit in the period in which it is spent; most organizations will need to employ the services of an outside market research firm to help; and it is not intuitively obvious how one measures elusive concepts such as corporate image and corporate reputation. Any of these reasons is generally sufficient to kill the idea of measuring corporate reputations—especially year after year.

For Fortune 500 companies that get rated in the annual America's Most Admired Companies survey or its equivalent,[1] there is a temptation to use this as a measure of corporate image. Don't! There are three reasons for this advice. First, recall from Chapter 1 that *Fortune* measures corporate image across eight attributes such as product quality, investment value, community and environmental friendliness. Over the years researchers have discovered that all eight attributes are highly correlated with each other (> 0.60) and when factor analysed, they produce only one factor.[2] That is, a company tends to rate high, or average, or low on all eight attributes. In practical terms, this means that you could get an equally reliable measure (or ranking) of America's most admired companies by simply getting people to rate each company on one scale such as:

Very Poorly Respected   1   2   3   4   5   6   7   Extremely Well Respected

Hence, the *Fortune* measure of corporate image gives very little diagnostic information to a manager.[3] Consequently, it is a *scorecard measure*, and hence my reference in the Introduction to the overall study as a beauty contest. This measure is good for some types of academic research studies, but not much good for helping you improve your corporate image and reputation.

The second reason for not using these publicly syndicated measures is that most do not discriminate among the images of different stakeholder groups. Readers who have come this far through the book are probably comfortable with the idea that different groups will hold different images and reputations. Hence, they need to be measured separately.

The third reason is that they do not distinguish between a measure of corporate image and corporate reputation. Recall (from Part 1 of the book) that the components of image are what a manager can seek to change, while a stakeholder's values act as the benchmark to calibrate the corporate image. Hence, measuring how a company rates on a set of image attributes does not really provide a measure of the reputation, or super-brand value of the company. The Chevron case study at the end of Chapter 7 illustrated one approach to linking corporate image to corporate reputation via the segmentation of stakeholders based on their values, namely, the inner- and outer-directed groups. This chapter describes a more comprehensive approach.

WHAT ARE WE TRYING TO ACHIEVE?

If you are going to spend the time and money doing research, collect as much of the following information as your budget will allow:

- (a) a detailed measure of the images and reputations held by various stakeholder groups;
- (b) similar, although often less detailed, measures of competitive organizations; and
- (c) an indication of the characteristics of an 'ideal' organization in your industry.

These measures must be designed for diagnostic purposes, not just as a scorecard.

Many researchers and practitioners suggest that any measure of corporate image and reputation be compared against those of other organizations—particularly competitors. There are two reasons to prefer comparative measures. One comes from customer satisfaction research, where it has been shown that relative satisfaction (*us* versus *them*) has a much stronger relationship with sales than satisfaction with *our* product/service alone.[4] A second reason is that it can help managers better understand which of the attributes of corporate image are related to changes in the industry, and which are related to their efforts. An organization whose corporate image is tied closely to that of the industry faces a different challenge to one that is not.

The idea of asking people about an ideal organization is an interesting one. As we will see later in the chapter, what this entails is that stakeholders are asked to rate a fictitious 'ideal' organization on the same set of attributes that are used to describe your organization and its competitors. Your organization can then be compared to the ideal on each attribute, and the gaps between these ratings suggest what needs to be improved. This type of gap analysis is valuable information for benchmarking an organization's strengths and weaknesses.

Few organizations spend the time and effort required to achieve all three of the objectives listed above. What most organizations measure is the level of awareness of their company (and its major competitors), and some broad indicators of the quality of advertising, products, prices, and customer service. To this list may be added a couple of questions about social responsibility and management quality. This is all useful information, but it lacks structure and is thus difficult to interpret. It fails what I call the 'so what test'. This test is expressed by managers in comments such as: 'This information is interesting, but how do I use it?'

THE STRUCTURE OF MEASURES OF CORPORATE IMAGE AND REPUTATION

Chapter 7 stressed the importance of awareness—if the target groups of stakeholders do not know about the organization then it has a problem. Let us assume that these people know something about the organization and the task is to construct a measure of the corporate images and reputations. To do this in a structured way, it is necessary to build a measurement model of corporate reputations. In Chapter 3 the models used (Figures 3.1 and 3.3 to 3.5) were designed for managers, to enable them to ascertain what factors drive the images that people hold of the organization. This time, the model is for researchers. However, it starts with a brief from management.

The role of corporate reputation is to help stakeholders make decisions about whether (a) to use the organization (e.g., buy its products and services, work for it, etc.), (b) to recommend it to other people, (c) to trust the organization to do things on their behalf or on behalf of their community, and (d) to help reduce the perceived risk which arises from these activities. Hence, a good corporate reputation helps the stakeholder develop trust and confidence in the organization, and if the circumstances are appropriate, leads to support such as in (a) and (b). A crucial point here, which is developed in the academic literature on trust,[5] is that the value of a corporate reputation will be contingent on what type of relationship a person wants with the organization. For example, a consumer who buys ready-to-eat breakfast cereal probably does not want any type of relationship with the manufacturer—hence, the potential value of a good corporate reputation will be small. However, an investor in a mutual fund may need to develop a relationship with the fund manager in order to have trust and confidence in the portfolio of fund investments. Here the potential value of a good reputation will be quite high. The outcomes of corporate reputation are shown in Figure 10.1.

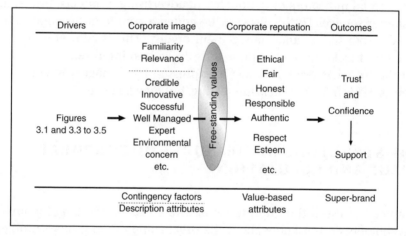

Figure 10.1. What to measure

Figure 10.1 lists some of the more important attributes of corporate images and reputations that are also common across various stakeholder groups. Familiarity and relevance are labelled contingency factors. The notion here is that an organization must have some relevance for a person before he or she will form a relationship-based image or reputation of it. Listed under these two factors are some of the attributes that can be used to describe the images people hold of organizations. The set chosen for measurement will depend on the stakeholder group and the role of corporate image in adding value to the organization. Within these constraints, corporate image attributes should be selected to represent stakeholders' shared beliefs about what is distinctive, central, and enduring about the organization.

Next, the corporate reputation attributes are value-based descriptors of the organization and are designed to reflect stakeholder values. Consider the notion of corporate responsibility. In 1996 President Clinton asked 100 leading businesspeople to the White House to discuss Corporate America's lack of social responsibility to US employees.[6] It seems that many politicians and social commentators considered that some of the new management practices (like outsourcing, re-engineering, and performance-based executive compensation) were changing the fundamental social contract between business and the workforce. Let us unpack this example to illustrate the logic in Figure 10.1.

Over the last century the relationship between workers and companies has ranged between hostility and harmony (i.e., trust, confidence, and support), depending on how responsible, fair, caring, and so on organizations were perceived to be. These attributes have in turn been driven by the management practices of the organizations. Hence, how do you get a trusting, confident, and supportive workforce? Move left to right across Figure 10.1. Embed, in the vision, formal policies, and culture of the organization, management practices that employees feel are ethical, fair, honest, and responsible. This just sounds like common sense doesn't it? And it is!

This process of creating a super-brand reputation is illustrated in Figure 10.2.[7] If an organization is familiar and relevant to a person, what makes it stand out is that it is successful, authentic, and different. Success is important because most of us like being associated with winners. It is also important for an organization to be seen to make a contribution to the economy and/or society, that is, to fulfil a stewardship function. Being authentic and different are two attributes of what some managers refer to as the 'personality' of the organization. A company's authenticity is often related to its honesty and reliability. Companies with all these attributes are the ones most respected and held in the highest esteem—they have the best reputations and can evolve into super-brands.

When using the frameworks in Figures 10.1 and 10.2, there are likely to be differences in the relative importance of the image and reputation attributes across different stakeholders and companies in different cultures. For example, stockmarket analysts tend to place the highest importance on (financial) success. Kevin Keller suggests that Japanese companies place the highest priority on being successful (as driven by their innovations), and socially responsible (i.e., a stewardship function).[8]

The power of the models in Figures 10.1 and 10.2 derives from their practical usefulness. First, they help to track the effects of changes made inside the organization. Second, they provide a blueprint for measuring corporate images and reputations. Measures need to be taken of image attributes, reputation attributes, *and* outcomes. Managers need to be involved in the selection of image attributes to ensure that they can be linked back to things that can be changed inside the organization.

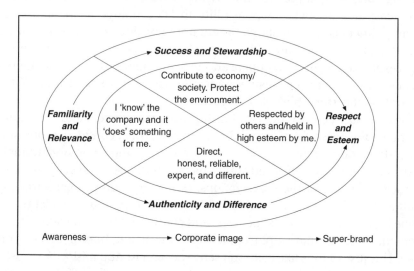

Figure 10.2. Creating a super-brand

THE MEASUREMENT PROCESS

This section outlines how to measure corporate reputations. Most organizations employ the services of a market research firm to ensure that the findings from one technique are appropriately integrated with those derived from other techniques. At the conclusion of this brief review, a stylized example is presented showing some measures of various organizations' images and reputations.

The following three-stage research approach is a good way to conduct a corporate reputation study. First, use qualitative research techniques to discover the attributes of corporate image and reputation, the relevant free-standing values, and the outcomes relevant for various stakeholder groups. This information should be presented to management to ensure that it can use the findings of the study to make changes to the corporate image drivers (viz., Figures 3.1 and 3.3 to 3.5). Second, design a survey to have stakeholders rate the company and its competitors. A profile of an ideal organization will also be developed during this stage. Third, do some statistical number crunching to quantify the corporate images and reputations, and to calibrate strengths and weaknesses. The next two sections elaborate this three-stage procedure.

Qualitative research—understanding images and reputations

Qualitative research is the best method for uncovering the characteristics people use to describe their image and reputation. The most popular qualitative research methods are: (a) management introspection, (b) in-depth interviews with key individual stakeholders, and (c) focus group interviews with selected groups of stakeholders. Each has its particular merits and problems. The method of choice depends on how much is already known about stakeholders' perceptions of the organization. The best approach is to use all three techniques. However, in practice management introspection and a few focus groups tend to be the most widely used combination.

When using in-depth interviews and focus groups, it is important to select the people to interview carefully. They should present the range of characteristics used to evaluate the organization by the stakeholder group. It is a good idea to include some people who are very familiar with the organization and some who are not so familiar. Those who are less familiar with it often rely more on country, industry, and brand images than on their knowledge of the organization to form their evaluations. It can also be a good strategy to interview some people who are favourably disposed to competitors. They are more likely to explain what is wrong with the organization than are loyal supporters.

The validity of in-depth interviews and focus group findings is largely dependent on the questioning and interpretative skills of the interviewer, or to use the more formal term, the moderator-analyst. The interview typically starts with a few broad questions that are followed by more specific questions focusing on the organization(s) of interest. For example, the initial questions may ask people about the role of the industry in which the organization operates, and whether or not they think that organizations from various countries are better or worse at carrying out these operations. When these broad topics have been explored, the questions become more focused on competitors and the focal organization. For example, respondents can be asked about which attributes make them seem to be similar to and different from each other, and what attributes would characterize an ideal organization. The analogy of a funnel is a good one for thinking about the sequencing of these questions. Figure 10.3 illustrates how a typical interview might proceed.

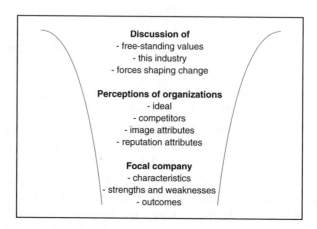

Figure 10.3. Sequencing questions in exploratory interviews

In-depth interviews and focus groups are both designed to produce 'rich' insights into the way (different groups of) stakeholders think about organizations. (Producing generalizable findings is the province of quantitative surveys.) After a number of interviews or group sessions (often only five or six), the main characteristics of the company and the range of opinions about them will become clear. This is the point at which to terminate interviewing and compile the results. The moderator-analyst will describe the range of characteristics using the 'language' of the various stakeholder groups. It may also be possible to identify some distinct clusters of similar characteristics. Care should be taken to search for linkages between the organization and its country of origin, its industry, and high-profile brands—the sources of marketing leverage discussed in Chapter 9.

A good moderator-analyst will also search for the benefits that stakeholders feel are offered by the company, and the emotions that energize them to respond to the organization. If these motivational 'triggers' are not found, then qualitative research has not fulfilled one of its most valuable functions. In the terminology of Figure 10.1, the moderator-analyst must seek to understand how people evaluate the organization's characteristics (the corporate image), and link these to their values to form a corporate reputation.

The moderator-analyst should brief managers who will be responsible for implementing any change. It is important to get their support and to try to avoid failing the 'so what' test mentioned earlier. Also, the moderator-analyst must submit a written report containing his or her interpretation of the foundations of the organization's images and reputations, and a profile of an ideal organization.

Quantitative research—describing images and reputations

The second stage of a corporate image and reputation measurement programme usually involves some type of survey. Well-designed surveys can provide reliable estimates of the number of stakeholders who hold particular types of image and reputation. That is, rather than rely on subjective evaluations, this research attempts to quantify the findings of the qualitative research. This phase of research is very important because the respondents in the qualitative phase were not selected to provide a representative picture of the organization's images and reputations, but rather the spread across these. Hence, without some quantitative research, it is difficult to know which perceptions represent the significant views.

Although thousands of surveys are administered each year, their design is still somewhat of an art rather than a science. We know more about the pitfalls associated with selecting respondents (sampling) and methods of administering questionnaires (by mail, phone, and personal interview), than the biases caused by poorly worded questions (such as ignoring the stakeholder language uncovered by the qualitative research).

While survey research is a complex activity, it is worth while for managers who must interpret research findings to develop some understanding of a few of the key aspects of surveys. Without a good feel for how robust (i.e., scientific) the research procedures employed are, it is easy to ascribe too little or too much significance to the results of a particular survey. There are several issues that directly affect the generalizability of the findings.

Let us start with sampling, that is, selecting a representative sample of people from each stakeholder group to interview. The best (i.e., most representative) sample is one in which every stakeholder has a known and equal probability of being selected. This is known as a 'simple random sample'. Often, however, it is not a simple matter to select a random sample of some types of stakeholders. For example, selecting a simple random sample of employees is straightforward if the personnel department has an accurate and up-to-date list. All employee names are given a number and some type of lottery (random number) system is used to draw names for inclusion in the sample.

Now consider trying to draw a simple random sample of customers. Is there an accurate list of *all* (potential) customers? The answer is probably no. Hence, any sample drawn will not be perfectly representative. The more difficult it is to get an accurate list of people from which to draw the sample, and the further the researcher departs from using a random number system for drawing the sample, the less representative the sample will be. Big sample sizes do not compensate for poor respondent selection. That is, if a researcher samples from only a subgroup of people, then it does not matter how many of these people are questioned, they will still not provide representative findings. Market researchers and pollsters use various techniques to try to overcome this problem and their help in drawing a sample is recommended.

Sample size is determined by how accurate the results need to be, and how confident one wants to be about them. It has little to do with how many people are in a particular stakeholder group! It is a common misconception among many people that, the bigger the stakeholder population, the bigger the sample needs to be. Sampling theory (which should be avoided by the faint-hearted) shows that if there are, say, 5,000 employees in the organization and 500,000 customers, then one would need a simple random sample of the same number of people from each group to be 95 per cent confident that the measures of the organization's images and reputations were equally precise.[9] What sampling theory also shows is that there is not a linear relationship between sample size and the degree of confidence or the level of accuracy of the survey results. For example, to double the precision of measures of the organization's images one needs a simple random sample four times as large. Sample selection is probably the most technically difficult aspect of survey research. Hence, my recommendation is to seek professional help.

The same advice applies to questionnaire design, and to selecting the mode of administering the questionnaires. When surveying hundreds of stakeholders, the approaches commonly used by market research firms are preprinted questionnaires sent through the mail and telephone surveys. Face-to-face interviews, which provide better-quality data, are generally too expensive for most organizations. Often combinations of these methods have proved to be successful in gaining respondent co-operation. For example, one procedure is to phone potential respondents asking them to participate in the study (and sometimes offering a gift or monetary inducement), and to follow this with a questionnaire sent by post, and then with a reminder letter or phone call. Each method, or combination of methods, has its advantages and disadvantages for gaining access to the selected sample of stakeholders, and getting them to provide their opinion about an organization. In choosing the most appropriate method, one should be guided by an experienced researcher.

The mode of questioning and the topics covered in the questionnaires play an important part in determining the response rate to a survey. It is a common observation that response rates for most types of surveys are falling. While there are numerous reasons for this, one of the most common is the simple fact that most surveys are boring and uninteresting to many people! This pessimism notwithstanding, the question remains as to what is a reasonable response rate to expect. If the survey is administered to long-haul air travellers at 30,000 feet above sea level halfway between New York and London, one would expect close to a 100 per cent response rate if passengers are asked to complete it at a sensible time during the flight. On the other hand, if a telephone survey is administered during mealtimes in a household, or late on a Friday afternoon to office workers, then no more than a 10 per cent response rate would be likely. As a general rule of thumb, for the type of research discussed in this chapter, a response rate of less than 80 per cent for employees, 50 per cent for financial analysts, and 30 per cent for customers would cause concern. In any case, the research firm administering the survey should report the response rate achieved, and an analysis of the reasons for non-response. It is then possible to estimate how generalizable the findings are likely to be.

The final pitfall is question wording. It takes considerable skill and experience to compose an interesting questionnaire (from the respondent's point of view) which gathers the type of data that can be analysed to produce a profile of the organization as it compares with other organizations. Most advice about designing questions comes in the form of admonitions: 'Don't ask leading questions' and 'Don't ask ambiguous questions', and so on. This advice is easy to give, but more difficult to follow—even for the professionals. So what happens in practice is that each questionnaire is pre-tested with a small sample of stakeholders before it is administered to the larger sample. This pre-testing is crucial to ensure that respondents understand the questions (and think that they are sensible), and that their responses show enough variation to facilitate subsequent statistical analysis.

In general, the simpler a rating scale question is for a person to answer (e.g., a 'yes' or 'no' answer as against one asking the person to 'rank order the following 7 items'), the more sophisticated the statistical data analysis will need to be to extract the maximum amount of information from the data gathered. Again the researcher must make trade-offs, and these can have a significant impact on the quality of the data collected, and the types of analysis that can be conducted. For example, telephone interviews have to be short (no more than ten minutes) and simple (many yes/no answers). Face-to-face interviews with sophisticated respondents like financial analysts can last an hour or more, especially if they are paid for their time.

Figure 10.4 summarizes the overall research methodology outlined above. It recommends starting with an analysis of past research and management experience, and then proceeding with exploratory research to gain a rich understanding of the characteristics that stakeholders use to form their images and reputations about the organization. The next stage is descriptive research, to quantify how widely and strongly these images and reputations are held within each stakeholder group. The figure shows two feedback loops. The first (solid) loop suggests that a periodic monitoring of these images and reputations be conducted (say, ever year—and regularly during a crisis). The second (dashed) loop indicates that further qualitative research may sometimes be needed to help clarify unexpected or ambiguous survey findings.

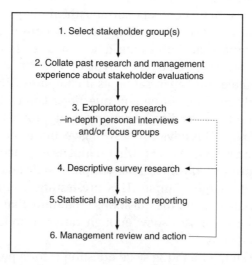

Figure 10.4. Steps to measure corporate images and reputations

A STYLIZED EXAMPLE OF CORPORATE IMAGE AND REPUTATION RESEARCH

The following example is based on an actual study conducted by a market research firm. It has been selected because country-of-origin and brand issues were not relevant (to simplify the presentation). It also illustrates some of the issues discussed above and some common practices (i.e., shortcuts) when doing this type of research. I have disguised the organizations to protect the innocent and the guilty. This example is not presented as the only way to conduct this type of research. (The following section outlines some other approaches.) It is used to highlight some novel aspects of this type of research, which produce more insightful results than the *Fortune* beauty contest type of measure.

Background

The research was undertaken to track the effects of a corporate identity change programme on the perceptions of two groups of customers. The corporate identity programme incorporated a new logo and was supported by a new advertising campaign. Prior to the launch of the new identity, the company commissioned a benchmark study to measure what customers thought of the organization and its competitors. Six months after the launch of the new identity campaign, a second measurement of these organization images and reputations was conducted.

Research design and methods

In major cities across the country 2,000 telephone interviews were conducted. Residential consumers were selected using what is known as systematic random sampling, where every nth name from the telephone directory was contacted. If the person in the telephone book was not available, then the adult over 18 who last had a birthday was selected for interview. Two callbacks were used to minimize sample bias. The response rate was 65 per cent, and the demographic profile of the respondents closely matched that derived from census data.

Of the 2,000 interviews, 300 responses were received from business users of the sponsoring company's products and services. This group was selected from company lists. Each of these respondents evaluated up to six organizations, which always included the sponsoring company and an ideal company, on fifteen characteristics. There were seven image attributes (such as a company 'whose products and services are expensive', 'that is technology driven', 'well managed', 'an industry leader', etc.), four reputation attributes (e.g., honest, respected, etc.), and four outcomes (e.g., confidence, trust, etc.). Each respondent was asked whether or not each characteristic described the organization. A 'yes' or 'no' response was all that was required, and respondents only evaluated organizations they were aware of. For these samples, it was estimated with 95 per cent confidence that the overall percentage of yes/no ratings for each characteristic was accurate to plus or minus 3 per cent of the reported percentages.

The fifteen characteristics on which each organization was evaluated were derived from the market research company's past research experience. This research company 'introspection' was supplemented with a series of in-depth personal interviews with the sponsoring company's managers. (In effect, the questionnaire was pre-tested using previous clients' research studies, and the management interviews were used as an 'insurance policy' so that no important characteristics were omitted.)

Findings

Table 10.1 shows the percentages of business respondents, before and after the new identity campaign, who said that each characteristic described the sponsoring company. (The respondents are two different samples of approximately 300 people.) Percentages in boxes are statistically significantly different at the 95 per cent level of confidence. We see that for seven out of fifteen (or 47 per cent) characteristics, the two groups had different evaluations. In most cases, the direction of change is favourable. The one exception is that after the identity change and advertising campaign, businesspeople thought that the company's products and services were more expensive! (Are businesspeople really as astute as this result suggests?)

The research firm presented another finding from this survey that is of interest, namely, the number of characteristics used by each person to describe the company. The average numbers of these are shown at the base of Table 10.1. They indicate that six months after the identity campaign, businesspeople were using three more (of these fifteen) characteristics to describe the company. In effect, the new logo and the new

Table 10.1. Pre- and post-advertising and identity changes in evaluations (per cent)

Characteristic	Businesspeople who agree that company is:	
	Pre-campaign	Post-campaign
Image attributes		
1. Well managed	37	39
2. Expensive products/service	35	44
3. Technology driven	58	71
4. Successful	38	50
5. Innovative	55	58
6. Customer focused	42	49
7. Internationally competitive	57	58
Reputation attributes		
8. Industry leader	47	57
9. Honest	58	58
10. Good corporate citizen	58	68
11. Respected	36	38
Outcomes		
12. Confidence	56	65
13. Trustworthiness	54	55
14. Support	65	67
15. Positive WOM	56	58
Average number of characteristics used	7	10

advertising campaign had stimulated businesspeople to think about the company using ten rather than seven characteristics. (For this conclusion to hold, it is necessary to assume that there was no significant change in the company's services, and that publicity or some other factor did not change people's perceptions.)

Once data have been collected they can be analysed in many ways. Table 10.2 shows how the three sets of variables in Figure 10.1 were related to each other at the end of the change programme. The top portion of Table 10.2 indicates that the company's image and reputation are quite closely associated. Also, each of the correlations makes intuitive sense. However, because this study did not measure the free-standing values of the businesspeople who provided these evaluations, it is difficult to probe below superficial explanations. For example, while a majority of respondents thought that the company was internationally competitive (see Table 10.1), why did this not impact on any of the reputation attributes?

Table 10.2. Significant correlations—post campaign*

| | Reputation attributes | | | |
Image	Leader	Honest	Corp. citizen	Respect
Management	+			+
Expensive products			−	
Technology	+			+
Success	+		+	+
Innovative	+			+
Customer focus		+	+	+
Competitive				

| | Outcomes | | | |
Reputation	Confidence	Trust	Support	+ WOM
Leadership	+			
Honest		+	+	+
Corporate citizen				
Respect	+	+	+	+

Notes: WOM = word-of-mouth.
  * Businesspeople.

The technique of perceptual mapping is often used to help answer the question about which of these characteristics discriminate between the various organizations. An example is shown in Figure 10.5 using only the reputation attributes and outcomes in shown Tables 10.1 and 10.2. These maps show the set of characteristics (the arrows) which discriminate among five of the organizations evaluated by respondents. The closer two organizations are to each other, the more similar they are perceived to be on the set of characteristics evaluated. For example, competitors C#2 and C#3 are the two most similar organizations, and the focal company and C#2 are the least similar. Longer arrows indicate more powerful discriminating ability of the characteristics. In effect, these arrows are statistically derived measures of the relative importance of each characteristic. The vertical and horizontal axes show that 41 per cent of the variance in respondents' evaluations occurs in a North–South direction, while 21 per cent occurs in the East–West direction. (The remaining 38 per cent is not explained by this map.)

As noted earlier, there are many different ways to analyse and present the results of a corporate image and reputation study. Each market research company has its own preferred approach (which it will always claim is better than any other company's approach). It is most important

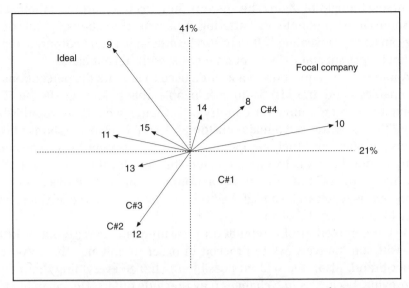

Figure 10.5. Perceptual map of corporate reputations and outcomes
Notes: The numbers refer to the characteristics in Table 10.1.
C = competitor.

for the researchers to use statistical procedures that make (intuitive) sense to the person commissioning the research, and for them to provide analysis of (and guidelines for) what should be changed in order to make desired improvements. Also the person commissioning the research should insist on being given a data file, in order to run extra analyses if desired. (Newly recruited MBAs enjoy showing off their analytic skills.)

Because there are so many ways to develop an insight into corporate images and reputations, the next section briefly notes some other techniques that may be considered.

Other measurement techniques

A colleague told me of an interesting study conducted by American Express in Asia some years ago that reversed the traditional logic of asking questions about companies. As the example in the previous section illustrates, most stakeholders are asked what *they* think about a company. American Express asked such a question and then asked its inverse, namely, what the respondents thought that the American Express company thought of them. The answers they received surprised them, and in some cases were not very flattering. This type of relationship questioning can be very revealing.[10] It may also be crucial if a good corporate reputation hinges substantially on building trust with stakeholders.

Another type of question that is often used to tap into the perceptions of companies (and brands) is to ask people the following: 'If the XYZ Company was an animal (or country or car, etc.), what type would it be? Why?' I once witnessed a major customer describe his perceptions of one of his suppliers and their competitors to a management team. The company in question was like an elephant—big and lovable, but ponderous and happy to crash around in its environment (market). Projective questions of this type can be a useful adjunct to the more sterile attribute surveys frequently undertaken.

At the completion of a reputation measurement exercise one is often left with alternative ways to proceed in order to enhance the corporate super-brand. Also, it is seldom possible to change everything that needs improving, because some changes may preclude others. Hence, managers are often reluctant to make the next move. One way to proceed is to construct a set of hypothetical scenarios that reflect possible changes and have stakeholders evaluate the desirability of each one. If these scenarios are designed in a particular way, it is then possible to decompose the respondents' evaluations and estimate the value (or part-worth utility, to use the technical term) of each level of each characteristic used in the scenarios. In essence, one can determine how much better the reputation would be by improving respondents' perceptions of particular image characteristics. The technical name for this type of exercise is conjoint analysis. It is one of the most widely used quantitative measurement approaches in market research.

Finally, many CEOs and CFOs would like some estimate of the value of their organization's images and reputations. Sometimes the accounting concept of goodwill is used as a surrogate measure. Other companies prefer to use the ratio of stockmarket value to the book value of the firm. Alternatively, more direct valuations of brand and company images have been proposed. These have aroused considerable debate as to their usefulness and robustness. They are, however, intriguing to many managers. They have also been included on the balance sheets of some companies (most notably in the United Kingdom). The Interbrand Group plc of the UK is an experienced advocate of valuing brands. Its approach could be easily adapted to valuing 'the corporate brand'.[11]

Conclusions

Measuring corporate images and reputations is a complex and sometimes difficult process, but its value lies in discovering what stakeholders actually think. This chapter operationalizes the theoretical framework outlined in Part 1 of the book. It does this by suggesting how to measure an organization's various images and reputations within this framework. When the research techniques reviewed here are linked in the fashion suggested in Figure 10.4, it is possible to derive a good measure of stakeholder images and reputations. If you decide to supplement this approach with one of the techniques outlined in the previous section, then you may gain added insight into how stakeholders perceive and react to your organization.

The stylized case study given in this chapter is typical of many commercial studies of corporate image or reputation research. It is presented precisely for this reason. Measuring 'slippery' constructs like corporate image and reputation requires many compromises in terms of balancing the amount of information one would like to collect versus what it is realistic to obtain. The crucial points to consider are:

(1) Use a professional market research firm.
(2) Use exploratory research and the theoretical guidelines outlined in this chapter to develop a broad list of descriptive characteristics of the organization.
(3) Measure both the importance and performance of each characteristic.
(4) For external stakeholder groups gather data about both the absolute and relative standing of the organization.

Remember that each stakeholder group may use a different set of characteristics to evaluate the organization. Hence, a number of research studies may be needed to fully profile the images and reputations held by all stakeholders. To get the full value from these studies, it is advisable to use a small core set of descriptive characteristics in each study. These characteristics can then be used to provide a partial comparison of the images and reputations across the various groups.

NOTES

1. For example, in Asia *Review 200* (published by the *Far Eastern Economic Review*) publishes a survey of the ten leading companies in eleven Asian

countries and ninety multinationals based outside Asia that do business in the region. Also, Landor Associates of San Francisco do surveys of the strength of major corporate, service, and consumer brand names across international markets.

2. B. Brown and S. Perry, 'Removing the Financial Performance Halo from Fortune's Most Admired Companies', *Academy of Management Journal*, 37 (1994), 1347–59; C. Fombrun and M. Shanley, 'What's in a Name? Reputation Building and Corporate Strategy', *Academy of Management Journal*, 33 (1990), 233–56; J. McGuire, A. Schneeweis, and B. Branch, 'Perceptions of Firm Quality: A Cause or Result of Firm Performance', *Journal of Management*, 16 (1990), 167–80; P. Roberts and G. Dowling, 'Corporate Reputation and Sustained Superior Profitability', Working Paper, Australian Graduate School of Management (1997).

3. The technical term for this type of measure is that it is a 'formative' index. These measures are constructed by the researcher defining a set of attributes to represent the construct. In this case the *Fortune* researchers say that eight attributes measure corporate image. The other way to measure a construct is to create a 'reflective' measure. Here the researcher builds a theory that guides the selection of items in the scale. Measures of intelligence are examples of this approach.

4. A. Griffin and J. Hauser, 'The Voice of the Customer', *Marketing Science*, 12, 1 (1993), 1–27.

5. R. Bhattacharaya, T. Devinney, and M. Pillutla, 'A Formal Model of Trust Based on Outcomes', *Academy of Management Journal*, 23, 3 (1998), 459–72.

6. 'Civics 101', *The Economist* (11 May 1996), 73: J. Waner, P. Dwyer, J. Rossant, and J. Templeman, 'Writing a New Social Contract', *Business Week* (11 March 1996), 38–43.

7. The logic of this diagram is based on Young and Rubicam's *Brand Asset Valuator* measure. See, for example, D. Aaker, *Building Strong Brands* (New York: The Free Press, 1996), 110–14.

8. K. Keller, *Strategic Brand Management* (Upper Saddle River, NJ: Prentice Hall, 1998).

9. The statistical purist will note that I have assumed, when making this statement, that the variance of each group's responses to the measurement scales is the same .

10. M. Blackston, 'A Brand with an Attitude: A Suitable Case for Treatment', *Journal of the Market Research Society*, 34, 3 (1992), 231–41.

11. There is a brief description of Interbrand Group's approach in M. Birkin, 'Assessing Brand Value', in P. Stobart (ed.), *Brand Power* (London: Macmillan, 1994), 209–24.

11

Managing and Changing Corporate Images: It Can Be Done

We have now reached the moment of truth. Is it possible to actively manage the information stakeholders use to form their images and reputations of an organization? As the title of this chapter suggests, the short answer is yes. The title also suggests that you try to change the images people hold, not their reputations. Recall that the reason for this is that it is unlikely that you can change people's basic values. What you can do is to try to change their perceptions and beliefs, and/or link these to the current values of stakeholders.

This chapter outlines some alternative approaches to managing and changing an organization's desired image. Each approach will work, and the choice depends on three factors. The first is the style of the CEO, because ultimately CEOs put their stamp on corporate images. Second, what the organization's current images are—since you build on your current position. Third, how decisions regarding change are usually implemented within the organization—it is necessary to follow the normal decision-making process.

Chapter 2 proposed that the best way to analyse an organization's activities is from the stakeholders' point of view. That is, what needs does the organization help its stakeholders fulfil? Chapter 7 built on this framework by examining how organizations communicate that they can fulfil stakeholders' needs. In essence, this discussion focused on communicating what I call the organization's 'Value proposition'.

Value propositions are what organizations offer to their stakeholders. It is important to understand a value proposition from the stakeholder's point of view, and to be able to distil it down to its essence. Advertisers often call this a core benefit or a USP—unique selling proposition. For example, employees at a major financial consulting organization summed up their firm's value proposition to them as 'Hell with a BIG bonus'. Many full-time MBA students describe what their business school offers as 'Hell with a better job at the end'.[1]

In the 1960s and 1970s IBM's value proposition for its mainframe computers was 'superior reliability of your data processing system'. The managers who bought these systems translated this into their own value proposition, namely, 'Nobody ever got fired for buying IBM'. In its early years, one of the key factors for the Apple computer company's success was that it designed a computer for individuals who wanted the value proposition: 'easier access to applications software', that is, a relatively friendly personal computer. Many customers were prepared to trade off computer speed and processing power, and pay a higher price to achieve this. Apple's products were so successful that they established a completely new category of computers—'personal' as opposed to 'small' computers. Today there are many such personal electronic products—Walkmans, mobile phones, PDAs (personal digital assistants), and so on.

Value propositions differentiate one organization from another, and play an important role in shaping stakeholder images and reputations. An outdated value proposition, strongly held by customers, can be the prime stimulus for an organization to change its advertising and/or identity symbols. For example, in the late 1960s Continental Airlines was the USA's fifth-largest airline. It was well regarded by both customers and employees for its efforts to live up to its advertising slogan: 'the proud bird with the golden tail'. After deregulation of the US airline industry, Continental was acquired by Frank Lorenzo and got into financial difficulties. It also developed an image as a no-frills airline for the masses. By 1990, however, Continental was offering better service than its no-frills image implied, and management wanted to move the airline's image up-market. In came the identity consultants (Lippincott & Margulies) who set out to realign travellers' perceptions with the airline's new customer service-based strengths.[2]

Continental Airlines acted in the same way as many other companies which come to the realization that their external images do not fit their current or desired offer to the market—they outsource the change programme to a consultant. The outsourcing option has a number of advantages, not the least of which are:

- an expert leads the change process;
- management can concentrate on routine activities;
- it is often easier for an outside consultant to transcend internal politics and get agreement on things such as a new corporate identity;

- the project can be handled as a (big) line-item in the budget; and
- an outsider can be blamed if it all goes wrong.

The outsourcing option, however, has two primary disadvantages. First, as the early chapters of this book indicate, corporate images are driven more by internal factors (such as vision, strategy, formal policies, and organizational culture) than communications directed to external stakeholders. Any external consultant, no matter how good he or she is, will struggle to influence these internal drivers. (The good consultants understand this and tread gently in these areas.) Hence, most consultants tend to focus more on external communication strategies and devices, such as identity, sponsorships, public relations, and advertising.

The second disadvantage is one of ownership. Does it make sense to outsource the design and change of one of the company's key intangible assets to somebody who does not have to live with the consequences of the change? In many cases the answer is no. Recall that when customers buy the company as well as the product or service, corporate image/reputation is one of the key differentiating, and value-adding factors, in customers' minds. Thus it is too important to be outsourced.

External consulting firms are efficient and effective for visual makeovers. Their senior, experienced partners can also play a valuable role as mentors during the process of corporate image redesign. But, when the images of a company are one of its key differentiating attributes and its reputations one of its core strategic assets, management and change must be directed from inside the senior management team. It is too important to be left to anybody else. This is the option discussed in this chapter.

The next section briefly outlines four approaches that the Chief Executive Officer (CEO) can adopt to build a desired image. Following this, a simple approach to choosing among alternative desired images is outlined. I then return briefly to the topic of positioning the organization against its competitors. The chapter concludes with some suggestions about how the CEO can lead the required change in his/her organization.

BUILDING A DESIRED IMAGE

The strategic management literature has identified a variety of approaches to implementing change.[3] While the focus of this research has typically been on major organizational change and restructuring, it does provide insight for changing desired corporate images. For example, one of the major researchers in this field, John Kotter of the Harvard Business School, suggests that there are four key elements:[4]

(1) To lead change you can't just change things. There are a lot of warm-up steps to be taken.
(2) Change is about leadership, not just management.
(3) Cultural change comes at the end, not the beginning.
(4) Wasting time and money on superficial things is worse than doing nothing.

In the context of changing an organization's desired corporate image, Kotter's advice puts the focus squarely on the CEO and his or her leadership style. Others—like Warren Buffett, the investor with probably the best track record in US history—agree. His opinion is that 'People are voting [in the *Fortune* 'Most Admired Companies' survey] for the artist [the CEO] not the painting [the company]'.[5]

The following discussion illustrates how a CEO can integrate his/her organization's internal activities and co-ordinate these with its external communications to project a desired image. These 'Pathfinder', 'Commander', 'Change', and 'Vision' models of change are summarized in Table 11.1.[6] The selection of a particular approach, or a combination of approaches, will be contingent on the history and size of the organization, and the personal decision-making style of the CEO. It should be no surprise to discover that I like an approach that incorporates the vision model. (Recall Figure 3.1 in Chapter 3.)

Table 11.1. CEO roles in building corporate images

Model	The CEO's question	The CEO's role
(a) Pathfinder	'How do I create an organization to fulfil my dreams?'	Leader
(b) Commander	'How do I engineer the best company?'	Rational analyst
(c) Change	'I have a different company in mind, how do I create it?'	Architect
(d) Vision	'How do I get top management and other employees to commit to a shared vision and thus our new image?'	Co-ordinator
	'How do I involve the whole organization in implementation?'	Mentor

Source: Based partly on J. Bourgeois and D. Brodwin, 'Strategic Implementation: Five Approaches to an Elusive Phenomenon', *Strategic Management Journal*, 5 (1984), 241–64.

The pathfinder model

Pathfinders in business are often entrepreneurs, company founders, or company reorganizers. Some (in)famous examples are Sam Walton of Wal-Mart; Bill Gates—who co-founded Microsoft; Steve Jobs—one of the founders of the Apple Computer company; Anita Roddick—founder of Body Shop; Maurice and Charles Saatchi—Saatchi & Saatchi advertising; Akio Morita—co-founder of Sony; Thomas Watson—founder of IBM; and Richard Branson—Virgin. The emotion, conviction, and public profile of these leaders helped ensure that employees, customers, other stakeholders, and the general public knew where the company wanted to go, and what it stood for. The role of a pathfinder CEO is to convince other people that his/her dream is worth while, and to lead them down this path.

The commander model

Commander CEOs are often rational analysts. Extensive analyses of the environment, market conditions, and competitors are conducted before any action is taken to change the strategic direction of the organization. Often one of the big management consulting firms will play a key role in this process. As an outcome of this strategic review, a working party is given responsibility for re-engineering a new company and thus a new ideal corporate image. Robert P. McNamara (Harvard MBA, Ford Motor Company senior executive, one-time Secretary of the US Department of Defense) is a person who had a personal reputation for being the archetype rational analyst. He could reportedly absorb and process vast amounts of information before issuing directives about the most rational course of action to follow. Harold Geneen of ITT was another domineering commander. His amazingly accurate memory, speed reading ability, and capacity to absorb large amounts of information allowed him to intellectually dominate most of his subordinates. During his era he used these skills to mould ITT into one of the largest companies in the world.[7]

Many commanders are typically 'hard' men (not women), who drive themselves and who create 'hard' companies. For example Andy Grove was reported to drive Intel through stringent methods combined with a mix of personal paranoia, obsessiveness, and doggedness. Stories of the combative style of Jack Welch (of General Electric), using financial measures to 'test' his senior managers, are typical of this type of CEO. (Welch also embodied some aspects of the change model discussed next, when, in 1992, he introduced a 'Change Accelerating Program' to develop a new breed of manager able to manage in a 'boundaryless organization'.)

The change model

In the change model the CEO is an architect and is often, but not always, a charismatic person. These people will tend to use the resources and control mechanisms of the organization to mould its activities and culture to shape a new desired corporate image. This type of CEO, like the rational analyst commander, may drive the desired corporate image out of the formal planning process and/or the employee performance-appraisal scheme. Lee Iacocca of Chrysler Corporation, Lord King of British Airways, Jan Carlzon of Scandinavian Airlines, Robert Goizueta of Coca-Cola, and John Sculley of Apple Computer used many aspects of this approach for changing the desired corporate image of their companies.

The vision model

The vision model is a shared decision-making version of the pathfinder model. The first stage of the image-building process occurs when the CEO brings together a group of top executives to design a vision for the organization. The vision statement summarizes the purpose and basic values of the organization and thereby guides the creation of internal value for employees and external value for customers. A good vision statement should also ensure that the organization does not clash with the values of most other stakeholders. Chapter 4 provided an extensive overview of the contents and role of a vision statement. As a catalyst for building an organization's desired image and reputation, the vision statement must be 'sold' throughout the organization by the CEO.

The four approaches outlined above and summarized in Table 11.1, differ with regard to the nature of the CEO, and how he or she uses their organization's culture and formal procedures to design a desired image, and get the commitment of managers and employees. In practice the demarcation lines between these four approaches are often blurred and CEOs will adopt a hybrid approach to strategy development and thus to image design and management. This is illustrated in Exhibit 11.1. As

Exhibit 11.1. Two Europeans—Carlzon of SAS and Barnevik of ABB

When Jan Carlzon took control of Scandinavian Airlines System in 1981 the airline was a mess. SAS was a bureaucratic company constrained by both internal and external barriers to creativity. These included a philosophy and management style that revolved around standardized operating procedures, and highly 'regulated competition' in the European market. In response to increasing oil prices, a recessionary environment, and a stagnant travel market, SAS went on a cost-cutting binge. This nearly cut the heart out of the airline, and it created very unhappy employees and customers. In short, SAS had a terrible image.

Jan Carlzon's leadership style differed from that of many of his Scandinavian counterparts, and that of SAS's previous two CEOs. It was outgoing and bold, and he had a flair for publicity. This highly visible style of leadership became a symbol of the change he sought for the airline. Carlzon's turnaround plan hinged on convincing employees that the airline was in the service business, not the airline business. He stressed to every employee and potential customer that SAS's only real asset was a satisfied customer. This meant listening much more to front-line employees and increasing their responsibility and authority.

After a team of US strategy consultants performed an analysis of the market, Carlzon settled on the strategy of becoming the preferred airline for the full-fare, business frequent-flyer. SAS adopted the corporate slogan 'The Business Airline of Europe'. The strategy succeeded handsomely and Carlzon attained guru status around the world. His book, *Moments of Truth*, became required reading for managers in every service industry. He blended the Visionary and the Change models of corporate image redesign.

If Europe had a management superstar in the 1990s it was Percy Barnevik, the CEO of ABB (Asea Brown Boveri), an electrical engineering giant. In 1988 Barnevik fashioned the company from two century-old competitors—the Swedish Asa and the Swiss Brown Boveri. ABB has twice been voted Europe's most respected company. Although Barnevik has now retired, the company as it exists today reflects Barnevik's vision of a big but small, multicultural multinational. In 1996 ABB consisted of 1,300 separate companies divided into 5,000 profit centres, and run by an élite cadre of 500 global managers.

Percy Barnevik signalled his leadership style when he took only six weeks to merge Asea and Brown Boveri. Since then, he was particularly successful running a company that operates in forty countries. He forced all employees to read his 'bible' (Vision statement) and he made English the official language of the company, although only 30 per cent of the 18,000 employees speak it as their mother tongue. A lot of what held ABB together, it seems, was Percy Barnevik's own relentlessness. His staff said that he could get by on only four

cont.

Exhibit 11.1. *cont.*

hours' sleep each night, and that he was familiar with every nook and cranny of the organization. Barnevik seemed to be an interesting blend of the Commander and the Visionary.

Sources: Derived from: *Scandinavian Airlines System*, Harvard Business School, Case 9-487-041 (1986); J. Carlzon, *Moments of Truth* (New York: Harper & Row, 1987); 'The ABB of Management', *The Economist* (6 Jan. 1996), 68.

discussed later in this chapter, the particular blend of pathfinder, commander, change, and vision will also depend on the resources the CEO can call on to obtain the required information to make a quality decision. This however begs the question of what a quality decision regarding the design of a desired image is.

CHOOSING A DESIRED IMAGE

Figures 10.1 and 10.2 in Chapter 10 provide an important part of the framework for answering the question of what a 'quality desired image' is. They suggest that stakeholders think of an organization in terms of its familiarity and relevance; authenticity and difference; success and stewardship; and respect and esteem. Get high ratings on these attributes and the flow-on effects are: confidence and trust; support; and positive word-of-mouth communication. Link the desired corporate image to stakeholder values and you are well on the way to creating a corporate super-brand.

Focusing communication on one, or a cluster of, related corporate image characteristics is what differentiates one organization from another. These characteristics should be based on the strategic position, and hence desired image of the organization, relative to its competitors. George Day, a noted corporate strategy thinker, argues that the organization's positioning theme is the critical link in the chain of activities needed to gain a competitive advantage.[8] His simple three-link chain is: (1) choose a generic strategy (as outlined in Chapter 5—Table 5.1), (2) favourably distinguish the business from competitors, and (3) devise a marketing strategy to support the positioning theme. Day's approach to searching for a (new) positioning theme around which strategy can be hinged is also a three-step process:

Step 1: Identify alternative positioning themes.

Step 2: Screen each alternative according to whether it:
   (a) is valuable to customers (and other external stakeholders),
   (b) is feasible given the organization's distinctive competencies and customer perceptions of what it is capable of achieving,
   (c) is competitive—superior or unique relative to competitors, and difficult for them to match or exceed, and
   (d) helps meet long-term performance objectives.

Step 3: Choose the position that best meets the criteria in Step 2, and which generates the most enthusiasm and commitment within the organization.

The key step in this process that can have a significant impact on the quality of the desired image adopted is Step 1. Researchers studying the quality of decision making have discovered that better decisions result from the choice among a number of good alternatives, rather than assessing the strengths and weaknesses of just one or two alternatives.[9] The best decision-making approach is to generate at least five or six desirable image positions which the CEO and his/her top management team can evaluate. The decision then becomes which one of these to choose using the criteria outlined in Step 2. Before implementing the chosen position, the organization should commission research to measure reaction by customers and other stakeholders to this theme.

POSITIONING THE ORGANIZATION

Many CEOs are comfortable with an image/position based on their company's distinctive competencies (e.g., we have the best technology) or long-term objectives (e.g., we will only be number one, two, or three in our markets). They are far less comfortable, however, with a position based on customer value. One reason for this stems from the fact that most organizations know a lot more about themselves than about their customers—production, budgets, and formal planning absorb a great deal more time and money than customer research. Also, many management fads in the 1980s and 1990s have largely ignored customers (e.g., employee empowerment, entrepreneuring, JIT, quality circles and TQM, time-based competition, benchmarking, business process re-engineering, the learning organization, downsizing, the virtual corporation, strategic partnering, and so on).

Chapter 7 provided the essential guidelines for developing a positioning statement. While many alternatives were identified, only a handful will be feasible given (a) the screening criteria outlined in Step 2 above, and (b) the organization's past history. What stakeholders come to believe about an organization constrains its next move. While it is tempting to redefine the desired corporate image/position in one bold step, old and wise advertisers often suggest that evolution is better than revolution. Figure 11.1 illustrates the evolutionary approach used by the giant Dutch Philips Electronics company. Its Centurion programme involved some fundamental changes inside the company, which were reflected in their 'positioning staircase'. It also graphically illustrates how becoming focused on a contemporary management movement can assign customers to secondary importance.

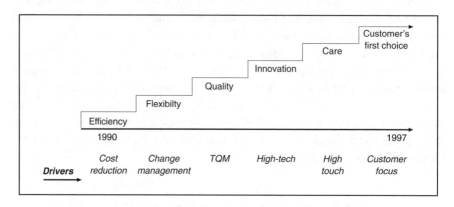

Figure 11.1. Philips Electronics Centurion corporate positioning

It is important to use research to find out what stakeholders think are the attributes that attach to an organization's size and market standing, and to its competitors. Good positioning strategies start with what stakeholders already believe. The idea is to build on any perceived strengths, rather than argue against a perceived weakness. More good advice from those masters of strategic positioning, Al Ries and Jack Trout, is not to choose a position based on corporate aspirations.[10] The famous Avis position of 'We're number 2—We try harder' is much better than Avis saying that they want to displace Hertz and become number 1 in car rentals. It's a believable proposition for customers that the market challenger will offer better service in order to become the market leader. This is also an example of how a potential weakness (being number 2) can be transformed into a strength by insightful market research and creative thinking on the part of the advertising agency.

When an organization tries to reposition itself, it usually does so by changing its advertising, the mix of its products and services, and/or its name. For example, Kentucky Fried Chicken changed its name to KFC to move away from the unhealthy associations of fried food. The Amatil cigarette company in Australia got out of cigarettes and into soft drinks and snack foods, and changed its name to Coca-Cola Amatil. Minnesota Mining and Manufacturing changed its name to 3M to break the position described by its name. When the computer companies Burroughs and Sperry merged they changed their name to Unisys, and used the advertising slogan 'The Power of 2'. This is another example of repositioning a potential problem (merging two, well-established companies) into a strength (the power of 2).

A good example of what not to do when repositioning an organization is illustrated by the giant oil company BP.[11] In 1989 BP ended one of Australia's longest-running corporate advertising success stories—'The Quiet Achiever' campaign. This campaign drew an analogy between the Australian characteristic of quiet achievement and BP's hidden technological achievements and low-key, but reliable customer service. The campaign was started in 1981, and by 1988 the company claimed that the advertising had positioned BP as the most responsible oil company in Australia.[12] In the United Kingdom during this era, the theme of the domestic campaign was 'Britain At Its Best'. Market research in the UK showed that this campaign successfully positioned the company as British, and a provider of quality products. Both these campaigns used a parochial theme to achieve considerable success.

By the late 1980s it was argued by BP's UK management and its advertising agency, Saatchi & Saatchi, that the company and the world had moved on. The time was appropriate to update people's perceptions of the company using a new advertising campaign. The new campaign was to be used around the world. It was based on the theme—'For All Our Tomorrows', and incorporated three messages: environmental concern, community help, and research-based product development. There is nothing wrong with arguing that BP's desired corporate image should reflect these three characteristics. In fact, it is difficult to think of any oil company that the community would like not to embrace these goals. And this represents BP's positioning blunder. It threw away two of the most successful and powerful parochial positions in the history of petrol company retailing for an untried position that competitors like Chevron, Mobil, and Shell could, claim, with equal legitimacy.

BP is not the only big company to walk away from a successful position built by advertising because it, or its ad agency, got sick of it. Remember Coke's great position—'It's The Real Thing'. Coca-Cola seems to change its advertising slogans (positioning statements) fairly regularly—'I'd Like to Buy the World a Coke', 'Coke Adds Life', 'Just For The Taste Of It' (Diet Coke), and 'Always Coca-Cola' are a few which followed 'It's The Real Thing'. Occasionally, however, Coke reverts to a variation on its most memorable position: 'Can't Beat The Real Thing', and 'Coke is *it*'. Maybe Coke managers have a memory after all!

Sooner or later, managers have to choose a positioning theme. Thomas Kosnik (of the Stanford Business School) advises using the CRUDD test to screen any feasible positioning alternatives.[13] This asks: is the position Credible, Relevant, Unique, Deliverable, and Durable?

The CRUDD criteria are self-explanatory and complement those advocated by George Day, which were outlined earlier in this chapter. They are useful, however, because they elaborate Day's Step 2(a) by focusing explicitly on what is important to stakeholders. A short example for the Australian international airline Qantas illustrates how they can be used to choose a good positioning theme.

Qantas has (at least) three credible positioning alternatives. One was broadcast to the world by Dustin Hoffman in the movie *Rainman*—'The World's Safest Airline'. (Qantas has a perfect safety record.)[14] The second is to position Qantas as *the* specialist long-haul airline. The basis for this position is that it is a long way to Australia regardless of which country you come from. The third position is the parochial theme summarized by the Qantas kangaroo logo and the slogan 'The Spirit of Australia'. All three positions pass the CRUDD criteria. Each is credible to travellers and other stakeholders, and deliverable by the airline. The safety theme is relevant to all air travellers, while the long-haul specialist and Australian themes are valued by many Australian travellers and overseas visitors. Two of the themes are unique to Qantas, namely, safety and Australian. The parochial theme, however, seems to be the most durable of the three, and also the one that Qantas can exploit most easily. The reasoning behind this selection is that airlines do not explicitly advertise their comparative safety records (rather, they advertise a surrogate, namely, the young age of their fleet), and nor do they tend to advertise that it takes a long time to reach your destination. Also, few travellers would fly on any long-haul airline if they considered it was unsafe. Hence, the Australian position gets the best overall rating on the CRUDD criteria. It is also the one that taps into a powerful free-standing value among its employees and Australian travellers.

CHANGING YOUR ORGANIZATION'S IMAGES

Two little quotes in my diary from that famous author, Anonymous, provide some insight about this task:

To put one's thoughts into action is the most difficult thing in the world.

Tomorrow's success is founded on today's preparation.

With these thoughts in mind, the seven-step approach to changing an organization's images outlined in Figure 11.2 has proven successful for many companies.

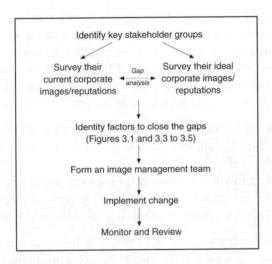

Figure 11.2. Changing corporate images

Imbedded in Figure 11.2 are five management tasks:

(1) Internal evaluation.
(2) Stakeholder research.
(3) Design and implementation.
(4) Internal and external marketing.
(5) Audit.

While the management of these tasks will be the primary responsibility of the CEO, their implementation will often be delegated to a committee of senior managers. Candidates for inclusion in this cross-functional group are: the CEO (as chairperson), and the senior managers responsible for marketing and publicity, production or operations, strategic planning, customer research, human resources, and a project officer to get the other managers organized. I label this group the Image Management Team (IMT). This label is meant to remind the group that co-operation is needed to reshape an organization's desired image, and while the formation of the team may have been triggered by a need for change, there is an ongoing need to manage the organization's images.

Internal evaluation

Figure 3.1 in Chapter 3 shows how an organization's vision (statement), formal policies, and culture are crucial in shaping the images and reputations of any organization. Hence, a good place to start the process of image repositioning is by auditing the driving forces behind the development of the organization's images. Two broad questions should guide this assessment of vision, formal policies, and organizational culture:

(1) Is there a tight 'internal fit' among the sentiments expressed in the organization's vision, formal strategy, and control mechanisms, and the invisible web of culture?

(2) Do the organization's capabilities support the desired image? That is, can the organization deliver on its promised desired corporate image? (This is sometimes referred to as achieving 'external fit'.)

My experience suggests that it is the link between employee performance-appraisal schemes and the formal expectations of organizations that often undermines internal fit. For example, the revenues of most university business schools are driven by teaching excellence, yet the academics are promoted more often for their scientific research. If you want to get promoted in many top business schools, an efficient and effective strategy is satisfactory teaching and great research. What often undermines external fit is the adoption of goals that exceed capabilities. For example, more and more companies have discovered the rewards that flow from being more innovative. In order to create a more innovative organization, goals are set such as the following: 'Thirty per cent of sales must come from products and services introduced in the last five years'. It takes years for most companies to learn how to do this. In the meantime, managers may be forced to launch many minor new product variations or underdeveloped new products (such as the original Apple Newton PDA) to meet these goals.

Stakeholder research

The first three steps in Figure 11.2 focus on the organization's key stakeholders. Which groups are of primary and secondary importance? What are their current perceptions? How do they describe an 'ideal' organization? The IMT needs to explicitly answer these questions because they impact directly on the choice of a desired image position. It is unlikely that a desired image will perfectly fit the expectations of every type of stakeholder. Hence, a trade-off will be necessary in favour of the more important groups.

Chapter 10 outlined how to research the images and reputations that stakeholders hold of an organization. Few organizations, however, seem to collect this information on a regular basis, for example, annually. The IMT can create a budget for this activity and thereby imbed it into the formal monitoring procedures of the organization. The research design (data collection and analysis) is best contracted out to a market research firm. When the data gathered from various stakeholders are analysed, it is crucial to compare the organization's images and reputations across different groups, and across competitor organizations for these groups. This type of comparative analysis can often reveal sources of potential trouble. For example, if the images held by journalists are less favourable than those held by other stakeholders, then the media reports of this group could change the opinions of other groups. This is a popular complaint of most organizations battling a media crisis. (See Chapter 12.)

Design and implementation

In the design and implementation stage the task is to integrate all the factors discussed in Chapters 4 to 9. In effect, the IMT takes on the role of architect. Like a good architect, the IMT must balance the sometimes conflicting effects of the image drivers to form a blueprint of the organization's desired image. A technique I have used successfully on a number of occasions to capture the essence of the organization's image position is to create a three-ringed diagram to represent the offer to stakeholders. The outside ring of the diagram contains the main products, services, and activities of the organization. The middle ring contains the stakeholder benefits and/or solutions to problems provided by the elements in the outside ring. The internal ring reflects the core benefit or *raison d'être* of

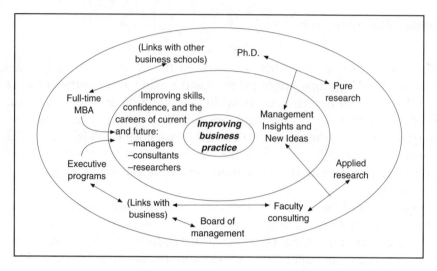

Figure 11.3. Graduate school of management

the organization. Figure 11.3 shows such a diagram for a hypothetical business school that offers full-time MBA and Ph.D. degrees, and executive
programmes designed for companies and individual managers. It suggests
that students, external stakeholders (like the government, business, and
the general community), and internal stakeholders (the academics, programme managers, and support staff) are all really striving to enhance the
capability of the business.

If the CEO and/or IMT feel uncomfortable with the complexity of the
change task, they can use the services of an external consultant to adopt
the role of mentor for the team. As will be clear from the previous discussion in this book, I do not recommend the use of a design consultant,
advertising agency, PR firm, or a market research firm for this role. Their
skill base tends to be too limited around their primary function. If a consultant is invited in to work with the IMT, then he/she needs to appreciate
how all the factors that shape an organization's desired image and reputation are kept in balance. This person can also help select an advertising
agency, market research firm, graphic design firm, or other specialists to
implement parts of the new image change programme.

Knowing if and when to call in outside assistance is a critical factor in
the successful design of an organization's desired image. In order to help
think through this problem, Figure 11.4 presents seven questions structured in the form of a decision tree. Table 11.2 then describes eight options
(or decision problems) to which the yes/no answers to these questions

lead. Each option is identified by a number in Figure 11.4. Table 11.2 lists a set of decision strategies that are appropriate for each of these decision problems and describes each of these decision strategies. The rationale behind each decision strategy is fully described in the original research which led to this decision tree.[15] Working through Figure 11.4 is worth the effort. It is based on what is known as the Vroom–Yetton model of leadership decision making, and is one of the most useful pieces of management research I have ever seen. CEOs or other managers responsible for actually deciding on a particular desired image position will welcome the clarity of the advice incorporated in this figure and its accompanying table.

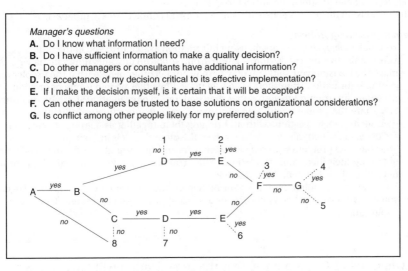

Manager's questions
A. Do I know what information I need?
B. Do I have sufficient information to make a quality decision?
C. Do other managers or consultants have additional information?
D. Is acceptance of my decision critical to its effective implementation?
E. If I make the decision myself, is it certain that it will be accepted?
F. Can other managers be trusted to base solutions on organizational considerations?
G. Is conflict among other people likely for my preferred solution?

Figure 11.4. Deciding how to decide

Internal and external marketing

A crucial step in the change process involves *selling* the (new) desired image position first to employees, and then to external stakeholders. It may not surprise you to learn that change managers often do a poor job of explaining (or marketing)—to both internal and external stakeholders why the organization is trying to reposition itself. It is not uncommon for the IMT to work in isolation from most other managers and all other employees. Often, the first time front-line employees hear about the idea of image management is when they see a new advertisement for their organization

Table 11.2. Recommended set of leadership decision styles

Decision type	Recommended method
1	A1, A2, C1, C2, G*
2	A1, A2, C1, C2, G*
3	G
4	C1 or C2**
5	C1 or C2
6	A2, C1, C2, G*
7	A2, C1, C2, G*
8	Bring in a consultant

Notes:
* G is recommended only if the answer to Question F is yes.
** If the decision maker can cope with (i.e., legitimize) conflict, use C1, otherwise use C2.

Alternative decision strategies
A1   You make the decision yourself, using information available to you at the time.
A2   You obtain the necessary information from subordinates and other managers, then make the decision yourself. You may or may not tell other people what the problem is in getting information from them. The role played by other people is one of providing the necessary information to you, rather than generating or evaluating alternative solutions.
C1   You share the problem with relevant managers and subordinates individually, getting their ideas and suggestions without bringing them together as a group. Then you make the decision, which may or may not reflect the other people's influence.
C2   You share the problem with relevant managers and subordinates as a group, collectively obtaining their ideas and suggestions. Then you make the decision, which may or may not reflect the other people's influence.
G   You share the problem with relevant managers and subordinates as a group. Together you generate and evaluate alternatives and attempt to reach agreement (consensus) on a solution.

or when the CEO announces that the organization will have a new name *tomorrow*! The IMT can usually come up with some good reasons for not sharing their ideas with employees. The usual ones are that they do not want to signal the organization's future plans to competitors, or that they could not involve everyone in the decision process because they could never reach a decision. Either way, it is insulting to many employees to find out about their organization's new direction in the media, and it can reinforce feelings that senior management do not trust the people who work in the organization.

John Kotter's research and the chapter in this book on organizational culture suggest that it may take considerable time to get all employees enthusiastic about contributing to their organization's (new) desired image. Also, the present chapter argues that an organization will have real trouble projecting any type of clear image if employees do not feel that it is in their best interest to co-operate. Hence, internal marketing and gaining the commitment of employees *must* precede any attempt to signal a new direction to external stakeholders. Customers and other external stakeholders become very cynical of an organization which says in its corporate advertising that it has improved its service, product quality, or whatever, when in fact it is merely *trying* to do so. Ask the customers of Australian banks what they thought of the advertising claims that said 'You can trust your bank' when they saw their government having to appoint a bank ombudsperson to adjudicate all the fights between customers and their banks. Ask the American customers of the Ford Motor company what they thought about the company advertising that 'Quality is Job 1', and then a couple of years latter confessing that Ford's quality standards had only then just reached those of its Japanese competitors. People might respect companies with good aspirations, but they have more respect for those companies that achieve quality outcomes.

Audit

Many organizations go through the first four steps of the image change process and then *stop*. A feeling develops among members of the IMT that 'we've now fixed up the organization's image problems and it's time to move on to something else'. Image management is, however, an ongoing process. Corporate images take a long time to form, and they can be damaged quickly in the event of a crisis, as we will see in the next chapter. Also, the actions of competitors will have an impact on the organization's relative position in stakeholders' minds. Hence, current images need continual monitoring to detect changes in stakeholder perceptions, and in the factors that combine to form them (Figure 3.1 in Chapter 3).

Keeping track of the organization's reputations over time usually requires an annual, or sometimes a biannual, survey of stakeholder perceptions. It is also recommended that an annual organizational culture survey be undertaken. The collection of these two pieces of information should be budgeted for in the annual planning process. The IMT should meet once or twice a year to evaluate this new information and to review the organization's overall images and reputations and their fit with the firm's strategic objectives. If a crisis occurs, the IMT can provide important information to the crisis management team about its potential effects on particular aspects of the organization's desired image. This is crucial information for formulating an appropriate response to the media.

CONCLUSIONS

This chapter outlines a number of different approaches to building a desired image. What they all have in common is that they try to position the organization to offer value to its various stakeholder groups. The pathfinder, commander, change, and vision models are alternative ways for CEOs to drive change. In practice, elements of each approach are often combined to achieve the desired outcome. Forming an IMT is an effective way to review your organization's current images and super-brand status, develop a desired image, and manage the change process.

The single most important point made in this chapter is that the senior management team must become actively involved in designing a desired image for their organization. This positioning theme is the critical link in the chain of activities needed to gain a competitive advantage. If managers do not know what the organization wants to stand for, then it is unlikely that employees can communicate a desired position for the organization to customers and other stakeholders. In a competitive market, if an organization has no clear image and value proposition, it usually means that the organization's reputations will be of less use as a strategic marketing asset.

NOTES

1. P. Robinson, *Snapshots from Hell* (London: Nicholas Brealey, 1994).
2. C. Chajet, 'A New Image for Continental Airlines', *Design Management Journal* (Winter 1992), 71–5.
3. J. P. Kotter, *Leading Change* (Boston: Harvard Business School Press, 1996); D. Turner and M. Crawford, *Change Power: Capabilities That Drive Corporate Renewal* (Sydney: Business & Professional Publishing, 1998).
4. Reported in F. Simons, 'Transforming Change', *Australian Financial Review Magazine* (27–8 March 1999), 30–6.
5. Reported in T. S. Stewart, 'Why Leadership Matters', *Fortune* (2 March 1998), 39–50.
6. J. Bourgeois and D. Brodwin, 'Strategic Implementation: Five Approaches to an Elusive Phenomenon', *Strategic Management Journal*, 5 (1984), 241–64.
7. R. T. Pascale and A. G. Athos, *The Art of Japanese Management* (New York: Simon & Schuster, 1981).
8. G. S. Day, *Market Driven Strategy: Processes for Creating Value* (New York: The Free Press, 1990), ch. 7.

9. J. Edward Russo and P. J. H. Schoemaker, *Decision Traps* (New York: Simon & Schuster, 1989); J. Rossiter and L. Percy, *Advertising Communications & Promotion Management* (New York: McGraw-Hill, 1997).
10. A. Ries and J. Trout, *Positioning: The Battle for Your Mind* (New York: McGraw-Hill, 1986).
11. G. R. Dowling, 'BP Catches the Global Brand Fad', *Australian Institute of Management Magazine* (Feb. 1991, NSW edn.), 7–8.
12. N. Shoebridge, 'Goodbye Quiet Achiever, Hello Global Togetherness', *Business Review Weekly* (27 Oct. 1989), 94, 95, 97.
13. T. J. Kosnik, 'Designing and Building a Corporate Reputation', *Design Management Journal* (Winter 1991), 10–16.
14. The reasons for this are fourfold, namely: (i) very good maintenance, (ii) rigorous pilot training, (iii) most flying is done in good weather conditions, and (iv) flying is mostly in uncongested airspace.
15. V. H. Vroom and P. Yetton, *Leadership and Decision Making* (Pittsburgh: Pittsburgh Press, 1973). Summaries of this research can also be found in most good textbooks on leadership and decision making.

12

The Crisis: Communication Strategies to Protect Desired Images and Reputations

The Chinese characters for crisis denote two words—danger and opportunity. From the point of view of an organization's desired reputation, it is the danger component that is the primary focus of this chapter. While opportunities may arise as the result of a crisis, the effects on corporate images and reputations are mostly negative. Inevitably, the publicity surrounding a crisis undermines many of the attributes of the organization such as being well managed, and carrying out a stewardship function. This will degrade the corporate image. If the crisis also leads to the erosion of respect and esteem, and ultimately, trust and confidence, then the corporate reputation has suffered. In effect, many serious crises make a withdrawal from the organization's reputation bank account (recall Figures 10.1 and 10.2).

The impact of a crisis on the images and reputations people hold of an organization is a function of three factors. One is how favourable or unfavourable their current images and reputations are, a second is the magnitude and type of crisis, and the third is the amount and tone of media publicity. While the first factor can be measured, as we saw in Chapter 10, to date there are few published scientific studies of how a crisis (adversely) affects a company's images and reputations. Much of what (we think) we know is opinion based rather than well researched. For example, many managers believe that a good corporate reputation acts as a type of insurance policy the first time the company faces a serious crisis. Here are three examples:

Mr. Justice Mars-Jones said that the penalty would have been substantially greater if Shell had not had an outstanding record for conservation and for generous support for the arts and other worthwhile causes.   (*Daily Telegraph* report on Shell's £1 million fine for the Mersey oil spillage.)

We had a good reputation before Bhopal and we did not lose a single customer afterwards.   (Bob Berzok, Director of Corporate Communications, Union Carbide.)

The reputation of the corporation, which has been carefully built over 90 years, provided a reservoir of goodwill among the public, the people in the regulatory agencies, and the media, which was of incalculable value in helping to restore the brand. (Jim Burke, Chairman of Johnson & Johnson speaking about the Tylenol poisonings.)

If a company suffering a crisis handles the affected parties and the media well, then damage can be minimized. The archetype of this, which is outlined shortly, was Johnson & Johnson's handling of the Tylenol poisonings in 1982. Even in this case, however, temporary reputation loss, as reflected in Tylenol's market share and stock price, was substantial. At the time of the crisis, Tylenol was the market leader, with a share of 37 per cent. As the product was withdrawn from sale, market share fell to 7 per cent. It climbed back to a 30 per cent share within twelve months and 35 per cent within four years. In the fourteen trading days after the crisis, the stockmarket value of J&J fell by $1.13 billion, equivalent to 14 per cent of the value of the company.[1]

If the crisis is handled badly, as was the case with the grounding of the oil tanker *Exxon Valdez* in Alaska in 1989, then the damage to the company's images and reputations can be magnified. The company made no public comment about spilling more than ten million gallons of crude oil for a week, and the CEO did not visit the site until a month later. The early media communications were conducted from the *Valdez* site, which was remote and difficult to contact—just the sort of strategy to get journalists with tight deadlines offside. Exxon's media strategy was: denial, then playing down the incident, and then reacting indignantly to the media. This arrogant response was characteristic of the company's internal culture. In the 14 trading days after the crisis, the stockmarket value of Exxon fell by $3 billion, or 5 per cent of the company's market value.[2]

Subsequent events showed that this $3 billion stockmarket markdown was a good initial estimate of the financial burden the company would suffer over the next few years.[3] For example, it cost approximately $1.4 billion to clean up the oil spill; civil and criminal claims were settled for $900 million, and consumer boycotts probably accounted for the rest. (Thousands of customers cut their Exxon credit cards in half and sent them back to the company in protest.) American managers also showed their disapproval of Exxon in the *Fortune* 'Most Admired Companies' annual survey, as shown in Figure 12.1.

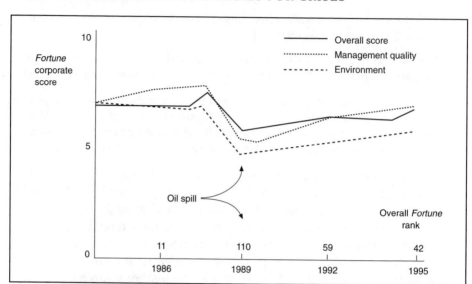

Figure 12.1. Exxon and the *Valdez* disaster

Arguably, one of the most damaging effects to Exxon was the effect on employees. Because the press made the company's inadequate action so visible and public, employees found that they were expected to defend the company's actions in social situations. When they identified strongly with the company, they often experienced these encounters personally. Also, as it became clearly evident that Exxon's management practices contributed to the circumstances that led to the oil spill, employees started to question their faith in the corporate giant.

While the press lampooned Exxon and some retail customers voiced their disapproval of the company, the initial evaluation of the Chairman of Exxon, Lawrence Rawl, turned out to be prophetic. At the time of the oil spill he said, 'I am confident that Exxon's traditional financial strength will not be impaired by this major accident'.[4] The share market seemed to agree, as Table 12.1 indicates.

Over the years, public relations firms have taken the lead in helping companies communicate with stakeholders during crisis situations. It is common practice for many organizations operating in high-risk areas such as chemicals, food production, mining, pharmaceuticals, and transport to have crisis communication plans which have been developed in conjunction with their PR advisers. Many of these plans, it seems, have been based on the famous Johnson & Johnson Tylenol crisis outlined in Exhibit 12.1.

Table 12.1. Exxon share prices, 1988–1997

Year	Price
1988	$22.00
1989*	$25.00
1989	$25.88
1990	$30.44
1991	$30.56
1992	$31.56
1993	$30.38
1994	$40.25
1995	$49.00
1996	$61.19
1997	$73.13

* Time of the *Exxon Valdez* oil spill.

Exhibit 12.1. Johnson & Johnson and the Tylenol crisis

In 1982, several people died after an unknown person tampered with some Tylenol capsules sold in Chicago. A crisis team was formed and immediately offered a reward of $100,000 for information about the person(s) responsible for the tamperings. Based on its Credo that is shown in Exhibit 4.2, J&J set out to protect the health and welfare of the families and doctors it served. It withdrew millions of bottles of Tylenol and developed a tamper-proof container for the product's re-launch, well in advance of government regulations.

J&J also immediately started a massive media campaign, including a toll-free hotline. There were separate PR programmes for consumers, employees, stockholders, politicians, and the media. A special communications programme for the medical community (key opinion leaders) involved putting 2,000 sales representatives on the road. J&J's chairman, James E. Burke, appeared in television advertisements and on talk shows explaining his company's actions. It was estimated that there were 80,000 news stories printed about the crisis, and a J&J survey later concluded that nine out of ten Americans knew of the deaths within a week. Other surveys revealed that J&J's long-standing reputation for truth-telling, aggressive customer-oriented actions, and easy press access helped it weather the storm.

The gold-standard practices of J&J were later followed by Union Carbide when, in 1984, an accidental lethal gas leak from its pesticide plant in Bhopal, India, killed approximately 2,500 people and injured 10,000 more. Since this time, the fast and open approach of J&J has set the standards by which many journalists judge the communications of organizations caught in a crisis.

Source: Based mainly on D. ten Berg, *The First 24 Hours* (Cambridge, MA: Basil Blackwell, 1988), ch. 2.

The fast and open approach of Johnson & Johnson, and advocated by most PR firms, is in stark contrast to the advice offered by many law firms. Good legal advice is public silence—words spoken now are facts to a judge and jury in a later court case. While silence is golden to a lawyer, it is often perceived as an admission of guilt by the public. The dilemma faced by managers in the middle of a crisis is to whom should they listen?

When two groups of different professionals offer conflicting advice, this is often a signal that the problem is more complex than first thought. Such is the case here. Much of the crisis management literature is anecdotal and prescriptive, and lacks a good theoretical underpinning.[5] The next section begins the search for some of the key factors that cause professionals to disagree. This discussion in turn should help resolve the dilemma posed by your legal and public relations counsels. The remainder of this chapter then presents a three-stage communication model that includes a number of alternative responses, from which an organization can select, to communicate its concern about, and remorse for, the crisis. Throughout this discussion I adopt the position that some type of contingency planning can and should be undertaken to develop guidelines for action in the unlikely event that a crisis occurs.

CRISIS CAUSES AND RESPONSES

Many crises are caused by two interacting sets of failures:[6] RIP failures in the organization's operating environment (Regulatory, Infrastructure, and Preparedness) interact with the HOT factors inside the organization (Human, Organizational, and Technological). For example, in 1991 the investment bank Salomon Brothers had a reputation for masterful trading in the US government bond market. However, its aggressive 'macho' internal trading culture, together with a more competitive market and some weakly enforced government regulations motivated the director of the government bond desk to make a series of illegal bids. When these were uncovered by the SEC and the Justice Department, Salomon was in a serious crisis.[7]

When an organization must manage a process that is made up of a large number of interacting events, disasters occur when either a RIP or a HOT factor is triggered by the occurrence of a number of low-probability events that become linked and amplified in ways that are incomprehensible and unpredictable.[8] Many air, factory, and transport disasters fit this scenario.

One way to classify crises is according to whether they are a discrete event or a recurring issue. For example, the Tylenol crisis involved two discrete events—the first in 1982 and then a repeat occurrence in 1986. While Johnson & Johnson knows how to respond to another such product tampering, this type of crisis is very different from those which are ongoing, and which involve one or more organized antagonists. A good example is the tobacco war which has raged for more than fifty years between anti-smokers and the medical profession against the tobacco companies and growers.

Most ongoing crises are overlaid with the values and morality of the affected parties, or those (self-)appointed upholders of public morality. This ideological context explains why some interest groups never withdraw from a contest with a company, nor will they compromise on the issue at hand—regardless of the chance of success. Classic examples involve environmental, health, and right-to-life groups. When the conflict can be presented as a 'David versus Corporate Goliath' struggle, plenty of press coverage and lawyers are likely to follow.

One of the most spectacular examples of a David versus Goliath conflict involved McDonald's. Two people (professional protesters) decided to hand out leaflets outside McDonald's outlets in the UK making a series of allegations about the company and its products. McDonald's decided to prosecute and the case evolved into the longest in United Kingdom legal history. During the course of the trial the amount of negative publicity was enormous, with the protestors broadcasting their views and those of other like-minded individuals on a website known at the time as McSpotlight. At the conclusion of the trial further publicity occurred when a television documentary went to air.[9]

There are many critical factors that must be taken into account before it becomes clear whether the fast and open approach pioneered by Johnson & Johnson, or the drawn-out legal approach of McDonald's, is the more appropriate one to adopt. For example, when it is obvious that the cause of the crisis was beyond the company's control, as is the case with an Act of God or a random criminal event, then fast and open may be the best response. Companies often frame their response as: 'It wasn't our fault, but we will still bear the loss for the good of all our stakeholders'.

However, when a small group of professional antagonists attack a company, a stand-up and knock-down fight may be the preferred option to signal to other such groups the company's resolve. Also, when it is or soon will be obvious that the company is at fault, and the crisis should have been avoided, it is not surprising that the corporate shutters go up. Corporate survival, personal reputations, and jobs are things which many people will fight hard to maintain. This is fertile ground for corporate lawyers and plaintiff attorneys to test their skill and nerves.

One of Corporate America's most feared corporate attackers is Dickie Scruggs—'counsel for the plaintiff'. He has been at the heart of many asbestos and tobacco suits. What makes him feared by many managers is his basic strategy when suing a company: 'I like to get the stakes so high that neither side can afford to lose'.[10] The tactic is then to settle out of court—it reduces the time and costs of both parties and, from Scruggs's point of view, it sidesteps the chance of an appeal.

A study by Indiana State University of 60,000 media transcripts found that the most common causes of crises are management failure, white collar crime, and mismanagement.[11] These are the types of crises that creep up on an organization. They are also the most difficult to detect and often the easiest to hide. However, they should be the most avoidable—with some foresight and built-in controls.

There are four other types of crises, which although not common, tend to have devastating consequences. One is when the operator of a large piece of machinery makes a major error—such as in many aircraft and train crashes. I label these 'Pilot error' crises. A second is the result of poor science and/or product testing, for example, the Ford Pinto's exploding fuel tank, Dow Corning Wright's leaking silicon breast implants, and Procter & Gamble's Rely tampons that were linked to toxic shock. I label these 'Poor science' crises. The third type results from poorly designed production processes and/or inadequate maintenance procedures. Many mining, oil refinery, and chemical plant disasters fall into this category of 'Poor production' crises. The fourth type of crisis is self-inflicted and occurs because of management hubris. A good example of this type of crisis is Benetton's exploitation of human suffering to advertise its clothing. These advertising campaigns routinely upset governments, pressure groups, charities, churches, potential customers, and often some of Benetton's own retailers. To see if they upset you, log on to www.benetton.com (At the time of writing Benetton had just launched a series of advertisements featuring people on death row in US prisons.)

Figure 12.2 bundles up the most common types of crises. While it might not present an exhaustive list, it is sufficient to indicate that more than one communication approach will be necessary, depending on the type of crisis faced. For example, single-event crises are probably more suitable for the J&J strategy. Alternatively, ongoing issues and disputes, by their very nature, are not amenable to a quick-fix strategy. Also, when a company has done nothing wrong, is it reasonable to suggest that it alone accept the responsibility for repairing all the damage done?

	Unexpected single-event	Ongoing Issues/Disputes
Act of God		
Act of an outsider		
Poor science Poor production Pilot error		
Management failure		

Figure 12.2. Types of crises

What is at the heart of any communication response to a crisis, is impression management (or spin doctoring, to use the more colourful terminology). This is the process which professionals use to influence other people's impressions of them. The skill of a good corporate spin doctor involves his or her ability to (a) understand to whom, or to what the audience will attribute the cause of the crisis, (b) assess the minimum acceptable level of punishment which stakeholders consider should be handed out to the guilty party, and (c) frame a credible communication strategy for salvaging the desired corporate image and reputation.

Attribution is an interesting phenomenon. The extent to which a person blames a company for a company-related incident results largely from how the person perceives the cause of the incident. Important pieces of information in determining cause and assigning blame include the perceived control of the company over the situation, and the likelihood of the incident recurring. Perceived cause and blame will be affected by the types of actions the organization takes, and the statements its officials make following the incident.

As many court cases and coroners' inquiries testify, when something goes wrong, especially when it takes human lives, people want to be able to attribute cause, and apportion blame. It is not uncommon to see victims and their supporters blame the courts if they do not convict a company involved in a crisis. It is difficult for many victims to live with a verdict that 'nobody was to blame'. The Japanese have a custom that if a company is found to be at fault for some serious, reputation-damaging incident, then the CEO will resign to accept responsibility. This tends to happen less often in American companies, where toughing it out is often the preferred response. For example, after the *Exxon Valdez* crisis, the last thing that was on the mind of Lawrence Rawl was resignation. (During a US Senate hearing on the accident a senator suggested such a course of action to Rawl—who laughed it off.) Also, in the Salomon Brothers crisis referred to earlier, it took the appointment of a new (interim) chairman— Warren Buffett (of Berkshire Hathaway and Salomon's largest share-holder) to remove the incumbent and most of his associates.

During the last fifteen years there has been some very interesting work done by psychologists studying the heuristics and biases that people use in their everyday and business decision making.[12] One such heuristic of particular interest to crisis communication is framing. This is a process we all use to simplify and structure the information we receive. In short, our frames influence the way that we 'see' our world. What makes these frames, and other aspects of decision making interesting, is that they are used to help interpret information about the crisis and thus affect people's evaluation of it. Exhibit 12.2 provides an insight into some of our common decision-making anomalies.

Exhibit 12.2. Decision traps

More than a decade ago a US academic, Robin Hogarth, made two insightful comments about our decision making that are still true today: (1) people are generally unaware of how they make decisions, and (2) they show little concern for the quality of their own decision-making process, although the failures of others are often noted with haste. To illustrate his observation, consider the following problem.

Suppose you were given the task of writing a marketing brochure for health insurance. One of the points you want to emphasize is that your company's policy covers hospital charges for all types of admissions. How would you word this benefit in the brochure, *and* would it matter?

Consider the following two options:

A. 'Our policy covers hospitalization for any reason.'
B. 'Our policy covers hospitalization for any accident or disease.'

Which description would you choose?

A research study suggested that some people were prepared to pay a higher insurance premium for Option B than Option A. Evidently, the explicit mention of accident and disease stimulated people to increase their perception of the chance that they might need to go to hospital. Hence, the attractiveness of the health insurance was increased.

This is not an isolated response to a minor change in the wording of information given to people to help them make a choice. Rather, it is one example of the growing body of scientific evidence that suggests that how a question is asked or how options are presented to people can change what they prefer.

The health insurance example illustrates what psychologists call the principle of 'unpacking'. If we unpack a category like 'death from an unnatural cause' into its components—fatal car accident, fire, plane crash, poisoning, drowning, homicide, crocodile attack, and so on, then people are reminded of possible causes that they otherwise may not consider. Making these more salient leads to a sort of double-counting of their likely occurrences. Unpacking generally increases the judged probability of an event.

Biases in the way in which we make everyday judgements have been known about for many years. Research is now confirming that we make the same types of mistakes in business decision making. Here are a few more examples for decisions based on beliefs about the likelihood of uncertain events. They have all been labelled 'representativeness biases'.

Consider the following description of a person you are about to meet: 'Steve is shy and sometimes withdrawn, always helpful, but with little interest in the world of reality. A meek and tidy person, he has a need for order and structure, and a passion for detail.' Which of the following is Steve's occupation: airline pilot, farmer, general practitioner, librarian, salesman, teacher?

You can make your choice based on two types of information—how Steve's description fits the stereotype of each occupation, and/or the base-rate frequency of these occupations in the community. Many people think that Steve is probably a librarian because he best fits this stereotype. However, there are many more farmers and salespeople in the community than librarians, and this fact should enter into any estimate of Steve's occupation.

Being insensitive to the prior probabilities of outcomes is a common judgemental bias. (Did you consider the base-rate occupational frequencies before making your choice?) However, this base-rate information is not always ignored in decision making. What the research shows is that it is highly sensitive to the way that the problem is presented to the decision maker. This information presentation problem was also illustrated in the first example in this exhibit. Let's consider another problem.

Assume that you are interviewing two university students who have just finished their first year of a three-year commerce degree. You would like to employ one of them in two years' time, and your decision will be based on their final grade-point average. The student with the best average grade gets the job. The first student has the following grades: B B B B B B, while the second student achieved: A C B B C A. They both presently have the same average. Which student do you think you will hire?

Many people will express more confidence in predicting the final grade-point average for the first student. Why? Because the internal consistency of a

Exhibit 12.2. *cont.*

pattern of inputs is a major determinant of one's confidence in predictions based on these inputs. This seems to make sense. However, a highly consistent pattern such as the first student's grades often occurs when the factors that determine the pattern are highly correlated with each other. This means that many of them are redundant for prediction purposes. A better forecast will be produced if you could obtain different types of equally reliable information that are uncorrelated with each other.

The overconfidence produced by the perception of a good fit between a predicted outcome and the input information is called the illusion of validity. It has been shown to persist even when the judge is aware of the factors that limit the accuracy of his or her predictions. For example, psychologists who conduct selection interviews and market researchers who pre-test the likely effectiveness of advertisements often state considerable confidence in their predictions, even when they know the fallibility of their techniques.

After reading about these types of biases, people frequently ask whether or not experts do better than novices. In many cases the answer is no! For example, other research has found that experienced retail buyers used the same heuristics, and displayed the same biases as novices when making sales forecasts.

While experience does not necessarily improve judgement, it seems that experienced judges do seem to be better at knowing which of their judgements are likely to be correct. In other words, they tend to know when they don't know. This is an important attribute that many managers, journalists, and business critics could acquire.

If expertise and experience are only of limited help, is there any way to improve your decision making? It seems that becoming aware of the various decision traps that may catch you is a good start. Also, there is some limited evidence that training can help. A better understanding of the way in which we make decisions is critical to better decision making.

Sources: Derived from: A. D. Cox and J. D. Summers, 'Heuristics and Biases in the Intuitive Projection of Retail Sales', *Journal of Marketing Research*, 24, 3 (1987), 290–7; H. N. Garb, 'Clinical Judgment, Clinical Training and Professional Experience', *Psychological Bulletin*, 105 (1989), 387–96; R. Hogarth, *Judgment and Choice: The Psychology of Decision* (New York: John Wiley, 1980); E. J. Johnson, J. Hershey, J. Meszaros, and H. Kunreuther, 'Framing, Probability Distortions and Insurance Decisions', *Journal of Risk and Uncertainty*, 7 (1993), 35–51; J. W. Payne, J. R. Bettman, and E. J. Johnson, 'Behavioral Decision Research: A Constructive Processing Perspective', *Annual Review of Psychology*, 43 (1992), 87–131; A. Tversky and D. Kahneman, 'Judgment Under Uncertainty: Heuristics and Biases', in D. Kahneman, P. Slovic, and A. Tversky (eds.), *Judgment Under Uncertainty: Heuristics and Biases* (Cambridge: Cambridge University Press, 1982); A. Tversky and D. J. Koehler, 'Support Theory: A Nonextensional Representation of Subjective Probability', *Psychological Review*, 101, 4 (1994), 547–67.

The importance of understanding human decision-making heuristics and biases is that having such knowledge allows managers to design their crisis communications in the best way to minimize the (adverse) impact on the organization's images and reputations. For example, if a corporate spin doctor frames the same incident in terms of some type of gain that will not be forthcoming (e.g., you will not be able to use the wetland for the next 12 months) as opposed to the loss that has been suffered (viz., the waterflow in the wetland has been severely restricted), then it will be evaluated quite differently by many people. I make no judgement about the ethics of such impression management. I just make the point that this is part of the trade of the corporate spin doctor. Using these heuristics and biases to your advantage is very much like practising (legal) tax minimization as opposed to (illegal) tax avoidance.

COMMUNICATION STRATEGIES FOR RESPONDING TO A CRISIS

This section outlines a simple three-stage crisis reaction plan. It is designed to help an organization (a) gain time to formulate a comprehensive communication response, and (b) select a strategy that helps the organization to express its concern about the crisis and demonstrate suitable remorse for any part it played in causing it. Managers who have been involved in an industrial crisis are quick to point out that every crisis is different. Consequently, a simple, yet flexible approach is outlined here which can be adapted to a wide range of situations. The overall aim of this strategy is to restrict the potential damage to the organization's images and reputations. There are other, more extensive, sets of crisis handling steps.[13]

Crisis communication should address both the cognitive needs (for facts and analysis) and emotional needs (for reassurance, sympathy, etc.) of affected stakeholders. It should also reinforce the organizational culture and procedures that keep the company operating.[14] Within this framework, responding to a crisis requires three sequential actions:

(1) The immediate communication response.
(2) Answering the three basic media questions.
(3) Demonstrating remorse.

The first action is designed to gain time so that when a spokesperson talks to the media (action 2) this more detailed response is an informed and credible one. If the first two actions are carried out well then the organization can implement a programme of corporate reputation damage control (action 3). If the three actions are implemented appropriately, it is possible for managers to demonstrate their competency and professionalism, and thus enhance their personal reputations.

The immediate communication response

Immediately after a crisis, or even during one (such as a factory fire), is the time when the media (especially television reporters) are at their most active (and potentially lethal). At this stage of a crisis 'facts' are scarce, and there is often speculation about the cause and effects of the crisis on the people involved and the general public. The 'game' some reporters play is to find a company spokesperson and ask a series of speculative and sometimes intrusive questions in the hope of obtaining a sensational/newsworthy story. While the journalism profession frequently denies these allegations, many nightly news and current affairs programmes offer evidence to counter such claims. From an organization's point of view it is best to be prepared for the worst type of media questioning. The decision about the type of statement to make about the crisis at this time is crucial.

If the organization is not ready to talk to the media immediately this can lead to two outcomes, namely:

(a) management personnel are perceived as confused, incompetent, or as withholding information, and/or
(b) the media will find someone else to interview, such as an eyewitness or an independent expert.

In the second case, management has let the agenda for the next round of communications be set by an external party. Management's next response will be reactive rather than proactive because the spokesperson will have to respond to the issues raised in the first media coverage. A better option is to have someone immediately available to show that management is in control. Such a strategy provides the tactical advantage of setting the crisis in the relevant context, and establishing the agenda and the timetable for future reports.

Implementing this proactive strategy requires answers to two questions, namely, (a) who should be selected as the company spokesperson and (b) what should he/she say? Answers to both questions are fairly straightforward. First, the spokesperson should be a (very) senior manager who has functional expertise in the area involving the crisis, for example, the Director of Finance for money-related issues; the Regional General Manager for a crisis involving a local facility, etc. Another equally good alternative is to have the CEO as the spokesperson—especially if he/she already has the trust and respect of the general public (e.g., Lee Iacocca of Chrysler) or the affected stakeholder group(s) (e.g., Warren Buffett had a 'Mr. Clean' image when he took control of Salomon Brothers). Journalists recommend against, if at all possible, (a) using someone from the PR department, or (b) claiming that your lawyers have advised that 'no comment' would be an appropriate response. Both of these options are likely to have negative credibility effects.

Whoever is chosen for this most demanding assignment should:

(a) have received media presentation training (or be a natural presenter), and
(b) remain as the spokesperson for the duration of the media coverage.

This person should also be part of any crisis management team that is set up (to ensure he or she is fully informed). The same person could also take the lead role in communicating with employees (to ensure that one consistent story is presented to everybody).

What should the company spokesperson say at this initial media encounter? The twin aims of this statement are to (a) establish the context and agenda for the information to be presented, and (b) try to ensure that the way the crisis is reported cannot further damage the organization. If the facts surrounding the crisis are not completely clear the spokesperson should make a statement to the effect that:

(1) Everything possible is being done at present to contain the damage, or minimize the effects of the crisis, etc.
(2) The spokesperson does not know all the relevant details at this time, so any statement now may be misleading.
(3) (Preliminary) investigations are under way.
(4) The spokesperson will be available to the media at a certain place and time with detailed information.
(5) The organization is extremely concerned about this issue.

At this point the company spokesperson should leave the reporters and say that his/her time is best spent managing the crisis and gathering more information. In essence, this is how Occidental International responded when an explosion and fire occurred on its Piper Alpha oil drilling platform in the North Sea.[15]

The time interval mentioned in (4) above cannot be too long otherwise it will lead to suspicion and speculation. On the other hand, it has to be long enough so that a clear picture emerges about the cause and possible effects of the crisis. Also, employees should be informed at this point if this has not already been done. The time interval chosen is a matter of judgement and some advice from the PR department or a friendly journalist can help in this matter.

Where management perceives that a crisis has the potential to expose damaging information about the organization, there is often a tendency to seek legal advice before making any public statement. As discussed earlier, advice from this source is often a two-edged sword. Lawyers are accustomed to studying matters thoroughly before making an opinion. Also, their opinions tend to err on the side of caution. Waiting for, and then relying on, such advice is likely to make it difficult for the spokesperson to take the initiative in any ensuing media dialogue.

This first response to a crisis can be critical. For example Dr Jean-Jacques Saltzmann, head of corporate safety and environmental protection for the Swiss chemical manufacturer Sandoz said that after his company polluted the Rhine river with water used to put out a chemical fire, the company handled the media poorly. The company, local authorities, and the government all made statements prematurely because of a lack of information. This degraded the reputation of the company, and the effects of the loss of reputation outweighed the material damage to the plant. The result was a loss of confidence for both Sandoz and the chemical industry.[16]

What to tell the media

In a crisis situation the media generally have three basic questions[17]:

(1) What happened?
(2) Why?
(3) What are you going to do about it?

Answering the 'what happened' and 'why' questions can be a factual recounting of cause and effect. These 'facts' should, however, be of the 'unshakeable variety' so that there is little chance that they will have to be modified at a later time. The way this information is presented should lead naturally into the organization's answer to the third question. A good discipline is for a carefully worded written statement (or statements) to be prepared for distribution to employees and the media. Then the spokesperson should insist that the media read the statement before they ask questions. If their subsequent questions can be answered by reference to the written statement then the spokesperson should refer them back to it. The spokesperson should resist the urge to answer a question by rewording what has already been stated. Such elaboration encourages reporters to continue this line of questioning and to make their own interpretation of the spokesperson's written response. In this exchange with the media the spokesperson must endeavour not to lose control of the situation. Such 'trial by media' can easily lead to the potentially damaging situation in which the spokesperson is forced to call an embarrassed halt to the interview when reporters are being filmed queuing up to ask more questions.

Public relations experts (either in-house or from a separate agency) can play a vital role during this stage of an organization's response to the media. Their understanding of media deadlines, the temperament of particular reporters, and their skills at drafting media releases can make an important contribution to the clear reporting of the organization's actions to resolve the crisis. They can also play a useful role in keeping the media away from all senior managers, and arranging times for the release of press statements and interviews with the spokesperson. If the crisis generates long-term interest, the PR group can monitor all the media coverage, and draft responses to any initial speculation or unfounded allegations. These are likely to occur when media interest shifts from wanting facts about the crisis to gathering human interest stories.[18]

Communication strategies for demonstrating remorse or salvaging the corporate reputation

Figure 12.3 lists some options for answering the media's third basic question—'What are you going to do to make amends for the crisis?' The twelve strategies reflect some very different corporate philosophies.

- *The aristocrat response.* This is: (a) don't explain, and (b) don't apologize. This was Intel's strategy when users found what the company thought was a rare problem in one of its early Pentium chips. The real problem, however, was that the users turned to Intel for help and reassurance. Initially, they were told nothing. Then they were told that there was a problem with the chip, but it occurred only under the circumstances that a demanding scientist would encounter. After

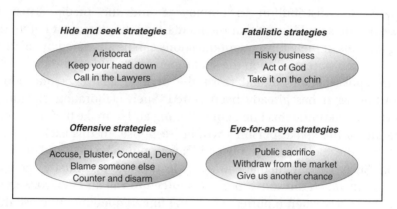

Figure 12.3. Communication strategies

more pressure from customers and PC manufacturers—notably IBM—Intel instituted a selective replacement policy. Finally, a no-questions-asked replacement policy was instituted. Commentators suggested that Intel's communication strategy (first, an aristocrat response, then an ABCD—accuse, bluster, conceal, deny—approach, and finally a take-it-on-the-chin response) reflected the personality of Andy Grove (the CEO) and the culture of the company.[19]

- *Keep your head down.* This approach calls for saying as little as possible, and waiting and hoping that the media's interest will be
  diverted to something else. A second aspect to this strategy may be to
  let the apportionment of blame for the crisis be determined by an
  independent body like a public inquiry or a court of law. Taken to the
  extreme, this approach is the classic 'no comment' strategy and relies
  for its (potential) success on the assumption that a lower visibility
  with the crisis will minimize the damage to the company's images and
  reputations. However, if the crisis involves a loss of life and the media
  develop a human interest theme, then the company will be vulnerable
  to receiving negative media publicity at any time when the victims are
  seeking due compensation. Also, if the findings of the independent
  body turn out to be perceived as unjust for some reason, then the
  media may criticize the company (again) for its part in the crisis, and
  seek a public statement about how it will compensate the victims. An
  interesting example of this scenario occurred after P&O's car ferry, the
  Herald of Free Enterprise, sank in the English Channel. The bow doors
  of the ferry were left open as it sailed from port, and with the front of
  the ferry open to the sea, it went down bow first. The English courts,
  however, acquitted the crew on charges of negligence, and for legal

reasons could not charge the company with manslaughter. The victims' relatives and the media then publicly criticized the company
and the legal system for their inability to apportion blame for the accident.

- *Call in the lawyers.* This is a strategy that is sometimes used when the
  company is being attacked by hostile outsiders (e.g., during a
  takeover), or when an employee leaks highly damaging confidential
  information. In 1991 the Australian bank Westpac used such a strategy
  to try to limit exposure of confidential correspondence from its solici-
  tors regarding foreign currency loans made by one of its subsidiary
  companies. The bank's lawyers issued injunctions against various
  individuals and the media to inhibit publication of the damaging
  material. One effect of this legal action was that the crisis migrated
  from the business press to the front pages of the popular newspapers
  and the television news. Human-interest stories about bank customers being forced into bankruptcy kept this crisis in the media for
  many months and gave it the name, 'The Westpac Letters Affair'.

- *ABCD (accuse, bluster, conceal, deny).* This was the strategy used by
  Mitsubishi Motor Manufacturing of America when it was accused of
  allowing widespread sexual harassment (sexist remarks, patting bot-
  toms, crude drawings on walls of women with their legs apart) in 1996.
  When the Equal Employment Opportunity Commission announced
  its case against the company, Mitsubishi opted for an in-your-face
  denial, including dispatching busloads of workers to picket the commission's Chicago offices.[20] If such an aggressive PR response makes
  people doubt the allegations against the company, or encourages the
  accusing party to settle on more favourable terms, then it may be considered to work—up to a point. However, there will always be a small
  negative mark placed before parts of the company's corporate image
  and reputation by many people, not the least by those who have been
  attacked.

- *Blame someone else.* In many crises the actions of another person,
  company, or local authority may play a (significant) part in causing
  the crisis. When this strategy is adopted the company states its case
  along such lines as: 'it followed all the regulations and guidelines,
  however they turned out to be inadequate', or 'the crisis was caused
  by the actions of other people outside its control', or 'it was really the
  victims' fault for letting themselves be exposed to a situation where
  harm could come to them', and so on. The risk of using this strategy is
  that it often stimulates a savage reaction from the accused party. Also,
  if the accusations are incorrect then the company's credibility can be

damaged when the full facts of the crisis emerge. Such a situation occurred to the London Transport Authority after a major fire in the King's Cross underground railway station. The transport authority speculated that the fire's severity might have been due to the use of a particular type of paint. Subsequent investigations established that this was a highly unlikely contributing factor to the spreading of the fire. Another example occurred when Audi blamed American car drivers for poor driving technique when some of its Audi 5000 cars were alleged to have a 'sudden acceleration' problem.

- *Counter and disarm.* This is a variation of the advocacy advertising carried out by some large corporations. The company involved in the crisis uses publicity and advertising to counter the claims made by another party and to state its own case. This strategy is often used during a hostile takeover. It is also sometimes used during an ongoing crisis such as an industrial relations dispute. For example, during the long-running 1989/90 dispute involving Australian domestic airline pilots, both the major airlines took out full-page newspaper advertisements to criticize the pilots' union for withdrawing their services, and to apologize to the travelling public. The media attack by Suzuki against the article in the American magazine *Consumer Reports* that its Samurai four-wheel drive car had a tendency to tip over is another example.[21]
- *Risky business.* This strategy is based on the fact that many industries are dangerous (e.g., mining, space exploration, etc.) and the 'law of large numbers' will sooner or later come into play. That is, no matter what precautions are taken, in some industries accidents will happen. The fallout from these crises will also contaminate the reputations of other similar organizations. For example, the nuclear reactor accidents at Three Mile Island in the America and Chernobyl in the USSR affected the image and reputation of the whole nuclear industry. The *Exxon Valdez* oil spill in Alaska had a negative impact on the reputations of all the oil companies. Implementation of this strategy often involves getting an industry association, a government body, an independent scientist, or some person with relevant expertise to explain the risks of doing business and lend their public support to the company in its time of crisis (i.e., referral to a higher authority).
- *Acts of God or 'we were just unlucky'.* This strategy is designed to appeal to the target audience's sense of fatalism or bad luck. For example, when Pan Am lost an aircraft in New Orleans in the early 1980s the company suspected freak weather conditions were the cause. To substantiate this claim it brought in independent meteoro-

logical experts to verify its suspicions (referral to a higher authority). The experts' reports were publicized to inform people that the cause of the crash was a unique weather condition, beyond the control of anyone.[22] This strategy could also be implemented by a company citing examples of similar crises occurring in its (or another) industry, or convincing people that when a company works at the leading edge of technology (in order to make advances for society) some problems are inevitable. If there really is a realistic chance that something dramatic can go wrong then it is probably wise not to have live television coverage of the organization's operations as NASA did during disaster involving the the space shuttle, *Challenger*.

- *Take it on the chin.* When the Piper Alpha drilling platform exploded in the UK's North Sea oil fields killing 167 men, the Occidental company chairman pledged fair and prompt compensation, and put £100 million in a fund to back up his intention.[23] When Perrier found traces of benzene in its mineral water and when Heinz found pieces of glass in its baby food, both companies recalled their products. The strong image of both brands and the quick reaction by the companies reduced the negative effects on both corporate reputations. (Perrier's initial responses to the media were made before they had all the facts about the cause of the contamination.)[24]

- *Public sacrifice of the guilty.* A good example of this strategy occurred after the British Midlands Airways plane crash on the M1 motorway in Britain. After an exhaustive public inquiry where pilot error was established as the major cause of the crash, the two surviving pilots were publicly dismissed from the airline. Another example occurred when the Chairman of British Airways, Lord King prematurely resigned in 1993 after BA was found guilty of conducting a 'dirty tricks' campaign against one of its small competitors—Virgin Airlines. Sir Colin Marshall, King's CEO, who many people thought was as much to blame as King, then took control of the airline.[25]

- *Withdraw from the market.* This is the fate of many faulty children's toys, unhealthy food products, and people in high-profile occupations who get caught in personality scandals—although not US presidents. While it is one of the more drastic strategies to adopt, it is often a logical outcome of the isolate and containment procedures used during the management of a crisis. Sometimes this strategy is adopted because post-crisis investigations show that the potential rewards from an area of business do not offset the inherent risks. In other cases, the decision may be forced on the company by adverse consumer reaction. This happened to the Pan Am airline after the sabotage and crash of one of its planes over the Scottish town of Lockerbie. Passenger numbers on Pan Am's flights from the USA to London fell to such an extent that the airline sold this air route to United Airlines.

- *Give us another chance.* Here the CEO publicly accepts all the responsibility for the crisis and asks that the company be given another chance. The apology may or may not be accompanied by the CEO's resignation. In the case of Japan Airlines President Yasumoto Takagi resigned immediately after the crash of one of its planes. Another example is Salomon Brothers, where the chief executives were forced to resign after the securities firm was found to have broken several laws regarding bond trading. This strategy is often adopted by political parties where a cabinet minister accepts responsibility for a mistake. The psychology behind such a strategy is interesting. The bigger the crisis, the more senior a person needs to be to accept ultimate responsibility in order for the public to think the sacrifice is appropriate. In large corporations, where it is commonly accepted that a CEO cannot know about (or be really held responsible for) the actions of people well away from the centre of control, use of this type of strategy can demonstrate concern, imply that changes will be made, and give the company another chance.

These twelve communication strategies are presented to reflect a range of options open to a company and to stimulate further thought. They are not presented as an exhaustive list, nor is it advisable for a company to try to pick the best one for a crisis situation. The idea is to evaluate the strengths and weaknesses of each approach, and then use elements from various strategies to design a suitable media strategy. In effect, these strategies present the raw materials for the design of a company's media response.

Crafting an appropriate media strategy is simple in theory but more difficult in practice, and will generally require the help of a PR expert. It involves designing a broad media crisis response for each potential disaster scenario developed during the organization's risk analysis evaluation. These can take the form of a short plan outlining the timing and sequence of actions to be taken in the event of a particular type of crisis, for example: (1) form a disaster team, (2) isolate and contain the crisis, (3) brief the PR team, (4) select and brief a company spokesperson, and so on.

The media strategy part of each crisis plan should be extracted and written as a 'concept statement' understandable to a member of the general public. In fact, a number of optional media strategies should be developed into concept statements for each major disaster scenario. Market research techniques can then be employed to determine the reactions of various stakeholder groups to each one. This idea of concept testing is common in the field of advertising when a new campaign is being developed. A short stylized example of such a concept statement is shown in Exhibit 12.3.

Exhibit 12.3. Sample concept statement for audience evaluation

Possible Disaster: Fire on the XYZ off-shore oil rig with loss of life, etc.

A. Company's initial media response
Chief Manager Operations issues a short press release stating:

  (a) cause of fire (not) known at this stage;
  (b) deaths and/or injuries have occurred but numbers unknown;
  (c) communications with oil rig disabled;
  (d) disaster recovery team being assembled;
  (e) will be available for further comment at 0900 hours the following day.

The Chief Manager will not answer any reporters' questions at this time.

B. Next media response
  (a) state known facts;
  (b) if cause known then state this; otherwise state that the investigation team is currently working to discover the cause;
  (c) state how company will address the concerns of employees, the public, and other affected parties;
  (d) will be available for further comment at XXXX hours.

A number of market research techniques can be used to evaluate stakeholder responses to a scenario such as that depicted in Exhibit 12.3. In-depth interviews and focus groups (discussed in Chapter 10) could be used to uncover (un)favourable reactions to this and other scenarios. Responses from these interviews would be content analysed to provide feedback on each media response. This type of information is essential to balance the opinions of senior managers and PR specialists against the information needs of journalists and stakeholders. In the aftermath of many crises, a common criticism is that the company appeared to be very arrogant. Recall that arrogance is a sure-fire way to discount a good reputation.

Technology is having a significant impact on crisis communications. The growth of the Internet means that crisis information can travel around the world within seconds. However, the Internet can also offer well-prepared companies the opportunity to talk directly to their stakeholders during a crisis. Some companies are preparing secure Internet 'dark sites' where they store material such as press releases and video statements for release during a crisis. Journalists around the world can also use these sites to keep up to date.

CONCLUSIONS

Business organizations encounter a wide range of unforeseen circumstances that have the potential to damage their desired images and reputations. A few are totally unexpected and outside the control of management (e.g., an earthquake), but most are directly or indirectly caused by management actions (e.g., white collar crime, hostile takeover, industrial relations dispute, customer service problems, faulty products, incorrect waste disposal, chemical spills and leakages, etc.). A crisis where management can be implicated provides fertile ground for investigative media reporting.

Unfortunately there is a natural tendency for many managers to think that a major crisis 'can't happen to our company'. Sometimes a lack of crisis planning, or the failure to implement existing plans, results from management overconfidence. For example, we know that space travel is a risky activity. As NASA's successes in space travel and exploration became legendary, in part due to the activities' effective self-promotion, the organization promoted live television coverage of its operations. However, when the explosion of the space shuttle Challenger was broadcast live to millions of people on 28 January 1986, NASA responded badly.[26] While it did have an emergency PR crisis plan, the years of promoting successes made the organization complacent. It was caught off guard. Also, at the time of the Challenger disaster, NASA's new acting chief administrator had been on the job for only a week.

The facts are that the media are reporting more and more disasters involving organizations. In many cases this publicity has damaging effects on the organization's images and reputations among employees, customers, the financial community, public policy makers, and the general public. This chapter outlines some of the communications options available to an organization when responding to a crisis. The variety of industrial crises noted here sound a warning that corporations should not become complacent about what can happen to their images and reputations if a crisis occurs.

Every organization should conduct a risk analysis, and then plan a reaction strategy based on the nature of the potential crises it may face, and how its images and reputations are formed. In the first few hours or days of a crisis, management generally sets the tone of how the crisis will be handled, and hence the potential negative impact on how the organization is evaluated. Damage to an organization's images and reputations after a crisis can be magnified because of media scrutiny and speculation. In fact, PR people say that it is the media which often escalate an incident into a crisis![27]

This book argues that if external stakeholders have a good reputation of an organization then this is one of the organization's most powerful strategic assets. The enhancement and defence of this asset is therefore a primary concern for senior management. In recent years the media, special interest groups, and politicians have increased their scrutiny of business, and have questioned the ethics, morality, effectiveness, and social cost of many business practices. As mentioned in Chapter 1, this increased public scrutiny has been a major factor in the decline of the overall superbrand status of many companies.

NOTES

1. C. Fombrun, *Reputation: Realizing Value from the Corporate Image* (Boston: Harvard Business School Press, 1996), 93–5.
2. Fombrun, *Reputation* (see n. 1 above).
3. In 1994 a Federal Court Jury ordered Exxon to pay $5 billion in punitive damages to a group of Alaskan fishermen, natives, and property owners affected by the spill. As expected, Exxon appealed against this decision.
4. P. Fries, 'Ripple Effect: 10 Years After the Exxon Valdez', *Australian Financial Review Magazine* (27–8 March 1998), 71–5.
5. C. Pearson and J. Clair, 'Reframing Crisis Management', *Academy of Management Review*, 23, 1 (1998), 59–76.
6. P. Shrivastava, I. Mitroff, D. Miller, and A. Miglani, 'Understanding Industrial Crises', *Journal of Management Studies*, 25 (July 1988), 285–303.
7. C. Fombrun, *Reputation* (see n. 1 above); R. Lowenstein, *Buffett* (New York: Doubleday, 1995), ch. 22.
8. K. Weick, 'The Vulnerable System: An Analysis of the Tenerife Air Disaster', *Journal of Management*, 16, 3 (1990), 571–93.
9. The court found that about half the protestors' claims were upheld.
10. T. Carvell, 'Counsel for the Plaintiff', *Fortune* (29 Sept. 1997), 97–102.
11. Reported in T. Cain, 'Why the old rules won't defuse a modern crisis', *Australian Financial Review* (15 Aug. 1997), 65.
12. For example, see: D. Kahneman, P. Slovic, and A. Tversky, *Judgement Under Uncertainty: Heuristics and Biases* (Cambridge: Cambridge University Press,

1982); J. Russo and P. Schoemaker, *Decision Traps* (New York: Simon & Schuster, 1989); A. Pratkauis and E. Aronson, *Age of Propaganda* (New York: W. H. Freeman and Company, 1991).

13. G. Meyers, with J. Holusha, *When It Hits the Fan: Managing the Nine Crises of Business* (Boston: Houghton Mifflin, 1986).

14. R. Kanter, 'Note on Management of Crisis', *Harvard Business School*, 9-389-054 (1988).

15. R. David, 'Damage Limitation', *Business* (April 1990), 88–91.

16. T. Nash, 'Tales of the Unexpected', *Director* (March 1990), 52–5.

17. See David, 'Damage Limitation' (n. 15 above) and Nash, 'Tales of the Unexpected' (n. 16 above).

18. See David (n. 15 above).

19. R. Hof, 'The Education of Andy Grove', *Business Week* (16 Jan. 1995), 50–2.

20. P. Annin and J. McCormic, 'More than a Tune-up', *Newsweek* (24 Nov. 1997), 50–2.

21. D. Kiley, 'How Suzuki Swerved to Avoid a Marketing Disaster', *Adweek's Marketing Week* (28 Oct. 1988), 27–8.

22. D. ten Berge, *The First 24 Hours* (Oxford: Basil Blackwell, 1988).

23. A good description of how the company managed this crisis can be found in ten Berge, *The First 24 Hours* (n. 22 above).

24. See ten Berge, *The First 24 Hours* (n. 22 above).

25. See Meyers with Holusha, *When It Hits the Fan* (n. 13 above).

26. See ten Berge, *The First 24 Hours* (n. 22 above).

27. See Nash, 'Tales of the Unexpected' (n. 16 above).

13

Recap: Avoiding the Twelve Most Common Traps

At the beginning of this book, I made the point that good corporate images and reputations have operational value—as reflected in the leverage they provide to the company's organizational culture and external marketing. I also identified that stakeholder confidence, trust, and support are the key outcomes of a good reputation. These good reputations define corporate super-brands.

The early chapters suggested that there are two types of corporate super-brand. Some companies achieve this status because of their great financial performance. Many of these appear in *Forbes*'s 'The A List' companies (www.global.forbes.com).[1] The other group achieve a status well beyond what their financial performance would predict (e.g., Body Shop, Qantas, Virgin). In this group we have companies that have an image that is linked to an important free-standing value in the community. Like the first group, many of these companies have a CEO who is a real leader and/or personality.

There is a small but growing group of companies that have achieved great performance in their industry and also tap into a core value of their stakeholders. Some that come to my mind are:

- The Walt Disney Company—making people happy.
- Berkshire Hathaway (and Warren Buffett)—high returns from an active, prudent investment strategy.
- Southwest Airlines—low cost, fun air travel.
- Wal-Mart (under Sam Walton)—branded goods, at everyday low prices.
- Nike in the 1990s—just do it.
- IBM in the 1970s and 1980s—the risk-free choice.

- Microsoft—PC software that empowers people and enriches their lives
- Harley-Davidson—live to ride, ride to live.

Which others can you identify?

The problem with corporate images and reputations is that they are invisible assets that reside in the heads of people. They are also fragile assets that can be damaged by information outside the control of the company to which they belong. And, like trust, they are based more on substance than on 'talk'. These factors make their management difficult. However, as the case studies referred to throughout this book testify, a good reputation affects everything a company does and says.

Carl Gustin, Kodak's Chief Marketing Officer, stated that prominent, well-defined corporate brands like AT&T, Coca-Cola, IBM, and Kodak will win and grow only if they continually provide value to their employees and their customers.[2] This nicely sums up the task facing companies which want to invest in building and improving their desired image. It also captures the essence of the problems currently facing Apple Computer as it fights for its survival in the fast-changing world of personal computing. Apple essentially created the modern personal computer. However, it slowed the pace of innovation (which was a founding attribute of its early strategy and which led to the development of a powerful reputation), and kept its prices high (which restricted the size of its installed base, and allowed its customer value proposition to be eroded by competitors). Nowadays, its image and market value are shadows of what they were, and of those of its major competitors Intel and Microsoft.

Since starting to write about corporate images and reputations, I have been invited into many companies to talk about corporate brands. I frequently find that many of these companies do not know what, if anything, makes them distinctive. Given that brand marketers have known for years that authenticity and uniqueness are key factors in a brand's success, it is surprising that this lesson has not been learnt by the managers of corporate brands.

Figure 13.1 summarizes the 'theory' of corporate reputation advanced in this book. It also provides a parsimonious description from which to discuss the major traps that catch managers as they try to enhance their organization's desired image among various stakeholder groups.

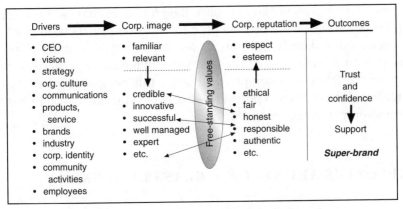

Figure 13.1. The task: creating a super-brand

THE SINGLE IMAGE/REPUTATION TRAP

This is the first, and potentially the most dangerous, trap. It catches senior managers, and often the CEO, who say that their organization has a good or bad image or reputation. When managers forget that they serve various groups of stakeholders, then one group, often customers or stockholders, tend to dominate the focus of attention. Everybody else gets secondary consideration. If this book makes only one contribution, let it be that of reminding companies and their advisers that they need to change their vocabulary—it is corporate image<u>s</u> and corporate reputation<u>s</u>.

THE UNBALANCED SCORECARD

This trap flows from the first. It says that organizations must strive for a balance across their major stakeholder groups. Some managers believe that customers are the most important group. Others argue that employees come first and customers (a close) second. I argue that both groups are equally important. I also believe that organizations that do well by their employees and customers will generally do well for the communities in which they operate.

Organizations get their images out of balance across various stakeholder groups when they do not tie their managers' and employees' performance appraisal to keeping them in balance. If senior management compensation is based mainly on financial and/or stock-market performance (via shares, options, and bonuses linked to profit), then it should come as no surprise that this performance will be their primary focus. The financial madness of the 1980s (junk bonds, greenmail, leveraged buyouts, asset-stripping takeovers, etc.) demonstrated how the power of money can quickly destroy the essential fabric of a company. Contrast this perspective with that of Body Shop. It has a triple report card—financial reporting, social reporting, and environmental reporting.

EMPLOYEES ARE SECOND-CLASS CITIZENS

The first three chapters make the point that employees are pivotal in the process of corporate image and reputation formation. As I write this chapter in America, the Saturn car division of General Motors is featuring its employees in its advertising. Advertisements where employees proclaim 'We enjoy making the car, and you will enjoy owning the car' are designed to personalize Saturn. Because many consumers like to meet the people who design and make their products, this tactic may add an extra attribute to both the company and its products. The overall strategy is summed up in the Saturn slogan: 'A different kind of company. A different kind of car.' Time will tell whether this strategy will differentiate Saturn from other car company brands.[3]

When companies 'advertise' their own employees, it generally has a big, positive impact inside the company. As Figure 3.1 (in Chapter 3) indicates, this is also likely to flow through to better images for customers. While advertising its employees is not the best strategy for every company, the idea of public recognition for employees is a sound idea. I once saw this policy put into practice at a business awards ceremony when the CEO and a check-out employee of a major supermarket chain both accepted a major award on behalf of their company.

In contrast, many companies seem to adopt the philosophy that adequate compensation for employees should be enough. For many who 'work to live', it might be. For those who 'live to work', however, it seldom is. Even in the world of merchant banking and consulting, where employees often joke about their work as 'hell with a big bonus', peer recognition is still important. Human resource people know this, but many of the rest of us forget it too often.

DELIBERATELY UPSET THE COMPANY'S CUSTOMERS

Research and common sense suggest that customers and other stakeholders will lose confidence in an organization which they perceive as:

- arrogant
- wasteful
- greedy
- stupid or
- discriminating between similar types of people
- having power over them or
- not trusting them.

At the time of writing, a good example of how to upset company customers has to be the airline frequent-flier programmes. Recall that these programmes are designed to create customer loyalty by offering points for every mile flown which can be converted later into upgrades, free flights, and other rewards. It sounds great in theory. However, for many people it breaks down in practice. Having given their patronage to an airline, customers hate the petty, restrictive, and complex conditions imposed on 'free' tickets.[4] When their expectations are not met, they blame the airline and degrade their image of it. Many also loudly tell their friends.

Every organization does a few things that (deliberately) upset some of their customers. Often these actions are merely small and inconsiderate, like scheduling events in hard-to-get-to locations or at inconvenient times. Others are more damaging, such as raising prices during holiday periods, or deliberately overbooking. While customer satisfaction research indicates that only a small percentage of the people who are offended will complain, everybody's image is lowered.

The way to avoid this trap is periodically to become your own organization's customer. You will often be surprised at how difficult your organization is to deal with.

COMPANIES AT WAR WITH THEMSELVES

Many companies seem to have a harmony that is obvious even to an outsider. Others are plagued by internal divisions which have the potential to disrupt operations and make work seem like 'hard labour'. Sometimes the cause of this disharmony can be traced to the conflict among different subcultures (Chapter 6). For example, in many business schools there is an underlying tension between those people who specialize in research and those who specialize in teaching. When it comes to making policy, the debate between the two schools of thought can be vigorous.

The case study at the end of Chapter 2 about Air-India illustrates how dysfunctional internal disharmony can become. The classic management versus labour disputes of the 1970s and 1980s, which often resulted in long, public, and emotionally charged strikes, are another example. A minimum condition for good images and reputations in most companies is that the organization can get on with its employees.

I found an interesting example of internal disharmony that has been designed into an organization in an Australian investment bank. It tolerates having various independent divisions competing for the same customers, and even encourages them to do so. There is no integrated key-account approach here. The bank likes to think that this internal competition focuses managers on customer needs and makes each division 'battle tough'. (It argues that if employees cannot hold their own inside the company, then they will have trouble with external competitors.) The senior managers are relatively comfortable with this internal competition (probably the result of self-selection), and junior managers can generally avoid the day-to-day effects of internal competition ('We just follow our division heads'). Also, in the world of merchant banking 'people get paid to compete'! Tension arises, however, because most managers get substantial performance bonuses based on divisional profitability.

There are some interesting side-effects to this internal competitive culture. One is that it keeps everybody on their toes. Another is that it has helped the bank to significant growth and profitability. However, when the bank recently became a public company and came under the scrutiny of the financial analysts and journalists, it did not fully appreciate how its culture would be interpreted when viewed from the outside. In a major article that reviewed the bank's first year of public performance, the financial journalists struggled to reconcile the quite different views expressed by senior executives as to why the bank was again successful. Independent, competitive senior executives, it seems, tend to have and to express different views about their success. This was fine when the bank was privately owned, but a common story needs to be told to outsiders if the bank wants to create a coherent, distinctive public persona.

THE 'LACK OF FIT' TRAP

While all the factors in Chapters 4 (vision), 5 (formal policies), 6 (organizational culture), and 7 (corporate communication) are under the control of management, it is surprising how difficult it is to get them aligned to support the organization's desired image. In Chapter 5 this problem was referred to as achieving both internal and external fit. Talk to any group of employees and they can quickly identify where things do not fit together. For example:

- Our aim is to have the best quality employees—*but* it is difficult to get training; and we don't pay above market salaries.
- We want to delight customers with our service—*but* front-line employees don't have discretion to fix a customer problem immediately; and the performance-appraisal system doesn't reward excellent service.
- We want to develop a relationship with our customers—*but* we don't really trust them not to take advantage of us; and our database is organized by transaction not by customer.
- Our mission is to grow by 20 per cent over the next five years—*but* we have just retrenched 10 per cent of the staff and initiated a cost cutting programme.
- Our strategy is to be more innovative—*but* we know little about new product development, and those people who have been involved in a past new product failure have had their career curtailed.
- We want to foster a team approach to our work—*but* we reward people on the basis of their individual abilities.

The list can go on and on. The point is that most organizations do a number of things that conflict with each other. When they involve employees, it is worth remembering that people have a tendency to do what is 'inspected' in preference to what is 'expected'. Also, when outsiders interact with different parts of the organization, and/or buy different products and services from the company, there is a good chance that they will get mixed messages. The giant Dutch electronics company Philips affords a good example of this last point. As noted earlier, it makes a wide range of products from light bulbs to consumer products to state-of-the-art traffic management systems and medical diagnostic equipment. The problem is that these vary so widely in their design and quality that Philips does not present a consistent brand image across its products.

THE CORPORATE BRANDING TRAP

There are many products and services that can benefit from being linked back to their maker. A good example is insurance. Here, the customer makes payments in the expectation that, if and when needed, the insurance company will cover the costs of the insured item or event. Thus, confidence in the company is an integral part of what is bought. The images and reputations that people hold of the insurance company are key psychological attributes of the insurance policy, and a key strategic asset of the company.

Yet even in this market, many insurance companies have a history of hiding from their customers. For example, consumer research routinely suggests that many people who buy their policy from an independent broker think that it is the broker's policy which they have just bought. The Australian division of one of the world's largest insurance companies did some market research in 1995 which showed that they had a market share which was higher than the level of awareness of the company among their current customers. (Awareness among potential customers was almost zero.) One can interpret such a finding in a number of ways. For example, customers trusted all insurance companies operating in Australia and did not care who stood behind the policy. (This explanation led to the conclusion that customers thought that insurance was a commodity and were happy to shop on the basis of convenience and/or price.) Or the independent brokers were more important to the customer than the insurance company. (This explanation led to the conclusion that the company had lost control of its customer base.) Either way, it was not a strong position from which to try to grow—especially when it built its website to deal directly with customers.

As Chapter 7 recommends, when the customers buy the company as well as the product, it is essential to make sure that they know about the company. Chapter 8 suggested that using the corporate name as (part of) the product name is one way of doing this. It is also worth while for a company to consider using corporate advertising and/or including the company in the product advertising.

CORPORATE IDENTITY TRAPS

There are many corporate identity traps! The most dangerous one is to assume that a change in corporate identity will automatically lead to an improvement in corporate image or reputation. It will, but only if it is accompanied by a significant change in the behaviour of the company— better products or service, a change in strategy or direction, a merger or partnership with another company, and so on. Remember that a change of corporate identity works best when it is interpreted as a signal that more fundamental changes *have* taken—not will take—place.

A second trap is to forget that many employees (especially the loyal, long-serving ones) may have an emotional attachment to the corporate identity symbols—especially well-known symbols. Imagine how employees would react to the idea of changing the corporate logos of Harley-Davidson or Nike. (Many customers would also feel upset.) Also, when the corporate identity is changed, many employees perceive it as an insult to be told about the change just hours before the news is released to customers and the public. (I once witnessed the launch of a new corporate advertising campaign to key account customers, managers, and salespeople at the same event. The ad agency ran the ads and the employees were left to support them to their customers whether they understood their rationale or liked them—30 seconds after they first saw them! They were not happy with either the ad agency or the corporate affairs department that organized the function.)

A third trap is to make a minor, evolutionary change to the corporate logo that is implemented as a big, quick-change project. Such changes often result in a significant cost since they involve tearing down all the existing signage, and reprinting letterheads, etc. Small changes are seldom noticed by outsiders and often not even by insiders. When there is a minor update to the corporate livery, then it is better to roll it out over time and not waste money.

If you are changing the company name then try to come up with a new name that has some intrinsic meaning. Product marketers have known for years that a good name starts the positioning process. Meaningless names require a substantial investment in advertising to become 'household names'. Another common name trap is to shorten a name to its initials—the Australian Graduate School of Management becomes the AGSM. Great if you are a faculty member or a student, but not so great if we are communicating with outsiders. If we had wanted a short name, we should have selected a short name when we named the school—not when we insiders got sick of saying our long name. The best time for a company to shorten its name to its initials is when outsiders are already doing it. For example, lots of people were calling Federal Express 'FedEx' before it became official.

The last of the identity traps involves the inconsistent presentation of the corporate name, logo, and so on. There are two strategies here. One is to bring in the design consultants to rework the corporate identity and issue a manual to ensure its consistent use. The other is simply to remind people that the organization has a single set of identity symbols that should be used in a consistent way. Design consultants often do a visual audit of a company's identity as a way of prising open a new assignment. It is easy to find inconsistencies in the presentation of corporate identity. The critical issue is whether key stakeholders notice these inconsistencies. If they do not, then you are untidy. If they do, then you may have a problem.

THE 'NO POSITION' TRAP

There are two versions of the 'no position' trap. One is the 'no awareness' trap. Very low levels of awareness can lead to the following chain of events—out of sight—out of mind—out of business. In the early 1990s in Australia Procter & Gamble was caught by this trap. P&G had been selling some of its brands in Australia for many years, and as in the USA, it did not prominently link the company name to the brand name. In Australia, unlike the USA, P&G maintained a very low corporate profile. When P&G decided to expand its operations, it was largely unknown among potential management recruits. The new CEO had to undertake a rapid awareness building programme, one part of which involved giving many talks to participants on MBA programmes, to executive seminars, and to professional society functions.

The second version of this trap often manifests itself in the form of the assertion that 'we are good, so we don't have to be distinctive'. It is important to people for companies to be distinctive because it helps them to think about and categorize companies. It helps them to simplify and speed up their decision making. In a society which is characterized by information overload, less really is more. If a company has an easy-to-understand position in the competitive marketplace this helps people remember who that company is. If this position can be linked to important free-standing values, the company may even become a corporate super-brand.

Companies need to articulate their customer value proposition and encapsulate this into their corporate positioning. Sometimes this is called value positioning. Terminology aside, if you are not known for something, you may well be known for anything, or worse still, you may be known for nothing.

THE MEASUREMENT TRAP

The measurement trap is really a double-barrelled trap. If you avoid the first part of the trap, you may still be caught by the second part. The first trap is to ignore any formal measure of this important strategic asset. Many managers are content to rely solely on their judgement as to the state of health and worth of this intangible asset. The second trap is to measure corporate images, but to use a poor measure. For example, many of the 'beauty contest' measures (namely, those rankings of companies published in business magazines) provide little or no insight into the subtleties of corporate images and reputations.

Few organizations have developed good customized measures of their corporate images or reputations that are used on a regular basis. Fewer still compare these across different groups of stakeholders. This is surprising given the effects that corporate images and reputations can have on marketing the company and its products and services (as outlined in Chapter 1).

There are three good reasons for developing a customized measure of corporate image/reputation. First, the process of developing the measures forces people to agree on what the drivers, attributes, and outcomes should be (see Figure 13.1). Also, it gets corporate reputations on the formal agenda of people's thinking, and it generates a budget. The second reason is that it stops people using their own peculiar experience and information sources to gauge the strength or weakness of this important strategic asset. It is not uncommon to hear managers from different parts of the organization express different opinions about their company's images and reputations. Third, once something is measured on a regular basis people tend to track it and there is a good chance that they will try to improve (measured) performance. We have seen this phenomenon with customer satisfaction surveys.

The measurement dilemma organizations face is nicely summed up in the following sayings:

If you can't measure it, you can't manage it.

And:

Not everything that can be counted counts, and not everything that counts can be counted.   (Albert Einstein.)

THE CRISIS TRAP

The crisis trap is to forget that during a crisis the set of actions that may be best for responding to the events at hand may well cause problems in other areas. For example, when you call in the lawyers to help resolve a crisis or its after-effects, this sends different messages to different stakeholders. Some people may interpret this decision as prudence while others may think that the company has something to hide.

One way to think about different stakeholder reactions is to check whether what is done during the crisis will diminish the key outcomes of a good reputation set out in Figure 13.1, namely, confidence, trust, and support. Also, check whether various stakeholders will perceive your actions in terms of the organization being arrogant, wasteful, greedy, stupid, or discriminating between similar types of people. Stakeholders quickly lose confidence in an organization that is characterized by these attributes.

THE CRM TRAP

At the time of writing, cause-related-marketing (CRM) is the latest fad to sweep the marketing profession.[5] The idea behind CRM is that aligning companies with causes that consumers feel strongly about, will create social capital and there will be a strong association between consumers and companies. A good example is the co-branded credit card of American Express and the World Wide Fund For Nature (formerly the World Wildlife Fund). The sales pitch is that the fund receives a small percentage donation of the sales from the co-branded credit cards to use as it sees fit. Also, American Express hopes to attract new customers. What a great idea. A win-win situation. So why is this scheme labelled a trap?

This type of scheme is a trap because of its superficiality. If the organization deems social responsibility to be important, then a fully integrated approach is likely to be a more effective way to enhance the desired corporate image for employees and external stakeholders. Consider the example of Levi Strauss & Co.[6] Many years ago Levi's set up The Levi Strauss Foundation to channel resources back into the communities in which the company works, and to support social causes. Each year the foundation receives a gift and a percentage of the profits from Levi Strauss & Co. to spend as it sees fit. The company also supports voluntary activities by employees in local community services, via its community involvement teams. Together these initiatives have made a major contribution to American society, as evidenced by the fact that President Clinton awarded Levi Strauss & Co. the first, annual Ron Brown Award for corporate leadership in 1998.

One last quote and we're done:

> The purest treasure mortal times afford
> is spotless reputation, that away
> men are but gilded loam or painted clay.
> (William Shakespeare, *Richard II.*)

NOTES

1. See *Forbes* business magazine (11 Jan. 1999), 44–80.
2. Interview reported in *Marketing Science Institute Review* (Fall 1997), 6–9.
3. Saturn will have to keep its advertising 'fresh', its employees happy (e.g., no long drawn-out labour disputes), and it will have to keep building good cars. Saturn also runs a separate series of advertisements featuring satisfied owners.
4. C. Murphy, 'Frequent Flier Tricks and Traps', *Business Review Weekly* (1 Dec. 1997), 46–52.
5. R. Burbury, 'The "Third Wave" of Branding', *Australian Financial Review* (15 March 1999), 15–16.
6. Levi Strauss & Co. corporate brochure (1998), and R. Mitchell with M. Oneal, 'Managing by Values: Is Levi Strauss' Approach Visionary—or Flaky?', *Business Week* (12 Sept. 1994), 38–43.

INDEX